What Philosophy Can Tell You about™ Your Cat

Also Available from Open Court

What Philosophy Can Tell You about Your Dog
edited by Steven D. Hales

What Philosophy Can Tell You about™ Your Cat

Edited by

STEVEN D. HALES

WITHDRAWN

To order books from Open Court, call 1-800-815-2280, or visit our website at www.opencourtbooks.com.

First printing 2008

Open Court acknowledges permission for use of the following pictures.
p. i: © iStockphoto.com/MaszaS;
p. 1: © Joaquim Alves Gaspar 2005;
p. 26: © iStockphoto.com/Photomick;
p. 43: © iStockphoto.com/kovalvs;
p. 62: © iStockphoto.com/DivaNir4a;
p. 74: © iStockphoto.com/JoeLena;
p. 88: © iStockphoto.com/kati1313;
p. 121: © iStockphoto.com/MaszaS;
p. 146: © iStockphoto.com/GlobalP;
p. 156: © iStockphoto.com/mchen007;
p. 171: © iStockphoto.com/MillerImages;
p. 228: © Pineo/Witherell 2008;
p. 238: © iStockphoto.com/ChrisAt.

Printed and bound in the United States of America.

Library of Congress Cataloging-in-Publication Data

What philosophy can tell you about your cat / edited by Steven D. Hales.
    p. cm.
    Includes bibliographical references and index.
    Summary: "Eighteen essays investigate philosophical aspects of the feline mind and the world of cats, illustrated by anecdotes about cats the authors have known"—Provided by publisher.
    ISBN 978-0-8126-9652-3 (trade paper : alk. paper)
    1. Cats—Psychology. 2. Cats—Psychological aspects.
    3. Human-animal relationships. 4. Cats—Philosophy. I. Hales, Steven D.
SF446.5.W47 2008
636.8—dc22

                      2008027046

Contents

III *The Fascination of Feline Minds*   121

IV *Metaphysics for Cats*   171

Catenations

STEVEN D. HALES

It's said that the domestic cat, *Felis silvestris*, is the tamest of all the cats, and the wildest of all the domestic animals. Living with a cat is certainly very unlike living with a dog. Donald Engels perceptively locates this difference in temperament to a philosophical difference. He writes that

> Whereas dogs are natural Stoics, cats tended to be Epicureans. According to this latter school of thought, which most Romans despised, the chance combination of atoms in a void explained everything else in the universe. There was no divine providence or purpose to the cosmos. Ethics were thought to be determined by the autonomous decisions of individuals, not by reference to a greater spiritual power. Humans were autonomous, independent, and ought to live like atoms, as unconnected as possible to the city's institutions or religions. "Live obscurely" was a favorite Epicurean motto . . . Epicurean values accord well with the cat. (*Classical Cats: The Rise and Fall of the Sacred Cat*, p. 93)

Cats have long been a part of human culture, and the bond between humans and cats has been more than tolerance, more than friendship, more than mouse-catching servant and cream-providing master. Engels connects feline values to the ancient Greek philosophy of Epicurus, but the ties are older than that. For four thousand years cats have been sacred and revered. The ancient Egyptians worshipped the cat-headed goddess Bastet, the lover and companion of the sun-god Ra, who represented the life-giving warmth of fire and the bringer of good fortune. Bastet was not the only feline divinity. The Egyptians also worshipped Sekhmet, a fierce lion-headed goddess of war, who, opposite to Bastet, symbolized the destructive power of fire and the scorching desert sun.

Many of our legends and myths about cats have their origins buried in deep antiquity. Take the association of black cats with bad luck and black magic, for example. Howey M. Oldfield argues that the black cat originally was not associated with witchcraft, but with the sacred feminine, tracing back its symbology through the Virgin Mary to Diana, Artemis, and Isis. "The black cat represents . . . not the darkness of evil but of the Uncreate, of the Great Deep, and the Unknown God. It is the Limitless, Formless, and Inexpressible . . ." (*The Cat in the Mysteries of Religion and Magic*, p. 70).

Even the Mother Goose rhyme "Hey diddle, diddle, the cat and the fiddle, the cow jumped over the moon" is no mere silliness for children, although we have mostly forgotten the original symbolism. The idea of a cat and a fiddle can be found in medieval times, and there are wooden carvings of cats playing fiddles to be found on the pews and other woodwork in medieval cathedrals. One such carving, of a cat surrounded by kittens and playing a fiddle, is in Beverly Minster Church, in Beverly, England. This carving is nearly identical to a seventh-century B.C. statue of the Egyptian goddess Bastet, surrounded by kittens, playing a bronze instrument called a sistrum. Although we won't let the details detain us, the cow and the moon in the rhyme aren't mere amusing touches added later, either, and the Roman historian Plutarch connects them to Isis and her sistrum.

Our long association with cats, from goddesses to ships' rat-catchers to the modern house tabby, lazing on a sunny windowsill, provides a fine opportunity to consider the lives that we have made with them. It is this occasion for reflection that is the natural pathway into philosophy. In the first Part of the book, our authors ponder the companionship of cats.

- **How can living with a needy stray help us to understand our relationships with cats in a way that pure abstract reasoning could never achieve?**

- **Cats have no set purpose, no obvious plan beyond, in the words of Friedrich Nietzsche, "prowling avidly about in search of spoil and victory." What can we learn from living with and loving such creatures?**

- **Would you give up your cat for a million dollars? How about giving up your best friend for a million dollars? Are cats truly our friends or just a saleable commodity?**

Appreciating cats isn't like the ordinary appreciation of art, books, movies, or what have you. You can't appreciate the book in your hands until it is completed, typeset, bound, delivered, and read. But cats are a work in progress, living, changing, and open-ended. Of course, we do not simply enjoy our cats—we also live with them and in many ways they are dependent on us, for our balls of yarns, our cans of tuna, our comfortable laps. In fact, the prophet Mohammed was such a lover of cats that he reputedly once cut off a portion of his robe to avoid disturbing a cat that sat upon it (Oldfield, *The Cat in the Mysteries of Religion and Magic*, p. 155). Mohammed was not the only religious leader who recommended kindness towards our feline friends. The non-canonical *Gospel of the Holy Twelve* (34: 7–10) relates the following story about Jesus:

> As Jesus entered into a certain village he saw a young cat which had none to care for her, and she was hungry and cried unto him, and he took her up, and put her inside his garment, and she lay in his bosom. And when he came into the village he set food and drink before the cat, and she ate and drank, and shewed thanks unto him. And he gave her unto one of his disciples, who was a widow, whose name was Lorenza, and she took care of her. And some of the people said, "This man cares for all creatures, are they his brothers and sisters that he should love them?" And he said unto them, "Verily these are your fellow creatures of the great Household of God, yea, they are your brethren and sisters, having the same breath of life in the Eternal. And whosoever cares for one of the least of these, and gives it to eat and drink in its need, the same does it unto me, and whoso willingly suffers one of these to be in want, and defends it not when evilly entreated, suffers the evil as done unto me; for as ye have done in this life, so shall it be done unto you in the life to come."

Our authors consider matters of feline aesthetics and ethics in the next Part.

- **Cat people vs. dog people is one of the great dichotomies (like Macs vs. PCs, shaken vs. stirred, tastes great vs. less filling, Sunni vs. Shiite). But what's the *real* difference between cat and dog folks?**

- **How is there a kind of artistry and beauty in ordinary spontaneous, uncontrived moments with your cat?**

- **Should we model veterinary care on human hospitals, or should we change human health care to make it more like veterinary care?**

- **If you truly love your very ill cat, do you euthanize her or do you spare no expense and effort to keep her alive? Which should you do?**

- **Why exactly is it wrong to be cruel to your cat?**

- **Do you have positive obligations of aid and care for your cat? Ought we to help beached whales? How about the hundreds of earthworms stranded on my driveway after a heavy rain? Are these cases different, and if so, why?**

The classic cats versus dogs joke is that dogs think, "my people keep me warm and dry, feed me good food, pet me, brush me, and play with me. They must be gods!" Cats, on the other hand, think, "my people keep me warm and dry, feed me good food, pet me, brush me, and play with me. *I* must be a god!"

But what's really going on inside that tiny, fluffy head? Do cats think about us? Are we regarded as more than catnip-fetching devices? Do cats *intend* to toy with mice, or torment the dog? Do they *believe* it's dinner-time? Behind that cool reserve, are they *thinking* anything? In Part III, The Fascination of Feline Minds, our authors consider just such questions.

- **Are you more rational than your cat? Or does your cat just care about accomplishing different things from you?**

- **What is it *like* to be your cat? Can you ever understand your cat's experiences?**

- **Does your cat *believe* that his food bowls are in the kitchen, *hope* for cheese to be in the bowl, or even have the concepts of "cheese," "kitchen," and "bowl"? What does your cat think about?**

- **Cats are able to solve familiar, routine kinds of problems, but are they capable of the sort of innovative creativity needed to solve new puzzles?**

The Greek historian Herodotus noted that if an Egyptian cat died a natural death in a private house, then all the inhabitants shaved their eyebrows in mourning. What's more, the Egyptians hoped that their cats would accompany them into the afterlife. According to Herodotus, when their cats died, they were taken to the city sacred to the goddess Bastet, called Per-Bastet, or Bubastis. There the cats were embalmed and buried in sacred repositories. Hundreds of thousands of cat mummies have been found in Bubastis. In the final Part, our authors take up the issues of whether there is a feline afterlife, what it is for our cats to survive over time, and the essence of catness.

- **If human beings have an immortal soul which survives the death of the body, then do cats as well?**

- **Can cloning bring back a beloved, deceased cat?**

- **If two cats exchange brains, did each cat get a new brain or a new body? How can we tell?**

- **Is there some sense in which cats are persons?**

- **Is there more to what makes a cat than some list of intrinsic properties? Does each cat possess a uniquely individual *catness* too?**

We do well to consider the richness, the depth, and the wonder that is occasioned by reflection on our life with cats. It's this contemplation that is the birth of philosophy. And so, enjoy the litter of philosophical kittens that follows, and see which one is the first to jump in your lap and purr.

I

The Companionship of Cats

1

What I Learned from a Cat that No Philosopher Could Teach Me

GARY STEINER

For about six months now, this cat has been working me like a rented mule. He receives my constant efforts—to provide him with the most delectable cat food, clean up after him, administer hourly love feasts, and generally treat him as an unqualified object of worship—as if these were his cosmic due and as if I should consider myself fortunate to be his indentured servant. Most anyone who lives with and has deep feelings for a cat will tell you the same thing, but in Pindar's case there is this difference: the day I took him into my home, the veterinarian recommended that I have Pindar euthanized instead.

It was a Saturday afternoon, and I was enjoying the combination of peace and loneliness that comes from recently having lost two cats to old age. Ajax and Cleo had insinuated themselves into my life as kittens, and had lived a very healthy and happy seventeen and eighteen years, respectively. They both conducted themselves like hereditary royalty, which naturally had wreaked minor havoc with my efforts to maintain an orderly household, keep my *de rigueur* academic black wardrobe free of cat hair, and manage frequent trips for academic conferences.

There's something humbling about a cat with a noble bearing; it serves as a constant challenge to the traditional human assumption of categorical superiority over the rest of living creation. When Cleo passed away, about a year after Ajax, I went into a state of mourning characteristic of the way in which people typically mourn for lost human loved ones. Even after two years in this state, I still did not feel ready to don the yoke and render myself subservient to another furry deity. But when my student Jessica called me on that Saturday afternoon, I found myself left with no choice.

Jessica had found a stray cat near the barn where she keeps her horse. The barn, like your typical barn in the Pennsylvania countryside, housed a contingent of cats whose service to humans consisted in controlling the rodent population. Pindar was not a regular at the barn; he simply showed up one day, and he showed up in dreadful condition. He was malnourished; he is a large cat, and we later learned that he weighed eight pounds. He had eye and ear infections. His paws were either cut or burned, and the wound on one of his forepaws had a tumor the size of a lima bean sticking out of it. Jessica had taken pity on him and had brought him up to school in a pet carrier, but she couldn't keep him because pets are not allowed in campus dormitories and she didn't have the money to take him to the vet. So she called me, since I am the faculty advisor to the Students Helping Animals group on campus and I am known to be an easy mark in situations such as this. I told Jessica to take the cat to the emergency vet hospital, and that I would pay the vet bills if she would find the cat a home.

So far so good. But then I got a call from Jessica a few hours later, informing me that in addition to everything else, blood work showed that the cat had FIV (feline AIDS) and feline leukemia, immunosuppressive conditions that (a) confer on a cat a life expectancy that can generally be reckoned in weeks or months rather than in years and (b) virtually guarantee that no human in his or her right mind would give this cat a home, due to the cost, grief, and inevitable sad outcome. Jessica told me that the veterinarian's recommendation was to "put the cat down."

Smelly Cat Becomes Pindar

Apparently it was also the vet's expectation that we would choose this course of action, because he expressed great surprise when he learned through Jessica that I didn't want the cat euthanized. When Jessica called and told me the bad news about the FIV and the leukemia, it immediately struck me as perverse and unacceptable to kill the cat. The first thing that ran through my mind was that we would never kill a human being who had comparable ailments. So why *kill* this cat? And on what grounds might someone consider it ethically acceptable to do so? Presumably the justification would be that we would be sparing the cat a great deal of pain and suffering and saving it from the likelihood of a gruesome death. But I couldn't help but wonder whether an unwillingness to spend the money, time, and energy required to care for a sick animal might be the deeper motivation—that perhaps people might simply prefer to be rid of the problem. In this case, the problem's name was Pindar.

But it didn't start out as Pindar. When I had Jessica make arrangements for me to pick up the cat at the veterinary hospital the day after she brought him there, she mentioned that she had checked this heretofore nameless feline into the hospital under the name "Smelly Cat." When I went to pick him up on Sunday afternoon, I immediately found out why: in addition to a panoply of ailments, he had a very strong odor for which the term 'funky' might well have been coined. The hospital staff loaded me up with an array of medications that I would need to administer for the next month, and I brought the patient home. For the first two weeks, even though he didn't range out of an upstairs bedroom, the entire house smelled terrible. And for the first month, I was administering four or five medications several times a day.

I remember asking myself one day, why me? And if I'm going to do a good deed like this, why couldn't I at least have taken in one of those regal, beautiful cats like Ajax and Cleo? Ajax in particular had seemed to know that his blood was blue; whenever I would carry him around the house, he would sit on top of my crossed arms, eyes half closed, looking about him somewhat in the manner of Alexander the Great surveying his worldly domain. The name of the game with Ajax was: 'Dig *me*'. It was almost as if Ajax just couldn't bear how great he was, and he was always up for a tour of the house with me as his human sedan chair. Cleo, too, was regal, but more in the traditional mode of an aloof cat who just doesn't have time to condescend to humans. This poor stray, on the other hand, was just a mess. And he didn't seem to have much in the way of personality.

Somewhere in the first few days, I hit on the name Pindar and it stuck. In spite of being dirty, scrawny, and a bit "sketchy" (as my students would put it), he was nonetheless a cat, and as such he had the potential to flourish in something approaching the manner in which Ajax and Cleo had so elegantly commanded my universe. Within about two months, Pindar's ear and eye infections had cleared up, his paws had healed, we had rid him of no fewer than three types of internal parasite, he had cleaned himself up nicely, and his weight had doubled from eight to sixteen pounds. Along with this dramatic improvement in his physical condition, his authentic personality manifested itself and I realized for the first time that my life had again been commandeered by one terrific feline.

I recalled with no little shame my having wished early on that I might at least have taken in a more beautiful or more interesting cat. Pindar had now emerged indisputably as a champion, a cat with a wonderful, loving, mischievous disposition. Inevitably, at some point he will contract a disease to which he will succumb. But it's been six months now, and you would never guess that Pindar has a seriously compromised immune system. So what about the suggestion six months ago that we simply "put him down"?

When my grandfather suffered a stroke some years ago and went into a steady final decline, nobody dreamt of suggesting that grandpa be "put down." We had the best care possible given to him, and we let nature take its course. By comparison, people are much more willing to consider euthanasia in the case of seriously ill companion animals. This willingness is supported and in some ways even encouraged by a long tradition of philosophical thinking in the West and by an Anglo-American tradition of jurisprudence that classifies animals as chattel, or in other words, as living property.

Animals as Possessions

There's a grand mythology in the Western philosophical tradition according to which the moral status of a given type of being is determined by that being's cognitive capacities. We have no direct legal or moral duties to rocks or other inanimate nature, nor to non-sentient beings such as plants. The traditional thinking is that because inanimate objects and plants are incapable of experiencing pain, there's no coherent sense in which these non-sentient beings can be said to be objects of direct moral or legal concern. Whatever moral and legal obligations we may have to non-sentient beings are at best indirect, which is to say that we should conserve nature, not for nature's sake, but rather for the sake of future generations of human beings.

Not all animals are thought to be sentient; bivalves such as oysters, for example, do not have central nervous systems and hence cannot experience perceptual states such as pain. But many animals do appear to be sentient, and one might expect that this fact confers upon them a moral and legal status superior to that of non-sentient beings. As it happens, the difference between the moral and legal status of animals and that of plants is relatively slight: From a legal standpoint animals have long been classified as property, which means that if someone comes into my house, abducts Pindar, and kills him, in principle I am entitled to monetary compensation equal to Pindar's fair market value—which, needless to say, is zero. In some recent cases, plaintiffs who have suffered the loss of a beloved companion animal due to a defendant's negligence or malice have been awarded additional damages for emotional distress, but such awards are very much the exception and are often reduced on appeal or judicial review.

A corollary of this devaluation of animals in the eyes of the law is our society's willingness to use animals in various forms of experimentation, the justification always being that the suffering and the potential welfare of human beings are more important than the suffering and the welfare of the animals upon whom we experiment—though much of this experimentation turns out to have no applicability whatsoever to human problems. The basis for this justification takes its bearings from the Western philosophical tradition, which has argued since classical Greece that the moral status of human beings is superior to that of animals inasmuch as human beings are rational and linguistic, whereas animals lack reason and language.

Even in the face of recent evidence demonstrating a wide variety of cognitive and communicative abilities in animals, we continue to demonstrate an unwillingness to challenge the conventional wisdom that the fact of animal suffering confers on human beings clear obligations to refrain from harming animals.[1] There still persists the tacit assumption that because human beings are more highly rational and linguistic than even the most cognitively sophisticated animals, our welfare and our desires are more important than those of animals—that it's morally permissible to sacrifice animals for the sake of human welfare.

---

[1] On cognitive and communicative abilities in animals, see Donald R. Griffin, *Animal Minds* (Chicago: University of Chicago Press, 1992); Susan Hurley and Matthew Nudds, eds., *Rational Animals?* (Oxford: Oxford University Press, 2006); Marc Bekoff, Colin Allen, and Gordon M. Burghardt, eds., *The Cognitive Animal: Empirical and Theoretical Perspectives on Animal Cognition* (MIT Press, 2002).

This same reasoning gets employed to justify the consumption of meat and other foods derived from or produced by animals, even though it's now beyond question that there is no biological need to eat such a diet. We eat meat, fish, eggs, dairy, and the like because they taste good. With the possible exception of a very few people on earth, no one needs to eat these foods. People eat them because of habit, pleasure, and convenience. This is made considerably easier by the systematic concealment of the conditions under which animals are raised to serve as food for human beings, and by the law's extremely permissive outlook about the use of terms such as "free range." Today in the United States, it is legally permissible to call a chicken "free range" even if it is raised in a gigantic warehouse and never sees a shred of actual daylight; all that is required is that the chicken have more than a certain amount of square inches in which to move about during its short life.

Seeing Animals as Inferior

What the great thinkers of the Western philosophical tradition never bothered to consider is that there's no logical connection whatsoever between a being's cognitive abilities and its moral status in relation to other living beings. Just because I can do math (after a fashion), just because I can form linguistic strings that observe the rules of English grammar, and just because I can contemplate the distant future and the remote past, whereas it appears that Pindar can do none of these things, it does not follow that I have the right to treat Pindar as property and perhaps even "put him down" rather than deal with the gritty realities of his health profile. Nor does it follow that human beings have the right to experiment on animals, or eat them, or use them as egg, milk, and cheese factories. It strikes me as the worst kind of anthropocentrism (human-centeredness) to suppose that the suffering of human beings "counts more" than that of non-human animals, or to suppose that because animals have no sense of their lives in the long run (no sense of the distant future) they have less to lose when they die than a human being has.

Some contemporary philosophers characterize this last difference between human beings and animals in terms of "opportunities for future satisfaction," and argue that because human beings are capable of abstract reasoning and contemplation, they have greater opportunities for future satisfaction than do animals. In effect, animals either don't know or have much less of a sense of what they stand to lose by dying than your typical human being has. Hence the life of a human being takes moral precedence over that of any animal; in a case in which we must choose between the life of a human and the life of animal, we ought to choose to spare the human being. Certainly our intuitions have been shaped to accept this reasoning, but I can't help but wonder whether it is ultimately based on self-serving considerations. In an emergency situation in which we had to choose, say, between saving our child or saving a companion animal, probably most people would without hesitation save the child, and they would presumably do so because of more intimate feelings of kinship with the child. But this is different than saying that we would be violating a moral obligation by saving the animal rather than the child. And if we want to argue that we do have a moral obligation to save the child, on the grounds that the child possesses greater rationality and linguistic ability, then we have to reckon with the question just how the possession of these capacities entails superior moral status. My own intuition is that, if my house were on fire and only Pindar or I (but not both of us) could be saved, most if not all humans would endeavor to save me rather than Pindar; but I don't see how I have more of a *right* to be saved than Pindar does.

I grew up in a major city, but for the past twenty years I have lived in rural Pennsylvania. I used to go jogging on a country road, and I was menaced by a particular young dog who would run off his companion human's property and chase me. I was vaguely under the impression that this dog didn't intend to harm me and was simply having a bit of fun at my expense, but that's the thing with an unfamiliar dog—you just never know. So I contacted the man who lived on the property and asked him to keep the dog from running out into the road. He said, "I hate to keep a dog on a line. Just throw some rocks at him, and he'll leave you alone." I said, "are you sure that's the best way to handle the situation?" Without any apparent irony, the man responded, "why?"

I hardly needed to move to the country to learn that most people in our society view non-human animals as fundamentally inferior to humans, and that most humans in our society are unhesitant about treating animals as commodities or mere annoyances. I like to think that there are not that many people who would seriously recommend throwing rocks at a dog when considerably more humane measures could easily be employed; for all that, however, the overwhelming tendency in our society is to view animals such as cats and dogs as amusement-delivery devices that may be neglected or discarded when the cost or effort of maintaining them becomes too great.

Our Bond with Animals

This attitude has always baffled me, particularly since Ajax and Cleo came into my life in the mid-1980s. Each of them had such a distinctive personality, such particular emotional needs, and such an unmistakable set of likes and dislikes that I was at least as fascinated by the ways in which they were *like* me as I was with the ways in which they were unlike me. Being a first-time parent to felines, I naturally (which is to say unwittingly) let them get the upper hand; they seemed to consider being waited on hand and foot to be their due in life. When they passed away within a year of each other, Ajax at seventeen and Cleo at eighteen, I experienced a sense of loss very much like the one I experienced when a beloved aunt of mine died a number of years ago. During Ajax and Cleo's latter years, I wrote an academic book on the moral status of animals that I completed shortly after Cleo's death; for me there was no question but to dedicate the book to their memory. In the dedication, I stated that Ajax and Cleo had "taught me more about the human-animal bond than all the philosophers combined."

My six months with Pindar have only reinforced the sense that the kinship bond between animals and humans can be grasped completely only at the level of direct interaction. It is through the cadences of day-to-day life, rather than through detached theoretical abstraction, that we become aware of the full extent of our relationship with animals. Of course, daily interactions are no guarantee that a person will achieve a felt acknowledgment of our kinship with animals; there are many people in the area where I live who have had much more direct experience with animals than I have but who feel strongly that animals are really nothing more than "dumb" animals. In a way it's like the appreciation of art: just as there is no guarantee that everyone will agree that Wagner is a great artist, there is no way to ensure that our kinship with animals will be universally felt and acknowledged by humanity. What's needed is a genuine openness to the prospect that there is something deep to be experienced in our encounters with animals.

I find cats particularly compelling in this regard. They exhibit a wide range of personality types and styles of living. Where Ajax and Cleo behaved like royalty, Pindar is much more the retired street fighter. When he started living with me, I became aware that he has a panoply of battle scars all over his body—which presumably accounts for the FIV, which is generally transmitted through fighting. Part of an ear chewed off, scar tissue lesions in various places on his neck and tail, an enormous scab on his nose when I first got him. These physical scars are placed into bold relief by his personality, which is substantially different than that of Ajax and Cleo. Pindar appears to have led a very rough, outdoor life for quite some time before he found his way to me. He's evidently not a feral cat; he is simply too friendly and human-identified to be feral. But there is a certain roughness to his conduct—even when he is expressing affection, he has a tendency to do it in a way that has me running for the alcohol and bandages. If Cleo was Ilsa Lund, Pindar is Stanley Kowalski.

People who have not experienced this sort of immediacy with animals tend to dismiss my way of looking at animals as anthropomorphism, the projection of human qualities onto beings that do not really possess those qualities: surely a creature with such relatively undeveloped cognitive abilities as a cat couldn't possibly have the sort of highly specific personality and preferences that I take for granted in Pindar. The charge of anthropomorphism is often made by people who follow philosophers such as the Stoics, Aquinas, Descartes, and Kant in supposing that only human beings are sufficiently intelligent to have rich subjective lives. The tradition followed this line of thinking as part of an effort to confer on human beings a special, privileged place in the order of things.

Who's Smarter?

The ancient Greeks, notably Aristotle, saw humanity as a form of life somewhere between divinity and animality. Aristotle argued that human beings achieve their highest potential when they seek to be as much as possible like gods and as little as possible like "beasts." This meant learning to regulate our passions by subjugating them to reason. For Aristotle and the Stoic philosophers after him, the possession of reason was the essence of ethical and political conduct; and to the extent that animals lack reason, they not only cannot be ethical or political creatures but also are not the sorts of beings toward which we have any ethical obligations—animals are excluded categorically from the sphere of justice.

Many years ago, a friend of mine announced one day that it is well established that "dogs are smarter than cats." I asked him on what grounds he believed dogs to be smarter than cats. He replied, "because you can train a dog to come when you call it, but you can't train a cat to do the same thing." I asked him why he thought that trainability to come when called counts as a sign of superior intelligence. His reply took the famous I'm-right-because-prove-that-I'm-wrong form of argumentation: "What else would you use as a criterion?" I proposed independence, resourcefulness in problem solving, or perhaps distinctive personality traits, but none of these were satisfactory; trainability was the gold standard. I think my friend just liked the idea of obedience in animals, and perhaps he was made a little indignant by the inclination of your typical cat not to care a whole lot about what people want. My friend was a proverbial dog person.

I have always taken my friend's attitude about cats to reflect the anthropocentric prejudice of the philosophical tradition: that human beings are unquestionably superior to all other living beings, and that the more a given being is like a human being the more intelligent that being is. Naturally the only way we can begin to contemplate the inner lives of animals is by analogy to our own mental lives. But we need to be careful not to dismiss as a lack of intelligence, or as a lack of sophistication in inner experience, characteristics in animals that we find difficult or impossible to explain by analogy to our own experience.

Cats are an excellent case in point. They engage in behaviors that, by the standards of human behavior, just seem irrational or pointless. Anyone who has observed a seated cat staring into a corner of the room for a long period of time has got to be baffled as to what is going on in the cat's mind, if indeed the observer is willing to entertain the hypothesis that the cat has a mind in the first place. I consider it beyond question that Pindar has a mind, even if his mind works differently than my own. I do not believe that cats (or most other animals) are capable of abstract reasoning or conceptual thought, but there is no mistaking the fact that the world *matters* to cats. We just can't comprehend the specifics of the cat's world view, beyond the obvious similarities between its own world view and our own—such as food preferences and the like. The philosophical tradition is right in supposing that at least most animals are incapable of rational thought; but the tradition has been wrong in assuming that the lack of formal reason deprives animals of the ability to have rich inner lives, and it has been wrong in assuming that a lack of rational capacity confers on animals a moral status inferior to our own.

What I wouldn't give to be able to talk with Pindar for just five minutes—to find out what his life was like before he came to me, why he kick boxes like a kangaroo when I so much as touch his hind legs, why he swings his tail rhythmically and forcefully back and forth when he is happy, why he occasionally likes to smack me on the side of the face with his paw for no apparent reason, why he absolutely loves to have me stroke him while he is eating, what is going on in that walnut-sized brain of his when he sits for hours in seeming contemplation. In particular, I wonder how his present consciousness is affected by the pain and adversity he must have experienced earlier in his life. I doubt that he can remember it at will.

One thing the ancient Stoic thinkers seem to have been right about is the proposition that animals can recall a past event or object when they experience something in present sensation that reminds them of it, but that animals cannot retrieve particular memories arbitrarily; Seneca says that, for example, a horse can recall a familiar road when it sees the road, but that the horse cannot recall the road when it is standing in its stall.[2] Even if Seneca went too far in supposing that animals are imprisoned in an eternal present, lacking any conscious relationship to the past or the future, there seems to be something right in the idea that animals cannot contemplate the distant past or the remote future; due to a lack of capacity for abstraction and predication, the conscious experience of animals appears to be confined within the limits of the present, the recent past, and the near future. This doesn't mean that animals have no relationship to the distant past or the remote future. Like human beings, animals such as Pindar seem to have a connection to past and future that does not take the form of conscious awareness; just as my personality has been shaped by events that I do not explicitly recall, Pindar's whole take on life, which differs so sharply from that of Ajax and Cleo, seems to have been influenced

---

[2] Seneca, *Ad Lucilium Epistulae Morales*, Volume 3, Latin with English translation by Richard M. Gummere (London: Heinemann, 1925), p. 445.

deeply by the challenges and the pain imposed by years of living paw to mouth—by the constant fighting, the daily need to find and kill his dinner, and a lack of the affection that he so evidently craves.

I feel toward Pindar as I would feel toward a fellow human who had been through so much suffering and adversity: I want to provide him with the most comfortable and enjoyable life I possibly can. That he repays my efforts with a great deal of affectionate regard is wonderful, but it is not my primary inducement for caring for him. Nor is it true that cats are creatures from whom we cannot learn to be better human beings. Living with a cat definitely puts you in your place: Where the ancient Greeks believed that we improve ourselves to the extent that we emulate the gods, I can't help but wonder whether I do not improve myself when I try to be like Pindar.

Cats exhibit such dignity and nobility, such independence and individual uniqueness, that they merit respect by virtue of their very natures. Every day it becomes clearer to me that it would have been a sin to have Pindar killed just because he failed to satisfy our culture's expectations for a feline amusement-delivery device.

2

What Your Cat Can Teach You about Philosophy

JOHN CARVALHO

Our first cat was a gift to my mother on her thirtieth birthday. Smokey was still a kitten when we brought her home, and her antics, which included climbing the drapes and leaping from the sofa to a stuffed chair to the head of whoever happened to be sitting in that stuffed chair were blithely tolerated and, even, encouraged.

For some time, we did not know what to expect next from the newest member of our household, nor did Smokey help us by obviously patterning her actions. From what we could tell, she seemed to exhaust herself in random series of activities punctuated by equally random—in no special place, for no fixed length of time—collapses into completely inert states. We learned quickly not to confuse these cat naps with sleep. Sleep was what Smokey did in the period just before we went to bed until some time well before we were ready to get up. On this plan, in what was the dark to us, Smokey carried out a share of her apparently patternless activities free from the bewildered observation of humans.

Cats mature rather quickly, which is to say they get larger, develop more robust appetites and slow down some within a year or so, but something of the kitten always stays with them, even into old age. Of the two cats we now care for, Poacher, who is nearly twenty, still suddenly dashes across the room, up the stairs and back down again in pursuit of something we would be inclined to describe as imaginary if it were clear that cats had an imagination or needed one to be transformed into these expenditures of evidently excess energy. From the beginning of their lives to the end, cats exhibit an *élan vital* or "vital impulse" that certain philosophers have proscribed for elevated states of human exis-

tence, noting that, in large part, ordinary human life suffers from
an absence of such exuberance. With these recommendations,
they depart from traditional philosophical preoccupation with
what is supposed to be most distinctive about being human—the
capacity to reason, use language, or make art, for example—and
focus, instead, on what human beings share in common with other
living things, including cats. Close attention to the vital impulse
exhibited by cats may gain us an insight into what these philosophers think is wanting in human life, and it may also give us an
insight into the philosophy that advocates the injection of such an
impulse into human being.

Élan Vital

Let's take a closer look at the term, *élan vital,* used above to
describe the expenditure of energy and life affirming exuberance
of cats. This French expression is usually translated as a "vital
force" or "vital impulse." The word "élan" is used in English to
denote an "impetuous ardor," and the whole expression, "élan
vital," is included in our English dictionaries where it is associated
with Bergson's philosophy and defined as "the creative force within
an organism that is able to build physical form and to produce
growth and necessary or desirable adaptations." This succinctly
translates the concept Bergson introduced in *Creative Evolution* as
a response to Darwinian accounts of evolution which he saw as
passive and mechanistic.[2] Bergson argued that no mechanism could
account either for sudden shifts in the evolution of a species or for
the coordination of the multitude of minor changes that necessarily came together to transform the structures of one or another
organism. Instead, Bergson theorized that an active, psychic dimension was at work in the adaptations of species, especially the
human species, which he termed *élan vital.*

  Could such a creative element have been at work in the evolution of the species *Felis silvestris* that has given us "domestic" cats?
The science about cats seems to corroborate Bergson's thesis that
evolutionary forces alone were not adequate to the task. *Felis silvestris* is the species of wildcat last to branch out from a long line
of the felid family that separated small cats from the big cats about

---

[2] Henri Bergson, *Creative Evolution* (New York: Holt, 1911).

nine million years ago.[3] In sharp contrast to domestic animals whose wild predecessors are extinct or endangered, millions of wildcats thrive to this day in habitats across Europe, Asia, the Near East, and Africa.[4]

While the shifting climate at the end of the Ice Age forced the wild ancestors of dogs, sheep, cattle, and horses into association with human populations whose fields and garbage they pillaged to supplement what their natural habitat no longer provided, wildcats expanded their habitats and adapted to new environs. Fifteen thousand years later, *Felis silvestris* is "the most geographically widespread member of the cat family, and the most adaptable." Adjusting to their "captivity" may be the most recent adaptation of *Felis silvestris,* but uniquely this adjustment has not produced nor does it appear to have been the result of a significant genetic difference.[5] The house cats, farm cats, and feral cats we call "domestic" differ by no more than five nucleotide substitutions from their wild counterparts which can differ from one another by as many as three substitutions in the chemical spelling of their respective DNA.

Cat Intelligence

Contrary to what Bergson says, the impetuous exuberance of cats does not appear to be evidence of a vital impulse at work when *Felis silvestris* split off from its nearest relative, *Felis margarita,* the sand cat, some two million years ago or when a sub-species of *Felis silvestris* began to make regular contact with human populations

---

[3] Stephen Budiansky, *The Character of Cats* (New York: Penguin Books, 2002), pp. 6–7.

[4] See Budiansky, p. 13, and the more recent study by Carlos A. Driscol, *et al.,* "The Near Eastern Origins of Cat Domestication,"published on line at *Sciencexpress,* www.sciencexpress.org, 28th June 2007, in advance of appearing in the journal *Science.*

[5] Budiansky reports (p. 15) that the biologist Juliet Clutton-Brock classes cats as "exploited captives" and not domestic animals since, unlike other domestic species, cats do not exhibit any of the genetic changes that map the domesticity of other species. See *Domesticated Animals from Early Times* (Austin: University of Texas Press, 1981) and *Cats, Ancient and Modern* (Harvard University Press, 1993). Driscol, *et al.,* citing an earlier study, note that "domestic cats appear to lack neotenous characteristics typical of other domesticated species."

some eight or nine thousand years ago.[6] The evidence suggests that involvement with humans is not the origin of your cat's *élan vital*. This vital impulse seems rather to connect house cats to their wild cousins whom we would not likely describe as exuberant or impetuous but rather as feral, fearsome, and fierce. We find the extreme behavior of house cats an exuberant will to life because it appears to us removed from a context in which it might function for wildcats as literally life preserving. House cats give chase and flee, they reach out and grab at quickly moving objects, they crouch low behind real or invisible screens and pounce on wine corks which, animated by the force of their "attack," induce even more chasing, pouncing, swatting and so on. In the wild, all these skills would be put to use in more serious affairs. In domestic environs, though, these activities are no less explicitly life affirming for your cat and, perhaps unexpectedly, a demonstration of your cat's intelligence.

What sense does it make to describe a cat as intelligent, and what is the connection of this intelligence to a cat's "will to life?" We ordinarily measure intelligence by the ability to solve problems or perform complex tasks. In humans, such abilities are often facilitated by critical or abstract or creative reasoning which on its own is taken to be a sign of intelligence (that is, apart from what problems or tasks are in fact solved or performed). By the same token, when a chimpanzee puzzles out how to get ants to eat by inserting a stick in an ant hole and making a meal of those ants that have climbed onto it or when a border collie synthesizes a wide array of different perceptions to perform just those actions which will herd many sheep to a single destination, we say the chimp or the dog demonstrates intelligence even if we hesitate to attribute reasoning to it. There is nothing in the way of problem solving or abstract reasoning that is comparable in cats. Contrary to the prevailing view, cats can be trained (to eat in a designated place or use a litter box where you put it), but they cannot be trained to perform tasks (roll over, fetch a stick, find a favorite toy). In clinical tests, cats show

---

[6] According to Budiansky, the earliest definitive historical evidence of domestic cats is found in Egyptian painting from about 1500 B.C.E., notably a wall painting from the tomb of a sculptor, Ipuy, in the time of Ramses II, dated *circa* 1272 B.C.E. (Budiansky, p. 11 and Plate II). Driscol, *et al.* argue that the remains of an eight-month-old feline discovered in 2006 with human remains at a Neolithic burial site on Cyprus, where there is no evidence of indigenous wildcats, proves that cat domestication occurred significantly earlier.

they can learn and even learn to learn, but they do not exhibit signs of what we ordinarily identify as intelligence. Why is that?

Well, it might be the result of our human prejudice against instinct and our tendency to oppose instinct to intelligence. It may be that we should be more willing than we are to recognize as intelligent behavior that does not ape what we take to be the special accomplishments of human being. What is instinctive comes naturally, we think, but intelligence requires reasoning or training, and reasoning or training don't come naturally but only after some practice and application. Instincts are also associated with the body, while intelligence is associated with the mind, and we have philosophers to thank for dividing the physical from the psychical and privileging the latter. Plato has Socrates make the following claim in the *Phaedo* (65e–66a).[7]

> Then the clearest knowledge will surely be attained by one who approaches the object so far as possible by thought, and thought alone, not permitting sight or any other sense to intrude upon his thinking, not dragging in any sense as accompaniment to reason . . . [the] one who gets rid, so far as possible, of eyes and ears and, broadly speaking, of the body altogether, knowing that when the body is the soul's partner it confuses the soul and prevents it from coming to possess truth and intelligence.

Simmias responds: "What you say, Socrates, is profoundly true," and this judgment was affirmed by late antique and medieval Christian appropriations of ancient Greek philosophy. The same insight, as it was restated in the seventeenth century by Descartes in the sixth of his *Meditations on First Philosophy*,[8] has had a profound effect on philosophy to the present day, but not every philosopher has accepted the truth of this claim.

Bodily Wisdom

In Descartes's time, Spinoza argued that mind and body were not distinct things at all but, as thinking and extension, two of the infi-

---

[7] *The Collected Dialogues of Plato* (Princeton: Princeton University Press, 2000).

[8] *The Philosophical Works of Descartes* (Cambridge University Press, 1975), pp. 131–199; "it is certain," Descartes writes, "that this I (that is to say, my soul by which I am what I am) is entirely and absolutely distinct from my body and can exist without it" (p. 190).

nite attributes of one and the same substance he called, alternately, Nature or God.[9] Closer to our time, Maurice Merleau-Ponty argued that the body, in its very corporeality, is the positive site of knowledge and intelligence and that we neglect this situation at our peril.[10] More precisely, in *Phenomenology of Perception*, Merleau-Ponty argued that the body situates the experience of consciousness in the world and that the body situates itself intentionally, that is to say, with a purpose or an aim in that world. On this view, the mind is inextricably embodied, and the body is ever mindful. "Whether or not I have decided to climb them," Merleau-Ponty writes, "these mountains appear high to me because they exceed my body's power to take them in its stride" (p. 440). At the same time, as I walk, "I have the experience of movement in spite of the demands and dilemmas of clear thought" (p. 269), which means my body finds its own way down a crowded urban street without abstract reasoning, in fact, without reasoning at all. For Merleau-Ponty, my body perceives, understands, and thinks. This is not a metaphor. This is not an argument for a special hybrid of the corporeal and the conceptual.

When Merleau-Ponty says that my body situates my awareness or consciousness of the world and situates it intentionally, he means that the body is already a thinking thing, a *res cogitans* in Descartes's vocabulary. The body is not an impediment to clear and distinct ideas, as Descartes thought, but the medium without which I have no ideas at all. When a talented athlete makes an exceptional play, it is not because her mind is working so quickly that her body enacts the movements required to execute it. Her body knows what to do on its own. There's nothing "subconscious" about this. It is rather unconscious in the literal not the psychoanalytic sense of the term (as when we say Venus Williams is unconscious when she slams a swinging volley for a winner in a close match). The mind is thoroughly embodied, the body thoroughly mindful, and in this picture of consciousness and action Merleau-Ponty argues for in humans is ably demonstrated and amplified in the awareness and activities of cats.

The cat's legendary ability to right itself in a fall and land on all fours, in fact, exemplifies the embodied intentionality, the body as

---

[9] See his *Ethics* (Book II, Proposition 13) in *A Spinoza Reader: The* Ethics *and Other Works* (Princeton University Press, 1994), pp. 123–24.

[10] Maurice Merleau-Ponty, *Phenomenology of Perception* (Routledge, 1962).

it is situated in the world, that Merleau-Ponty argues is the basis of all our experiences. There's nothing about the physicality of the cat's body that causes it to turn over in flight until all four paws are pointed to the ground. Nor is it something that is innate or hard-wired in cats' brains. It is an intentional relation that cats establish between their bodies and the force of gravity, an intelligent process of testing, judging, reassessing, and evaluation that cats conduct, taking into consideration changes in their bodies and their situations—the height of the fall, the different surfaces they will contact—as they are falling.

What appears natural in cats is really a learned behavior, a practice of the cat's body regularized as a kitten (between four and six weeks) and improved on in the course of the cat's life. Your cat has not learned this once and for all at six weeks. She learns it every time she falls, judging the rate of descent, the position of her body, adjusting her posture, preparing her landing. No two falls are identical. Her body is never exactly the same—she's just eaten or awakened from a nap or fresh from an attack or an escape—and her body responds to the circumstances. Over time what she learns is precisely this: that circumstances will never be the same, there will always be the need for adaptation, and that adaptation is not a mental process but a physical one.

The Will to Hunt

The cat's legendary abilities as a hunter, on the other hand, amply demonstrates how that embodied intentionality, as Merleau-Ponty argues, situates our experience and informs our intelligence. Cats possess a range of hearing (into the very high frequencies) and a capacity for visually tracking fast-moving objects (and discriminating from among those objects which are animate and those which are not) that are especially well fashioned for hunting rodents and birds. Beyond these sensory adaptations, though, cats also have exceptional abilities to judge spatial relations, specifically the distance separating them from prey and their potential for covering that distance before the prey eludes them. They have excellent eye-paw coordination, enabling them to strike at prey effectively and to grasp an object and draw it toward them. And anyone who has watched a cat pursue an elusive rodent knows not only just how fast cats are but also how capable they are of changing direction quickly and repeatedly, running at full speed through too-small spaces, leaping over or around seeming obstructions, and how satisfied they can still seem even if they haven't made a kill.

Everything a cat knows in these situations comes to her from the purposes of her embodiment in the world. This intelligence appears to us as instinct because we do not see in this activity anything a cat is obviously thinking or planning and, as it turns out, we get this much right. Cats do not plan to hunt. They are opportunists, dedicating less than an hour each day to hunting and pursuing prey as chance presents them. Yet, we miss something if we do not recognize the complex synthesis of psycho-physical powers that go into hunting as intelligence and the embodiment of such intelligence in cats as a special feature of them. Even cats fed regularly with store-bought "delicacies" will hunt and act out hunting practices in our company. In fact, all those apparently excessive expenditures of energy, that vital impulse, that exuberance discussed above are just so many examples of this acting out, and this is how your cat's intelligence is connected to her "will to live." In her wild European, Asian and African cousins, this intelligence no doubt serves a important, vital purpose—preservation—but there, as in the case of your domestic feline, it is, perhaps, also an expenditure of vital force that gives expression to a powerful and exemplary will to live.

Nietzsche says that the instinct for self-preservation is only an effect of just such a deeper and more profound will of every living thing to discharge its strength.[11] Every living thing, according to Nietzsche, strives for *more* living. It does not seek to preserve the life it has. It seeks, instead, to enhance its life and to discharge its strength in the service of that end. Nietzsche calls the state of tension that leads a form of life to discharge itself in this way, "life itself" as he understands it, "will to power," a commanding, vital impulse that directs a living thing to overcome its weaknesses and maximize its strengths.[12] This is not a will in the ordinary sense, a determination (to see things through, for example) or a striving (for what you do not already have). It is rather the basic instinct, the "intelligible character" from out of which the rest of our instinctive life has ramified and developed. Will to power is a will to more power and more power after that.

---

[11] Friedrich Nietzsche, *Beyond Good and Evil*, in *Basic Writings of Nietzsche* (New York: The Modern Library, 2000), section 13. See also *Will to Power*, section 650.

[12] *Will to Power*, sections 254, 668; *Beyond Good and Evil*, section 13.

Feline Self-Assertion

Cats are a wonderful and endearing expression of this basic instinct. Your cat never knows how high she can climb a tree until the day you need a ladder to help her down. Your cat never chases prey, or another cat, she does not expect to overtake. She never flees from another animal she does not expect to escape. He never knows how far he can roam until the day he roams so far your cat adopts a new human family rather than returning home. Your cat always believes you have nothing else to do with your time but let him out and let him in and let him out again and feed her. pet her, brush her, make a lap for her or make room for her on the bed, on the couch or on your chair. Your cat never tires of asserting himself at turns by purring away contentedly as he sits alone in a favorite sunny spot, by insinuating himself in the midst of a task you are trying to complete—dancing between your feet as you stand at a counter preparing your own meal, sitting on the stack of papers on your desk you are working from—or by completely ignoring you precisely when you want some attention from him.

These forms of self-assertion are closely related to another important way your cat discharges her strength and her will to live. Your cat is a tireless seeker of pleasure, and she takes her pleasure where she finds and for just as long as she wants without guilt or remorse about the pleasure she may be depriving you or any other companion animal. Your cat does not seek out the warmest spot in the house on a cold day but a spot warmed to her specifications. When she has had enough of your petting she will leave you without warning or, alternatively, after whipping around to claw and bite the hand that soothes her. In it this propensity which, added to her naturally regal bearing, marks your cat's nobility, the kind of nobility Nietzsche attributes to certain "sovereign individuals," those with an aristocratic bearing and a superiority of soul, those we admire because we also fear them. It is as if Nietzsche had cats in mind when he wrote *On the Genealogy of Morals* to elaborate on a form of human life that stands above and apart from the all-too-human norm.

These exemplary human types, Nietzsche says there, distinguish themselves by their "superiority in power" and "truthfulness" as well as their "superiority of soul."[13] Nietzsche goes so far as to

---

[13] Friedrich Nietzsche, *On the Genealogy of Morals*, in *Basic Writings of Nietzsche* (New York: The Modern Library, 2000), first essay, sections 5–6.

associate them with what is essentially good and "godlike" in human kind. Among themselves, he say, these types are "so resourceful in consideration, self-control, delicacy, loyalty, pride and friendship," but among strangers "they are not much better than uncaged beasts of prey" (Section 11).

> There they savor a freedom from all social constraints, they compensate themselves in the wilderness for the tension engendered by protracted confinement and enclosure within the peace of society, the *go back* to the innocent conscience of the best of prey . . . exhilarated and undisturbed . . .

This is the passage containing the infamous reference to "the splendid *blonde beast* prowling about avidly in search of spoil and victory" which has been correctly interpreted as comparing these noble types with qualities of the lion whose "hidden core needs to erupt from time to time, the animal has to get out again and go back to the wilderness."

The Superiority of Cats

Nietzsche may have held that after two thousand years of "slave morality" this mastery is unattainable by human beings, but that should not stop you from appreciating such nobility and something of this beast of prey in your cat. Among her equals and among those she has allowed into her life, she is refined and delicate, considerate and loyal, at ease with her propensity for outbursts and wildness, for sudden bursts of seemingly undirected activity, for excess expenditures of resources that can be recovered with a short nap, for a general exuberance that signs your cat's personal style. Among strangers she does not trust, among those who do not know how to handle her, those who are intimidated or put off by her unpredictability, she can be unfriendly and fierce. There's no real evidence that Nietzsche actually had cats in mind while writing this passage or any of the passages cited above, but there is an uncanny affinity between the qualities we appreciate in cats and the exuberant forms of human life that Nietzsche recommends for mere humans.

When your cat loves you, when he accepts you as his equal, he expects love in return: he anticipates your pattern of care for him, and he expects you to anticipate his needs. Much of this is organized around his feeding routines, covering not just a regular schedule of feeding times but also the offering of special meals on what are for you special occasions. It can also include some "rough trade," a risky variation on your cat's exuberance in which you provoke and endure your cat clawing and biting you knowing he will stop short of the kind of harm he could do if you were not a friend. In effect, you know your cat loves you when you can tell he accepts that you are up to the task of caring for him. Perhaps he shows this by butting his head against your arm or by rubbing up against your leg with his tail at attention or by curling up alongside you while you sleep, but this is no selfless love you get from your cat. Your cat loves you for himself, because you have made it possible for him to become the cat he is.

So, as you live with your cat, and care for her, and love her, there's also something you can learn from her about the meaning of living in a world with no set purpose, no obvious plan, adapting creatively to new situations, trusting the intelligence of instinct and the body, putting knowledge in the service of life (and not life in the service of knowledge), living every moment as if it were the only moment, discharging your strength without concern for your reserves, indulging your nobility, your truth, the strength of your soul, and loving completely out of a deep love for yourself.

If this draws an odd picture of philosophy, perhaps the reason is that philosophers have remained skeptical about the value of Nietzsche or, perhaps the reason is, trusting Nietzsche, we have labored for so long under one definition of the word. If Western philosophy has mastered the love of wisdom, what has it to tell us about the wisdom of love? Luce Irigaray notes that we call theology a discourse about God and metrology a science of measure but have never considered philosophy a wisdom of love. She does not doubt that the love of wisdom aptly captures the affection of philosophers from the earliest times, nor that philosophers have given considerable attention to the subject of love (she cites Plato's *Symposium*). She asks, nonetheless, what philosophy might become if, reversing the norm, it put wisdom in the service of love.[14]

Perhaps this is one more thing your cat can teach you about philosophy. In the company of our cats, are we not all students in the wisdom of love?

---

[14] Luce Irigaray, *The Way of Love* (New York: Continuum, 2002), pp. 1–12.

3
The Friendship of Felines

DIANE JESKE

I was once asked whether I would be willing to sell my cat for one million dollars. Without hesitation I replied that no amount of money could induce me to part with my cat. Since then, I have asked quite a few people—colleagues, students, friends, family— the same question, and have observed that responses tend to divide between those, like mine, of horror at the very thought of accepting the money and those of disbelief that *anyone* would refuse such an offer if it really came down to it.

Very different attitudes toward our relationships to our feline companions underlie these two types of responses. There are those who have affection for their cats, but who, nonetheless, regard their bond with their cat as something essentially replaceable, in the way that one could replace one's TV or car. And there are those who have affection for their cats and who view that affection as part of a unique bond to *this* cat as opposed to other cats (or other humans or dogs) and thus as irreplaceable.

The second attitude is the type of attitude that we take toward our bonds with our friends who are human persons. No one would find it surprising if I said that I would be unwilling to accept one million dollars in return for the sacrifice of my closest human friendship. In fact, if someone *were* willing to make such a trade, we would find ourselves questioning the extent to which a friendship ever really existed.

Someone I know decided to give his cat away, because he was trying to sell his house and his real estate agent told him that he could get a better price if the house were shown as being devoid of pets. How would we judge someone who was willing to give up a human friend in order to make a few thousand dollars? I think that most people would find such an action to be a morally heinous betrayal revealing a deep confusion about values. We expect people to be willing to make sacrifices for their friends, not to be willing to make a quick buck in trade for a friendship.

Admittedly, I have many relationships that generate obligations of care on my part (not to mention my more general moral obligations). In some situations, these obligations will conflict: suppose, for example, that I need one million dollars in order to provide my brother with life-saving medical treatment. I might then be prepared to sell my cat, or cut off all communication with a friend, for a million dollar payment. All the same, friendship, whether human or feline, places strong demands of care upon us, including a demand that we not treat or regard our friends as fungible in quite the way that cars and jewelry are fungible.

Cats May Be Our Friends

There are those who might say that we ought to be willing to trade away our bonds with our cats for gains that would not induce us to trade away our human friends. The people who think like this might insist that we're not friends with our cats, because the nature of cats precludes friendship.

But I say that at least some of us are friends with our feline companions and that this friendship has value for many of the same reasons that friendships with humans have value. This doesn't mean that any given friendship with a cat is as valuable as any given friendship with a human. But, then again, some human friendships are less valuable than others, and there may be some feline friendships that are more valuable than some human friendships.

I'm assuming that cats are not automata, as Descartes thought of them. Descartes claimed that non-human animals such as cats are complicated mechanisms created by God. Cats, according to Descartes, no more have mental states such as pain, pleasure, desire, or belief than do alarm clocks or thermostats. Descartes was willing to grant that the behavior of many non-human animals makes it natural to attribute mental states to them. But for Descartes, mental states require an immortal soul that will be sent either to heaven or to hell upon the death of the physical body. In order to avoid being committed to regarding cats, cows, and pigs, as moral agents deserving of eternal reward or punishment, Descartes strove to defend an alternative explanation of the behavior of animals.

I'm not going to answer Descartes's arguments here—some of the other chapters in this book do that. I'm going to take it for granted that we have enough behavioral evidence to be justified in attributing at least some mental states to cats—at the very least, they experience pleasure, pain, desires, as well as likes and dislikes—and that we have no counterbalancing evidence strong enough to undermine the theory that animals do have mental states. I'm not assuming anything about the level of complexity of cats' mental lives: for example, I leave open whether cats have second-order mental states, such as awareness of their pleasures or pains, desires that they keep, eliminate, or develop, first-order desires such as the desire to claw expensive furniture, and so on. If cats have any of these more complex mental states, then so much the better for my arguments in this chapter.

Seven Conditions of Friendship

Before we can answer the question whether we can be friends with our cat companions, we need to spell out what's involved in a friendship relation between two persons.

'Person' is a generic term that leaves open the biological species of the being in question. So Klingons, elves, and God, if they exist, are all persons, though none are members of the human species. Our conception of friendship is built on an understanding of human-human friendships, but movies and novels suggest that we are willing to extend our conception to include relationships involving non-human beings. Frodo and Sam in *The Lord of the Rings* trilogy are hobbits, not humans, but they are very clearly friends, as are Pooh and Piglet, who are clearly not human whatever they are. All of these creatures are modeled on humans, and so it remains an open question whether our cat companions can be our friends.

Aristotle held that genuine friendship requires that the parties to it be of virtuous character. My own view of friendship rejects this aspect of Aristotle's account, because I think that less than morally perfect persons can be friends. Only by rejecting that assumption of Aristotle's can we open the way for friendship with felines, given that cats are not moral agents, and so cannot achieve virtuous characters.

So let's try to pin down the idea of friendship.

Friendship Condition #1

First, it seems that if two persons—call them Lucy and Ethel—are friends with one another, they must have some sort of positive attitude toward one another that could appropriately be described as liking each other, loving each other, being fond of each other, having affection for one another, or caring about one another.

This seems obvious, and in fact, this first feature of friendship may be a necessary condition of any relationship's qualifying as a friendship. It comes very close to a contradiction, if it isn't one, to say that Lucy and Ethel are friends but they hate one another and don't care one whit about one another. Also, it's important that the type of positive attitude that Lucy and Ethel have toward one another is of a certain type: mere respect, admiration, or amusement, for example, are not of the right sort on their own (although their presence is perfectly compatible with friendship as long as affection or love is also present).

Friendship Condition #2

Second, the attitudes of concern, love, or affection present in the relationship must be *mutual* attitudes: the attitudes must be reciprocated, and Lucy and Ethel must be aware, or, at least, be in a position to become aware of, this mutuality in attitude.

Friendships are two-way relationships. Suppose someone avidly reads the tabloids, following every detail of Angelina Jolie's life. This fan may come to care deeply about Angie, feeling sad if Angie and Brad break up, taking joy in Angie's adopting a new child, and so forth. But if Angelina Jolie knows nothing about this fan, or knows about this fan only to the extent of wanting to take out a restraining order against her, then Angelina and the fan are not friends.

In saying that the attitudes of the parties to the friendship must be mutual, I'm not claiming that they must have precisely the same attitudes toward one another. Lucy may love Ethel more than Ethel loves Lucy, or maybe Ethel is merely fond of Lucy while Lucy's feelings for Ethel are much deeper and more intense. Some relationships (particularly those of a romantic nature) cannot withstand

significant disparities in strength of concern, affection, or love, but others can. Friendship requires mutuality in attitudes of liking or love, but not necessarily of the same sort or to the same degree.

I've said that Lucy and Ethel, in order to be friends, must each be aware of the other's attitude. If two people love one another from afar without ever knowing that the other reciprocates her feelings, we would not describe these two people as friends. However, it's true that some people are insecure, and, as a result, feel unsure about whether others care about them. I don't want to rule out friendships involving insecure people, so I have said that the parties to the relationship must be in a position to become aware of the other's attitude. If Lucy were to examine her evidence regarding Ethel's attitude to her without the filter of her insecurity, she would have a justified belief that Ethel cares about her. Insecurities are compatible with friendship, although if such insecurities become pathological, they can do great damage to relationships.

Friendship Condition #3

Lucy and Ethel must have a concern for one another that exceeds their concern for any person simply as a person.

Imagine hearing that some woman in Darfur died as a result of displacement resulting from civil war in that country. You might feel sad, angry, helpless, and outraged. But now imagine that you hear that a close friend who was working in Darfur has died. All of your feelings, of sadness or of anger, will be intensified. Further, those feelings will have a different cast or tone to them: the death of your friend constitutes a loss to you in a way that the death of the unknown woman does not. This personal loss that you suffer is not just a matter of losing benefits for yourself—I am not pointing to a loss that is to be understood purely selfishly. Rather, when your friend dies, it is the loss of this particular person that distresses you, not just the loss of human life as such.

Our ordinary practice of describing friends as close to one another captures quite well the point that I am trying to make. When I say that I am now close to my computer, in spatial terms, I am implying that most other objects are at a greater distance from me than is my computer. Similarly, people are emotionally close to one another only if it is true that most other persons are at a greater emotional distance. So friends have a *special* concern for one another.

Friendship Condition #4

Lucy and Ethel must desire to share time with one another.

Friends standardly enjoy one another's company and so desire to be with another. But we need to be careful here, because caring about someone can take many different forms. We do not always desire to share as much time with some of our friends as we do with others. However, we do desire to be 'in touch with' all of our friends in some way; further, we want more than just news about them—we also want to see or to speak with them directly. At the very least, we must want to see or speak with our friends at least occasionally. The existence of a friendship is surely called into doubt if Lucy and Ethel are always avoiding one another, and we can find no explanation for this avoidance other than an aversion for one another's company.

Friendship Condition #5

Lucy and Ethel must have actually spent some time in one another's company, or have causally interacted in some other relevantly similar manner.

What is being ruled out here as a friendship is a relationship entirely mediated by third parties. Most actual friends have been in one another's physical presence, but that is not necessary for friendship. We can imagine that Lucy and Ethel have been pen pals for years: surely they are friends before they ever meet or even if they never do meet. What is important is the interaction between Lucy and Ethel. A friendship is a relationship, and two people must have some kind of unmediated contact with one another in order to have a relationship.

Friendship Condition #6

Lucy and Ethel must share a history with one another that exhibits or evidences concern.

Even if Lucy and Ethel have interacted directly with one another, that interaction will not suffice for friendship if the inter-action has never been of a caring or loving sort. If Lucy reflects on her past with Ethel and that reflection reveals that Ethel has never demonstrated any concern for Lucy, Lucy will rightly begin to question whether Ethel is really her friend. Even if Ethel protests that she really does care about Lucy but that she has never done anything to show that concern, Lucy will be correct to charge Ethel with failing to be a friend. Friendship is more than mutual attitudes: friendship involves acting on mutual attitudes of concern.

Certain kinds of circumstances make it difficult for friends to show their concern for one another. Perhaps Ethel has been very sick or preoccupied with severe financial difficulties. In such cases, Ethel may not be able to show her concern for Lucy in ways that she wants to be able to. Deficiencies in one feature of friendship can be offset by others or by the nature of circumstances. Nonetheless, it costs little and takes little energy to convey our love to our friends: a kind word, a shared private joke, demonstrated interest in on-going projects can all carry a message of concern without great expenditure of effort. Evidencing our concern for another need not involve grand gestures: a pat on the back often means much more than any expensive gift.

Friendship Condition #7

Finally, Lucy and Ethel must have, or be making an effort to acquire, a certain level of knowledge about one another, a level that goes considerably beyond what a stranger or mere acquaintance would have.

We know our friends in ways that we do not know other persons. A friendship can be called into question when it is revealed that Lucy, for example, has not paid sufficient attention to acquire certain kinds of knowledge about Ethel or if Lucy and Ethel have never revealed various important features of themselves to one another. This doesn't mean that friends must tell one another everything, from their childhood dreams to their sexual fantasies.

How this knowledge is acquired is important. If two people read each other's autobiography, they may know a great deal about one another. Friends acquire knowledge of one another through interactions with one another. So the knowledge must be the result of some kind of direct contact with the other person.

Friendship with Cats?

Our paradigms of friendship involve two human persons. But nothing in the seven conditions that I have discussed in the previous section seems to require that the parties to the relationship be human. After all, if there were Klingons as depicted in *Star Trek*, there is no reason to suppose that humans could not form friendships with Klingons.

Religious persons often speak of being friends with God. Whether or not this is possible depends not only on the existence of God but also on the nature of the relationship between God and one of his human creatures. Friendship with God certainly does not seem to be ruled out merely because God, if he were to exist, would not be human.

Can humans form friendships, then, with felines?

Cats and Prize Possessions

The first three conditions of friendship described in the previous section involve concern: friends must have mutual positive attitudes of concern for one another, and those attitudes of concern must be greater than those that they have for any other person considered merely as a person. So if my cat Pi and I are friends, then she and I have mutual attitudes of special concern for one another.

I do care about my cat; after all, I wouldn't trade her away even for a million dollars. Someone might suggest that this does not demonstrate that I have the right sort of attitude of concern for my cat, because people often have prized possessions that they would not trade away for any amount of money. If my attitude toward my cat is like that toward one of my prized antique botanical prints or my by now ancient Winnie-the-Pooh stuffed bear, then it is not the right type of concern for friendship.

I don't think, however, that most of us who have feline companions view them as we view our favorite works of art or childhood teddy bears. My concern for my cat is a concern for her well-being that extends beyond her relationship with me. I want my cat to be happy and healthy, and if I became convinced that staying with me would undermine her health and happiness, I would relinquish her into the care of a trusted friend. I have enlisted a friend to be my cat's guardian if anything were to happen to me, and this enlisting of a guardian is a very different kind of act than that of leaving my antique prints to someone in my will. I want my cat to be well-off and not to suffer, while what I want is my own possession of my prints and my teddy bear. Thus, my concern for Pi is like my concern for my human friend Tracy: I care that both Pi and Tracy do well and avoid suffering, and I care about those ends independently of how their welfare or suffering affects my own selfish ends.

Someone might insist that I do, in fact, want more than just my own possession of my prints and my teddy bear. After all, I do prefer that if something were to happen to me, that my prized possessions be given to someone who will take care of them and treasure them in the way that I do. I value my antique prints, and want them to remain undamaged even after my own death. So it seems that I care about my prints beyond their relationship to me and role in my life. How, then, does my concern for Pi differ from my concern for my first-edition Redoute lily?

It differs in the same way that my concern for Tracy differs from my concern for my first-edition print: I regard Tracy as having an inner life of her own, of having concerns, interests, likes and dislikes. She is more than just the *object* of interest and concern, she herself is a *subject* of interests and concerns. Unlike the print, Pi is both the object of my concern, and a being with concerns of her own. Once I acknowledge this, my concern for her will inevitably be a concern about the quality of her inner life, just as my concern for Tracy involves a concern for the quality of her inner life. I need to take account of Pi's own perspective in my attempts to promote her well-being, whereas a print or a teddy-bear has no perspective on the world: this is why respect for a cat is a different sort of attitude than is respect for a work of art. My concern for Pi, then, is like my concern for my human friends, in a way that my concern for my prized, inanimate possessions is not.

Further, my concern for Pi exceeds the concern that I have for any other cat or human considered merely as a cat or a human. Whenever I hear about the number of cats languishing in shelters in need of homes, I feel distress. But my distress would be of a different order entirely if Pi were to become lost and I feared that she had ended up back in a shelter such as the one from which I rescued her. Similarly, I am upset whenever I hear about someone dying a premature death. But, again, if Pi, who is about five years old, were to die such a premature death, my grief and sense of loss would be of a different magnitude and type altogether.

Some people are appalled by the kinds of attachment that some of us develop toward our feline companions, complaining that the amount of attention and resources that we devote toward our cats would be better spent on charitable endeavors geared toward aiding needy humans. Such persons might very well find my great grief at the loss of Pi to be morally repugnant. Yet most of us also devote a disproportionate amount of attention and resources to our human friends and family, to the detriment of other humans who are far needier but unknown to us. I'm only pointing out that I have certain attitudes toward my cat companion that you and I also have toward our human friends. Such attitudes are typical of friendship, and I'm not making any moral claim about the appropriateness of these attitudes in *either* case.

I love Pi in a way that is different than the way that I care about just any other cat or any other human. This, I believe, is true for many people who have cat companions, as is evidenced by their grief at their cat's death and their inability to think that they can simply waltz down to the shelter and get a replacement. Eventually, a new cat companion can be loved and cherished, but no cat will take the place of the one who has been lost, any more than a new spouse can take the place of one who has died.

Some people recommend getting a new pet as a way of assuaging the grief experienced upon the death of a beloved animal companion. It's true that love for a new pet can help one overcome grief, although the efficacy of such a strategy varies greatly from person to person. But even for those who take such a course of action, getting a new pet will not be the same as getting a new couch. Upon getting a new couch, the old one will be forgotten in so far as it has been replaced. But a new cat companion is not a replacement. The new cat can shift one's focus to a new object of love, but love and appreciation for one's old cat remains—one only hopes to ease the pain of loss.

How Cats Feel about Humans

Does Pi care about me? And, if she does care about me, does she care about me in the right sort of way? Many will regard this as the obstacle to feline friendship. It will be said by opponents of feline friendship that our cats do not care about us in the right sort of way: our cat companions care about us, the objection goes, not for our own sakes, but only instrumentally. According to this view, Pi cares about me only as a means to the satisfaction of various desires that she has: her desire for a warm lap to sleep on, her desire for food on a regular basis, or her desire for play. In the crudest terms, then, Pi is using me to get various things that she wants that do not intrinsically involve me in any way.

One response to this objection is to point out that Pi does not seem satisfied with just any warm lap or provider of regular food and play. When I go out of town for several days, Pi gets access to my mother's warm lap, and my mother fills my role of food-provider and litter box-cleaner. Pi is certainly willing to take advantage of my mother's warm lap and yummy, satisfying kibbles, but she seems to remain less happy than if she were on my warm lap and eating the kibbles that I put in her bowl. So it seems that Pi misses me, even though her desires for food and other amenities are being satisfied.

The objector might insist that without my presence, one of Pi's most fundamental desires is not being satisfied, namely her desire for security and stability. Especially for former shelter cats, trust in the reliability and kindness of one's human companion is achieved only over time. So Pi's sense of safety is threatened whenever I leave our shared territory for longer than usual, and thus, her missing of me does not demonstrate that she views me other than as a means to getting her desires satisfied.

We could go on like this forever, disputing about the correct interpretation of Pi's behavior. But, given the behavioral evidence, which is similar to the behavioral evidence that we have for the claim that our human friends care about us, why should we give credence to alternative explanations of Pi's behavior? Given Pi's apparently contented meows when being cradled in my arms, her gentle stroking of my face as we drift off to sleep, and the relaxed swaying of her tail as she lies on my outstretched legs, we need some reason to back away from the obvious and simple explanation of her behavior as expressing a liking of me, not just a liking of what I provide to her in respect to the satisfaction of her desires.

But some people will insist that there's something about Pi that undermines the behavioral evidence, an aspect that isn't present in the case of our human friends: my cat is unable to care about me for my own sake, because she does not have the mental capacity to understand that I am a being with a welfare of my own, who can do well or suffer. If so, Pi simply does not have the capacity to care about me for my own sake, because she does not have the concept of me as a separate being with my own inner mental life, a concept that I have every reason to suppose that Tracy, my human friend, has.

Love or Cupboard Love?

There's something plausible about this objection, in so far as it's true that it is a significant cognitive accomplishment to have a concept of another person as a person like oneself with independent feelings, hopes, thoughts, and desires. Human children don't seem to develop such concepts for at least several years: they need to be taught that others feel the same way that they do when they are hit, they need to be taught that their parents have needs and desires and are not merely there to serve them, and that they themselves are not somehow unique in the nature of their mental lives. Psychopaths such as Ted Bundy seem never to develop a robust understanding of other people as distinct centers of experiences, which seems to be part of the explanation of why such people are unable to form intimate ties or to value others except instrumentally. So can we suppose that adult cats have an understanding of their human companions as beings with an independent good?

The evidence we have for thinking that our cats care about us for our own sake is precisely the same kind of evidence that we have for thinking that our human friends care about us for our own sake: the way that they treat us. The behavioral evidence is limited in the case of cats, given that they are unable to explicitly say 'I care about you'. But even in the case of human friends, these words aren't always spoken; however, actions often say much more than the mere words ever could. Pi often engages in behavior with respect to me the simplest explanation of which is that she is expressing her affection for me: when I stroke her, she will pull herself closer to me so that she can stroke or knead my cheek; when I'm reading in bed, she will come and lie on my chest and nuzzle her head against my chin or neck; when I come home in the evening, she comes running to greet me with a welcoming meow even when she still has food in her bowl. Further, these are behaviors that she saves for her interactions with me.

Are these just her cunning ways of trying to ensure that I continue to meet her selfish needs and desires? I don't think so. When I first brought Pi home from the shelter, I fed her and provided her with a warm, safe home, but it took a couple of years before she showed me affection in the ways that I have described. I think that she has developed affection for me through her interactions with me. And if she has the mental capacity to be so shrewd to behave as she does in order to manipulate me, then surely she has the mental capacity to care about me for my own sake: the former as well as the latter capacity involve an understanding of me as a being with an inner life independent of her own. We can never be certain how another being feels about us, be that creature human or feline. Still, I think that we have evidence that our cat companions do have the requisite attitudes toward us to qualify as our friends. We might be wrong about this, but then again, we might be wrong with respect to our supposed human friends as well.

At this point, I think that it is important to address the charge that many will make against me: interpreting feline behavior in the same way that we interpret human behavior is just egregious anthropomorphism. However, we need to remember that anthropomorphism involves an *inappropriate* or *unwarranted* attribution of human qualities to some entity or being. The question at issue here is whether or not such attribution in the case of cats is in fact appropriate or warranted. In order to answer that question, we need to consider cat behavior in its entirety and carefully compare it to human behavior. I have been arguing that cat behavior exhibits so many similarities to human behavior that we would need strong counterbalancing considerations (such as Descartes believed that he had) to deny that cats care about us for our own sakes. Such considerations might be like those that we have to deny that our appliances *intend* to make us miserable: we know how those appliances were constructed and can explain their often frustrating 'behavior' in terms of malfunction due to human fallibility. Knee-jerk charges of anthropomorphism assume that certain kinds of mental qualities are peculiarly human rather than constituting an argument against feline mental and emotional capacity.[1]

How Cats and Humans Interact

Friendship Conditions #4, #5, and #6 all concern the nature of the interaction between the friends. Friends have spent some time in one another's company, desire to continue spending time in one another's company, and have, during their time together, shown affection and concern for one another.

---

[1] Marc Bekoff, a respected animal behaviorist, effectively argues that certain kinds of supposed anthropomorphism can open up new and profitable areas of scientific study. See his *Minding Animals: Awareness, Emotions, and Heart* (Oxford University Press, 2002), especially Chapter 2.

Having established the presence of mutual attitudes of special concern between humans and their feline companions through an appeal to behavioral evidence, we have thereby established that cats evidence concern for their humans. Because humans live with their feline companions, they have spent quite a bit of time interacting with one another: Pi greets me at the door when I arrive home, she sits on my lap or stretches out across my legs, we play together with her flying feathers, strings, and stuffed mice, and she sleeps every night on her pillow which is right next to mine. I have every reason to believe that Pi desires to spend time with me just as I desire to spend time with her: as I said, she runs to greet me, she seems depressed when I am away on a trip, she follows me from room to room, apparently eager to be in my presence. Moreover, I love spending time with Pi—her presence makes me feel content, the sound of her purr soothes me, her warm weight on my lap is comforting and companionable, and her presence in the middle of the night helps me shake any bad dreams. I have learned to interpret her meows—her hunger meow, her scolding meow after I've been out late, her chatty, shooting the breeze meow, etc.—and find joy and comfort in her company. A gentle head butt or face rubbing can make all of the stresses of the world disappear. I have every reason to believe that Pi returns my love of her companionship.

Friends Know Each Other

Condition #7 requires that friends must either have or be making an effort to have a kind of knowledge about one another that goes beyond the knowledge that a mere stranger or acquaintance would have. Do cats and their human companions have this kind of knowledge of one another?

At one level, it seems obvious that they do. Cats and their humans spend a great deal of time together, sharing a home territory as they do. Yet is their knowledge of one another anything beyond simply knowing the habitual movements of the other? For example, Pi tends to go under the bed as I am getting dressed in the morning. Under the bed is her safe spot (she spent hours there when I first brought her home from the shelter), so she retreats there when she observes the signs of my getting ready to leave the territory for the day. Similarly, early in the morning, I know to look for Pi on the back of the comfy chair in the living room, because it is a good observation point in regards to the early birds seeking the worm and the bunnies seeking tender grass shoots drenched in dew. However, the knowledge friends have of one another needs to go deeper than merely being able to predict each other's movements. After all, if a peeping tom kept his binoculars trained on me all day, he could make excellent predictions of my movements, probably better than any of my human friends could. So do humans and their cat companions have a deeper level of knowledge of one another, a deeper level achieved via their mutual interactions with one another?

What's crucial is that cats and their humans know not only one another's movements, but also, as the example of Pi going under the bed reveals, the meanings and causes of those movements. I understand *why* Pi retreats to the bed as I am getting dressed in the morning—I understand the anxiety that underlies her need for her safe spot. I understand why Pi does not like being carried to the door—she fears being abandoned outside our territory, as she must once have been abandoned before ending up in a shelter as a stray. Why does Pi meow outside closed bathroom or closet doors? Because she likes to be able to check on all parts of her territory, making sure all is safe and secure. Our shared history has allowed me access to Pi's emotional life, and so I can use my understanding of that emotional life to explain her behaviors. There are numerous stories of humans knowing that their cat companions are ill, even when a vet tells them otherwise. We become attuned not only to our cats' movements, but to the emotional shades or tones that color those movements, allowing us to see what others, even supposed experts, cannot see.

Do our cats have the same kind of access to the emotional life underlying our movements? I am inclined to think that they may in fact have better access to our emotional ups and downs than do many of our human companions. Denied use of human language, those animals that have adapted themselves to human companionship rely on a sensitivity to the slightest alterations in our body language and moods. Body language can often be more revealing than our words, because we do not have as much conscious awareness of how we are expressing ourselves bodily as opposed to verbally. Our cat companions, then, may be able to penetrate to the heart of our emotional lives in ways that our human companions cannot. This is speculation on my part, but it is speculation backed up by experience of Pi's seemingly uncanny ability to give me a head butt just when I need it most, to hold off demanding play when I am tired, and to snuggle close when I require a reminder that I am not alone.

It remains true that cats are limited in their understanding of us because they do not have the same types of linguistic ability that we have. So Pi will never be able to understand the nature of my profession, my relationships to other humans, or certain crucial features of my self-conception. I am unable to convey these aspects of my life to her, and she cannot infer them from my behavior and moods alone. Does this fact undermine my claim that we can be friends with our cat companions?

Human friendships also exhibit great diversity: it's unreasonable to demand that one friend meet all of our emotional and intellectual needs. A rational adult person has a web of relationships, and she appreciates each friend in that web for what he or she can provide in addition to caring about each friend for her own sake.

To focus on the limitations of our friends is to fail to place due significance on how much each enriches our lives in his or her own special way. Likewise we must not expect of our cats what they cannot give. However, that does not mean that we should devalue what they do provide to us: something that few humans ever do, an appreciation and love of us that is independent of our contingent worldly status. Our cat companions call forth our best qualities—generosity, warmth, sympathetic understanding, tolerance, whimsical playfulness, joy in the moment—and force us to try to understand ourselves apart from how others perceive us in terms of career, weight, wealth, or marital status.

Not only, then, can cats understand us in a way that other humans have a hard time doing, they can help bring us to that kind of understanding and appreciation of ourselves. If our cats are to be faulted for not knowing us as our human friends can, similarly, our human friends can be faulted for not knowing us as our cats do. Rather than finding fault with either, we should recognize that each enhances our lives in a special way, providing us with value and understanding that is unique to our relationship with that individual, be she human or feline.[2]

---

[2] I thank David Cunning and Steven Hales for very helpful comments on earlier drafts of this paper, and Richard Fumerton for years of helpful discussions that have helped me to formulate and develop my views on the nature of friendship. Special thanks are owed to my mother, Barbara Franke, who urged me to open my heart to cats, and to Pi, who teaches me every day the value and reality of feline friendship.

II

Feline Aesthetics and Ethics

4

The Good, the Bad, and the Beautiful

RANDALL E. AUXIER

Picture if you will, the famous Mexican Stand-off in the Sad Hill Cemetery in Sergio Leone's *The Good, The Bad, and the Ugly*. But now, instead of Blondie, Tuco, and Angel Eyes, you've got a dog person, a cat person, and a horse person. Who draws first, and who is left standing? We'll get to the bottom of it before all is said and done. But it's good to remember that the stand-off occurs in the film not because the three antagonists don't *like* each other. That is irrelevant. They don't *trust* each other, and that is the problem.

Horse People

Cats are the choice of thinking people. Over dogs, I mean. Horse people are another story altogether. Something primal is going on there that I will never quite grasp. When I first saw *Equus*, I had a hard time following it, the idea being so far beyond my teenage imagination. And then I read about Catherine the Great, and then I got to know some horse people, and, well, I really don't get it. But I still have to say a few words about horse people.

As far as I can see, horse people are all about *eros*. This is about sex. I think that's fine, and I'm sure that horse people have the very best sex of *all* people. Horses are very big. They run really fast, and that's what they *like* to do. You can draw the analogies. I don't envy horse people, except for a vague feeling that I might be missing something—the thing they all seem to know that evades the rest of us. That's why I don't trust them. They know something I don't know, and are perfectly alright with the idea of being kicked in the head once in a while, and with suffering horrible injuries and even death just to go nowhere in particular *faster.* The world needs them, but they aren't my friends.

Dog People

I get dogs and dog people. They are people of action, and that's a good thing. The world needs people like that. Dog people aren't always dull-witted, but they aren't thinkers. Cat people probably understand dog people better than dog people understand themselves, just as cats understand dogs better than dogs understand themselves. This arrangement is fine with dog people and with dogs.

I mean, how much does anyone really *need* to know? Life isn't about knowing things; it's about doing things, from their point of view. And it's easy to see the attraction of an animal that adores everything you do and everything you are, whose sense of self depends entirely upon your next act. I have to think that dog people want to be admired almost as much as they want to go play Frisbee, which is apparently quite a lot. If I want to be admired for no good reason, I'll certainly get a dog. They are virtuous beasts, and their owners are usually dutiful people. But I don't trust them. There is a slight hint of the totalitarian mindset in them. They can be our friends, but don't go into business with one—unless you are also a dog person, in which case, I don't know why you are reading this book (gathering intelligence on the loyal opposition?).

Cat People

Cats don't admire us and they don't really need us. Oddly, they like us (after all, we constantly do their bidding, so maybe it isn't terribly odd). But cats are what they are with or without us, which is part of what we like about them. They choose us, for reasons of their own. Like many of you, I have spent decades trying to descry the feline and grasp the choice. Because they choose me, they are my life companions. I like people well enough to live with one of them—another cat person of course—but our four and a half cats currently outnumber us (the half cat is a Tom we've been feeding outside for several years, but he won't let us too close to him; many of you can relate).

I trust cat people, and I get them. Cats are more reliable than cat people, but neither is very reliable. Cat people will make promises they cannot keep, but at least it's predictable, so we cat people forgive each other. Dog and horse people cannot understand this, and they never forget, and they don't trust us.

I've figured some things out, I think. And some of those things are philosophical. I will present them in vignettes, but there is an overall point in this. I want to know why cats are the choice of thinking people, and I have some suggestions that are not, I hope, simply partisan generalizations proffered by a cat person. I aim to say things that even dog people would have to concede. Horse people aren't reading this, so we will never know what they think. They have other things to do with their horses and with each other.

Feline Phenomenology

A little over a century ago, some German and Austrian philosophers described a method of doing philosophy called "phenomenology." It's a fancy word for a fairly simple activity. Most of the time, when you are thinking, you are thinking *about* something, some object of your thought, say, breakfast, or a nap. Now, if you pause for a moment and consider not breakfast itself, but *how* you're thinking about it, you become aware that you can think about breakfast in a lot of different ways. You can remember past breakfasts, or you can be estimating whether you have time to cook this morning, or you can be rearranging the anticipated parts of the meal while sifting the contents of the refrigerator and cabinets in your memory. There's no limit to the variations in *how* you can think about breakfast, and yet, it's all still breakfast.

When you consider the variations themselves, and how you feel and think differently depending on how breakfast is "given" to your thinking, well, you are doing a phenomenology of breakfast. To give one example, thinking about breakfast feels very different when you're really hungry compared to when you aren't. Phenomenologists love to discover patterns in these differences and describe the general features of the patterns in long, boring treatises. I will explain more about phenomenology as I go, but I am putting you on notice that there is a method to the madness in what follows, and the madness flows from wondering *how* cats experience their world(s), meanwhile the method licenses us to pretend we actually understand what we're talking about when we offer answers.

To Will One Thing

I chose breakfast for a reason. The ways in which cats consider breakfast is astonishingly unified, by which I mean that the variations among them are not great. Cats never approach breakfast with studied indifference. It is the one time of day when they can be counted on to lose their natural detachment. With effort, a cat can be nonchalant about almost anything—a mouse scurrying across the floor, even a mid-day bowl of tuna juice (I have seen this with my own eyes)—but when it comes to breakfast, there is a noticeable unanimity of engaged concern. So I started thinking, because that's what I do, what is breakfast to a cat? How is it experienced?

Some (dog people) may say "well, their hungry, and that is controling them" (dog people can't spell and have poor grammar). That isn't right. Cats behave this way about breakfast even when they intend to take only a bite or two and wander away. This isn't about over-weaning hunger. It's something else. It has the power to unify cat consciousness into a single aim, just one possible course of action to the exclusion of all others. Breakfast takes a cat whole, possesses it, drives it into an anticipated future that simply cannot fail to come about. Breakfast is like an object of religious fervor and devotion for a cat.

In the morning, cats are like the little band of true believers waiting on a remote hillside for the Second Coming of Christ, and for them, you get to be Christ. If you wait too long, you'll be the Devil, but simply arrive within the appointed hour (actually, you have about fifteen minutes) and you're the Savior. It's not that the cats are hungry (they may be, but it isn't relevant), it is that cats are better at worship than their humans are, more faithful, more ardent believers. The ritual is simple, but it is of infinite significance. The act of feeding or being fed is sacred—the connection between the feline believer and the higher power, which they experience with a fervor that would shame any dog-loving Pentecostal.

Humans (even horse people) have nothing in their experience to compare with this perfect bliss. As I have contemplated what in my own life might approach a cat's level of unified consciousness in the presence of the breakfast communion, I can only imagine what beatific vision might be like—but I am not so pure in heart as to have seen God, and not so other-worldly as to wish to. The Danish philosopher Søren Kierkegaard (1813–1855) taught, following the Apostle James, that purity of heart is to "will one thing."[1] This is to say, that if a human being could ever succeed in drawing all of his or her disparate desires to be focused only upon one end, one idea, one object, that would be "to will the Good" in the purity of heart—to see God. I don't think Kierkegaard was likely to have been a cat person; if he had been, he would have realized that his thinking implies that, from a certain point of view, breakfast is God.

I do not believe cats have pure hearts, nor do cat people, but I do think that cats believe in the miracle of breakfast. Cat people believe in the believers in the miracle of breakfast. It's the best we can manage, in terms of faith. I have had cats who believed in other miracles as well—for example, I have one cat who believes that the flushing of the toilet is so impossible an occurrence that it has to be witnessed several times a day, at close quarters. There is an occasional immersion, so I take this cat to be a Baptist of some sort. But whatever denominations cats may fall into, they all believe in breakfast, and because their little hearts are so mixed (or impure) most of the time, the advent of breakfast is quite special. Dogs have religious experiences many times a day, and their hearts are pure most of the time. Unifying the will of a dog into one and only one future is so easy that it isn't even fun. The joy of a dog is saintly, which is to say, uninteresting at a distance and annoying close by. It is much more interesting to consider the pure thoughts of an inveterate sinner than those of a saint. I admit, it is still more interesting to contemplate the impure thoughts of a saint, but that is another story—one for dog people.

Kierkegaard thought that life can be divided into three stages: an aesthetic stage, an ethical stage, and a religious stage. A person's development has to move through these three before the heart can ever be pure, but it is easy to get stuck at one of the earlier stages. Most people do get stuck, and *no one* was religious enough to suit Kierkegaard, *including* Kierkegaard. Instead of growing spiritually, when we get stuck, we might instead commence refinements of the stage we're at, either the aesthetic or the (merely) ethical. So, for example, some people live their whole lives as though the edification of the senses, and the continual refinement of the pleasures they crave, can appropriately consume a whole life.

---

[1] See Kierkegaard, *Purity of Heart Is to Will One Thing* (New York: Harper and Row, 1938). The scriptural passage is the Epistle of James, 4:8.

This does not necessarily mean that such people are debauched addicts of some sort, as Kierkegaard thought—everything was a stark either/or for him. But he wasn't quite right, because people who remain in the aesthetic stage may spend their energies perfecting, for example, their palates for the tasting of the subtlest differences in wines or chocolates, without becoming alcoholics or gluttons. They may accumulate books and read for edification rather than for, say, moral instruction. They may acquire three or four cats without needing twenty or thirty. Yes, I think you see where this is going.

Kierkegaard was, by anyone *else's* standards, a religious guy. So he didn't think it was a good thing to get yourself trapped in the aesthetic stage of life. But cat people might take issue. It's true that we aren't driven by ethical concerns, as dog people are, but we admire the *beauty* of morality, which is something even dog people can appreciate from a safe ethical distance. And cat people *want* to be good, just not at the expense of pleasures, especially refined pleasures. We can point to the horse people and say "well, now those are hedonists, addicts, at least we aren't like *them* . . ." Cat people do something similar with the religious side of life, which is to say, they are prone to aestheticize it. A good liturgy, a well-formed sermon, rhetorically perfect, a Bach chorale sung with exquisite precision, and some nice stained glass windows—these make for a properly fulfilling worship experience. Kierkegaard would be horrified.

And yet, our cats teach something about the purity of heart that cat people can learn in no other way. We cat people never "will one thing," we will *many* things, all of them pleasing, and refined, and long-lasting. But with spiritual matters, we like paradoxes and puzzles, questions and doubts, and go to our various meditations and prayers with manifold sins and perhaps just a little wickedness, not knowing quite how or what to confess (they are such minor infractions in the grand scheme of things) and not feeling any special need of forgiveness. We leave the deep feelings of moral inadequacy before God to the dog people, who approach their God as if He were a scolding Master with a newspaper for their noses.

But our feline companions? They have pure hearts, precisely once per day, and we minister to their desires as bearers of the only kind of grace we can receive ourselves—the undeserved dispensation from above, the unmerited, unearned sort, but desired with as much ardor as we can gather. Our cats show us how to gather it, how to skip straight past the ethical stage of development and into, if not the Goodness of God, then the beauty of the Goodness of God, if He shows up on time. If God expects more from us than this, He should have withheld the wine, the chocolate, the books, and the cats when He was thinking up ways to compensate us for the sufferings of mortal life. If I must choose between a pure heart and my cats, I choose the cats. But surely God is at least as merciful as I am, in the morning when nothing matters except breakfast—or at death, which is when I plan to worry about salvation (and not before). If God strikes me dead for saying this, then I hope he will also feed me breakfast as I go (and punish the horse people for my spiritual education).

The Kitty Sublime

Returning to feline phenomenology, if we have understood that breakfast is the reward of the pure heart, and an aesthetic reward at that, a kitty communion bearing the mystery of Being behind the veil of the flesh, the further question arises: how do cats experience *us*? Roger Karas, the great cat-commentator, among others, has suggested that part of the reason we are able to co-habit with cats so easily is that our social instincts and theirs are *accidentally* compatible (so much for Providence). That is, cats are not so much domesticated and brought into our social order, as they are able to interpret *our* social order as being some version of *their own*. In short, cats experience us and interact with us as if we were simply larger cats. There is something to be said for this suggestion. I took it seriously and began interacting with my own companions in ways I recognized from their social behaviors—growling to assert dominance, butting heads as a greeting, stuff like that (no one has made a video of me doing this, I hope), and I find confirmation of Karas's idea. My cats seem to think I am a bigger cat.

But this looks inconsistent with the results of the last section, in which I was allowed to be a god. Perhaps it isn't, though. From an aesthetic point of view, one thing that makes God god-like is, well, God is very *big*. Philosophers use the word "sublime" to describe an aesthetic experience of something so big that we can't quite take it all in, such as when we look at the Grand Canyon, or the stars, or a great mountain, or yes, perhaps when we consider God.

The German philosopher Immanuel Kant (1724–1804) pointed out that when we experience something as beautiful, we consider its *form* (never mind what he means by that: trust me, it's a long boring story), but the experience of something as sublime, while also pleasing to us, is *formless*, because it is too big for our senses to take in a form. So, for example, where we might experience a Bach chorale as *beautiful*, because we can grasp the form, we will have to settle for an experience of the *sublime* in listening to Gustav Mahler's 8th Symphony, the so-called "Symphony of a Thousand," which premiered in 1910 with 850 singers and 171 instrumental musicians, and which strains the limits of musical form and tonality—you just can't quite take it all in (and that was Mahler's aim). Perhaps the stars and the Grand Canyon and Mahler's symphony and God do *have* form, but not adjusted to human sensory limits.

This brings me back to cats. Cats have fine senses, but their sensory limits are different from ours. For example, a moving automobile makes fair sense to us, and we can adjudge not only its speed and color, but also whether it is or is not a "nice" car, perhaps even a beautiful car (if it happens to be the sort from the early 1960s with big tail-fins). But to a cat, a moving automobile is simply incomprehensible. It moves too fast, makes too much noise, and is too large to be considered as anything except something to be avoided (and sadly, our kitties often fail to avoid them). Except for the small yip-yip dogs (which are not *really* dogs, and their owners are not *really* dog people; these are inferior cats with slightly perverse owners—I mean if you want a dog, get a *dog*, if you want a cat, get a *cat*, and if you can't make up your mind, let someone more stable choose for you . . . I don't know *what* a chi-hua-hua is, but it's closer to a rat than a dog), dogs are just big enough and just fast enough to be able to consider a car as an *object*, but a Greyhound bus is a little beyond them.

Now, Kant also says that whereas the judgment that something is "beautiful" comes from a *restful* state of mind and a consideration of its form, saying something is "sublime" involves the *movement* of a restless mind in trying to take in the formlessness of something, well, big enough to be awe-inspiring.

So think about this. Human beings are about ten times taller and weigh about ten times more than their cats. We are pretty big. When I imagine what it would be like to share intimate space with something *that* much bigger than I am, I imagine having, say, a Clydesdale draft-horse in my living room, and with a living room that was scaled to their proportions rather than mine. And here I am, this tiny thing, in the midst of all that clopping and neighing. Horse people *like* this sort of thing, which is why they spend so much time in barns. But it horrifies cat people.

I can't help believing that if I were a cat, I would be eager to seek places and surroundings a little more suited to my own size and the limits of my senses. Here is where cats teach their people something more than just how to worship God in the purity of heart. Domestic cats are not only *not* afraid of their people, they fearlessly wind around our legs as we walk, and they even look upon us as potential sources of amusement. I cannot easily imagine finding the courage to wind around the legs of a Clydesdale while it walks, or hopping between the horse and its food to see if I might want some. Even horse people know better than to try that. Whence this astonishing boldness among the cats?

Two Sublimities: With a Trip to the Grand Canyon

Let us back up for a moment and consider their experience again. Cats and dogs, and even horses, *experience* the sublime—for example, they all seem to agree that thunder is too big to deal with. But *their* sublime is not quite like *our* experience of it. The sublime pleases human beings, while it frightens our mammalian counterparts. But it doesn't please us all in just the same ways.

Kant says that humans experience the sublime in two different ways, one that inspires thinking and one that stirs our emotions. He calls the thinking type the "mathematical" sublime, because the paradigm case of it is what we experience in trying to consider things like an object with infinitely many sides, or a thousand planes, or the highest number. Such contemplations *are* aesthetic experiences, but they are not sensory experiences, they are *thoughts*, sublime thoughts. The other sort of sublimity he calls "dynamical," and it moves our innards more than it moves our thinking. This dynamical sublime is, for instance, what it feels like to see the Grand Canyon—which makes one physically dizzy. The expressions of emotion heard from astronauts as they first beheld the earth from space would be another keen example. (Cat people do not become astronauts; at most they calculate the trajectories, but more likely, read about it in a history book from the comfort of the living room. Dog people command the missions and horse people go out to do the space-walks.)

Cat people don't much care for the dynamical sublime, and they don't go to any great lengths to find experiences of it. Horse people, on the other hand, *love* it. Dog people remain fairly sober in the face of it—they're the ones most likely to be looking at the individual geological features of the Grand Canyon while everyone else is attempting to take in the whole of it. The horse people are wandering out to the rim to look down, the dog people are warning the horse people that the rocks may be loose, and the cat people are simply cringing and cowering at a more-than-safe distance— quite content to *think* about the idea of the Canyon rather than experience it first-hand, and to wonder when it will be time for breakfast.

Ah, but here we come to a point worth considering. When faced with a choice of sublimities, cat people will take the mathematical approach even to a dynamical opportunity. It's enough to *know* that one *might* experience such a thing as the Grand Canyon. That such a Canyon *exists* somewhere is interesting to think about. We like to be *told* about such wonders, by horse people and dog people who have taken the trouble to go. Conversations, stories, ideas, yes, these will do nicely. But not hikes down steep ledges on the backs of burros, no, not that—well, maybe just a little hike, once in a while, in a cozy wood with a well-worn trail, and not too many people, and no horses or motorcycles.

And cat people feel the same way about God. They don't want to *see* God, but are content to *think* about possible Gods that *might* exist and *might* be merciful, and might be seen by saints (we have never met a saint, and we aren't sure we even want to meet Kierkegaard, let alone someone *he* thought was adequately religious). Instead, cat people will settle in their minds on a satisfactory *idea* of God, something mathematically sublime, and defer their actual experience of said deity until it cannot be evaded any longer—which, most of them realize, may be *forever* (another mathematically sublime idea). If experience of God comes, it should definitely be mystical and affirming, and over as quickly as possible so that we can *think* about it while it is still fresh.

Cat people are in charge of the mathematical sublime, for the human race. This is not to say that they are in charge of *thinking*— all human beings do that, and horse people and dog people can be very, very good at it. What I mean to say is that cat people are in charge of the *aesthetics* of thinking, having sublime thoughts for their own sake. They have the same curiosity as their cats, which is to say, of a sort not terribly well-organized or purpose-driven. When experiences start to become actual, and big, cat people pass and stay home, to make sure *some*one is thinking all the thoughts: yet, they also serve who only sit and think. There are plenty of horse people and dog people to take care of thinking the practical thoughts, and running the government, and flying the airplanes, and whatever else needs doing.

Cats at the Threshold

It's impossible not to have noticed that cats pause at the threshold, between indoors and out-of-doors, especially. It takes them a moment to undergo the transition, to gird themselves up for the larger world outside or the smaller one inside. Sometimes they pause for maddeningly long stretches: "Hmmm, shall I go in, or stay out? I just don't know . . . on the one paw, there is food in there, but on the other paw, there are birds out here . . . hmmm." This is a third aesthetic experience, although Kant and Kierkegaard don't talk about it. It is "liminal," which comes from "limen," the Latin word for threshold or boundary. It's part of the word "sub-liminal," and "sublimation," as well as "sublime."

Cats are mistresses of the liminal, the borderland between the beautiful and the sublime; this region of experience is populated with things that have *some* form and *some* formlessness. This power of the threshold among cats comes from cultivating the parts of experience that are *almost* too big to handle, but not quite—like humans, but not moving automobiles—along with the parts that are *almost* too small to be significant, but not quite—like a cricket, but not an ant. The secret of feline detachment, and their forms of engagement with life, derives from their power of noticing and interacting with the liminal aspects of it. And so it is with their people, even if the scale is different. The *idea* of a horse is fascinating to a cat person. The horse itself is just too big, but the idea of such a beast, well, it is not something we cat people would have con-jured up, but it's not bad to imagine. That idea is on the edges. Horses. What a concept! Great big beautiful beasts you could ride at amazing speeds. What an experience that would be, for someone *else*. . . .

Dogs and their people are uninteresting precisely because there is nothing liminal about them. They both exist in a middle-sized world filled with middle-sized objects and middle-sized ideas. Dog people don't do metaphysics or mysticism, and they are content with Budweiser, Hershey's chocolate, and the television shows selected for them by Fox or CBS; by analogy, their dogs are content with rolling in putrified dead things, and searching the cat box for treats, followed by licking their masters' faces in a most undignified display of affection. A dog person's idea of a big aesthetic decision is whether to put the gun cabinet in the den or the living room. If they start imagining anything bigger, they become fundamentalists and neo-conservatives and the like. And that only happens when no one rubs their bellies. It is a good idea to rub the belly of your favorite dog person. You should create some middle-sized problem for him to solve and watch him fetch the solution like a nice middle-sized stick. Keep them all busy with that sort of thing and they will leave everyone else alone.

Horse people are downright scary. They want the dynamical sublime, way past the threshold, not just the idea of it. I hate to admit it, I mean I *hate* this, but horse people make the best leaders—dog people are more trustworthy on the whole, but they will not take your institution or business into new and daring frontiers. Dog people make good bureaucrats (and the world needs dutiful bureaucrats), but poor chief executives and presidents. No vision, little imagination, need too much belly-rubbing. Horse people, by contrast, may wreck your life, your health, and your business by trying foolish things, but they won't sit still and accept the status quo, and they will not busy themselves in pointless re-organizations of the staff—like cat people will. Don't put a cat person in charge of other people. We weren't made for that. The wise horse person will keep a cat person at the withers, to get liminal ideas and possibilities, and a dog person at the flanks, to get done what few of those ideas are actually worth pursuing into middle-sized forms. And the horse person will give the cat person liminal problems, being careful not to upset her with the prospect of *actual* things that are too big, while giving the dog person well-formed instructions, in full recognition that he is a problem solver and capable of great loyalty, service, and devotion.

It almost makes me cry to give first rank to horse people. They scare me. I don't understand them. They do things I wouldn't do –couldn't do. And why don't they ever give *me* a shot at carrying out a task? I mean, surely if a mere dog person can do it, *I* can. How much can there be *to it*? But I guess, when I think about it, I don't even always answer when my name is called, and then I pretend I didn't hear it when forced to answer. Not unlike my cats. Perhaps it would be unwise to trust me with something that requires a kind of loyalty I cannot find inside myself. Take it from an honest expert at sifting the liminal options, you horse people and dog people, you don't want to be in a fox-hole with me. I may have the courage it takes to think sublime thoughts, but my reality definitely should not include enemy soldiers charging my position.

And in this light, aren't horses and dogs, for all their insensitivities to the very finest things, astonishing in their bravery and fortitude? They can send horses and dogs into battle, you know, with full expectation of service to the death. Try *that* with a cat. Try it with a cat person. I think the wise general on horseback knows well enough that the cat people will do better at breaking enemy codes. But cat people are not cowards, I'm not suggesting that. It takes a kind of courage that both horse and dog people lack to, well, tolerate and work creatively with *profound* ambiguity. This is the threshold, the liminal part of life.

Cat people have tremendous, nay *infinite*, patience with ambiguity—both emotional and intellectual. That ability, and the kind of courage (and aesthetic understanding) that goes with it, astonishes dog and horse people. And it's on this account that they don't trust us. How can any beast stand on the threshold for five minutes, neither inside nor out? "Get on with it," the dog and horse people say. But the cat person pauses with the cat: "On the one paw, there is this . . . on the other paw, well, I guess I actually have *four* paws, come to think of it; well, I don't know, is a human *foot* really a *paw*? And if so, do cats sort of have *hands*? What about elbows? Do cats have elbows? And a waist, where is a cat's waist? . . . ."

High Noon in the Sad Hill Cemetery

I have promised, and I think, *delivered* an answer to the question why cats are the choice of "thinking" people. Faced with a choice between the dynamical and mathematical sublime, cat people will press everything in the direction of thinking, and then live at the liminal edges available there. There is both virtue and vice in it, both courage and cowardice. But these failings are mainly aesthetic preferences, not really moral principles. In Plato's *Republic*, Socrates says that in order to understand justice fully, we also have to understand injustice. I think Socrates is right. We have looked at some of the virtues of cats, dogs, and horses, and the aesthetic

virtues and failings of their people. But what happens when cat
and dog and horse people go *bad?* I don't mean aesthetically ugly,
I mean morally *bad.*

When cat people go bad, it's just as bad as when dog or horse
people turn vicious. When they are good, they are as good as the
best people. Cat people make fine advisers, faithful companions,
even fine teachers of, if not the purity of heart and the seeing of
God, at least the *ideas* associated with these matters. And when any
situation requires a high tolerance of ambiguity, well, the dog needs
to ride the horse to the nearest cat house. But what of badness?

I also promised a solution to the Mexican Stand-off, didn't I?
You know, cat people don't always keep their promises. But I suppose I will, *this* time. The first thing to bear in mind is that all three
of our principal characters in that film are *bad,* very, very bad. And
they are all devilishly smart, and utterly ruthless, and quite fearless
in their own ways. But even among the very, very bad there are
important differences.

I haven't studied the facts of the matter (that would be boring),
but I think Sergio Leone was, almost certainly, a cat person. In the
famous stand-off, Tuco's gun wasn't even *loaded* and Blondie
knew it wasn't, since he took the bullets the night before. Some
would say that this is cheating the audience of the "real" Mexican
Stand-off.

The people protesting are dog people, I assure you, and they
should go watch Tarantino movies instead; there's plenty for them
there. The cat people, on the other paw, just love this contrived
Sergio Leone stuff. The horse people simply could not sit through
five minutes of theme music waiting for someone to draw a gun,
no matter how great the music is. But the cat people could wait
longer than anyone, like a cat outside the mouse-hole. The waiting
is liminal. It's the perfect joining of the beautiful and the sublime.
There *might* be a mouse—we certainly aren't waiting for enemy
soldiers here. Maybe no mouse, ah, but the *idea* of the mouse, now
that is enough to hold us in the moment, indefinitely. Leone gets
this. The dog people are complaining, bitterly, that they were
cheated; sure, but he gives them a bone. You'll see.

If you watch the stand-off in the film closely, you will see in Eli
Wallach's eyes—what a beautiful performance he gave—that Tuco
knows he has no business *whatsoever* in this god-forsaken stand-
off, and no desire whatsoever to do anything but run. This stand-
off is not liminal, this is the real thing. Tuco is a cat person. Not a

very nice one, but a cat person. He cannot prevail in such a confrontation, and he would do well not to try, as he knows very well.

He faces two others. After having so flattered the horse people above, I must now report, and they will have to accept, that Angel Eyes, Lee Van Cleef's character, is a horse person who has gone very, very bad. We could spend many pages on how horse people go bad, but suffice to say that there is no possibility of reprieve or repentance when it happens. When a horse person goes bad, the kindest thing to do is, well, shoot him—unlike dog people, who will sometimes beg forgiveness holding nothing back, and cat people who will at least grudgingly admit a mistake, if they *must*. But cat people are very bad at admitting mistakes, and moral failings they will admit least of all—they invent all sorts of aesthetic excuses, some quite convincing. Horse people not only don't admit mistakes, they don't even *believe* in them. You'll get no justifications from a horse person, especially a very, very bad one. And Angel Eyes has crossed the line, has no conscience, no fear, and no limits. He is off the map.

Blondie, Clint Eastwood, knows very well who *is* dangerous and who *is not*, standing in that cemetery. Perhaps he took Tuco's bullets so that he wouldn't have to kill Tuco later (since saving Tuco's life is actually what Blondie does for a living in this story). And Blondie is counting on Angel Eyes to make the mistake of thinking Tuco is just as dangerous and unpredictable as any of them is.

You may now be thinking Blondie is the dog person, and I think that is right, although you may be vaguely remembering a scene in which he spits on a dog rather than petting it –something *no* dog person would *ever* do, nor ever *forgive*. Even to imagine it is the work of a liminal imagination—but that was a different movie. The dog people win the stand-off, precisely because they live in a middle-sized world; they are restrained, indulging neither their imaginations nor their desires, neither fears nor hopes, and nothing liminal. The situation just is what it *is*, and nothing else. The horse person draws first and is certain he is faster. But he is wrong, if for no other reason than because Blondie already knows who he does and doesn't have to shoot. You may not believe me about all this now, but you will in a moment.

In the scene just before the stand-off, Tuco is running through the Sad Hill Cemetery, looking for the grave of one "Arch Stanton," where Tuco believes there is buried gold. The cemetery is round and has thousands of graves; as Tuco runs the scene swirls into a dizzying sublimity—where is the grave, where is the gold?

Sergio Leone did not tell Eli Wallach what he intended to do, but as the scene began, Leone released a *dog*, yes a *dog*, into the cemetery, so that when Wallach saw the dog, he would be *genuinely* surprised. The cinematographer, Tonino Delli Colli was instructed to capture the liminal moment when Tuco sees the dog. Wallach's whole body seizes up for just a moment, and, professional that he is, he stays in character. Only a cat person would have imagined such a foreshadowing of the impending stand-off.[2]

Blondie is a dog person; no matter how smart you are, he can best you if you get too far away from the practical world yourself, failing, for example, to make sure your gun has bullets. And, yes, dogs are smarter than cats as surely as Blondie is smarter than Tuco. And so Blondie will win the stand-off *because* he is a dog person, and Tuco will be surprised when he shouldn't have been. The cat just never takes the dog's intelligence seriously enough. It's a fatal weakness in both cats and their people. The one appearance made by a cat in the film is when Blondie is sitting in a war-scarred town and hears a gunshot across the way. He is petting a *kitten*, yes, a *kitten* (a very cute one), and this is completely gratuitous and out of place unless Leone means it as a symbol. As Blondie sets the kitten down, he tells his momentary companions that he has recognized the sound of Tuco's gun. Tuco is the kitten. It takes a pretty keen ear to discern individual gun sounds—something well beyond the abilities of cats or horses, and cat people and horse people would never attach significance to learning such a thing.

The final proof comes when Angel Eyes is (mercifully) dead from the stand-off, and Tuco has, at gunpoint, dug all the gold from the right grave. Blondie has fashioned a noose for Tuco in the meantime, and orders him to climb atop a rickety cross, put the noose around his own neck (this is payback for something similar Tuco did earlier in the story). If Tuco slips, it will cause his (well-deserved) hanging—at which point, being a cat person, it will finally occur to him to worry about salvation. And then—now pay close attention—*Blondie leaves half the gold for Tuco.* That has always been their arrangement, to split things fifty-fifty. And it's atonement for Blondie's having taken all the money and left Tuco

---

[2] The second shot of the entire movie (shot, not scene), is a dog sauntering across a dusty, deserted street. Talk about foreshadowing . . .

in the desert earlier. Then, as the film ends, Blondie shows Tuco a kind of loyalty that Tuco hasn't earned by shooting the rope from a distance and freeing Tuco from his predicament. As Blondie rides away, the last line is Tuco screaming after Blondie that he is . . . what? Do you remember? Tuco screams that Blondie is a son of a bitch. The movie ends as it begins, with a dog.

There's your bone, you dog people, so stop bitching. You win, okay? I know that's very important to you. And Tuco, instead of being grateful to Blondie for the reprieve, screams hateful canine epithets. If there's one thing dog people can't abide, it's ingratitude. Recall my saying that you cat people shouldn't go into business with a dog person? Well, dog people won't cheat you, but don't be surprised when they leave you with your half of the business because you were ungrateful and whiny just one time too many.

Now, a dog might rescue a cat, or a horse, but it would be the rare horse or cat that would rescue a dog—or another cat or horse for that matter. Dogs and dog people just dig beneath the ambiguities and find reasons to be loyal and good that the rest of us can't even smell. I still don't trust them, but I guess I should. But what can I say? It's not in my nature.

5

Cats and the Aesthetics of the Everyday

ALLISON HAGERMAN

We must begin at the beginning, and that is with the appreciation of cats themselves. My own living environment is deeply cat-saturated. Five felines currently reside with me and graciously provide me with ample doses of their presence. They vary in age, color, and temperament, and have established a symphonic order of relations among themselves (no boring stable hierarchical pecking order here). None were "picked" because of the way they looked—they all just needed homes.

At any given moment, I can walk into the two rooms in which the cats spend most of their time and witness varying arrangements of their napping bodies gracefully strewn about. In times of peace, I'll find three in a row on the vermilion-ish sofa, which has a special fray on the corners that you can only get just so from the surreptitious and naughty tugs of little cat claws. Sometimes they'll dazzle me with a white-cat-black-cat-white-cat arrangement, evenly dividing the sofa into thirds. Other times they get into more of an avante-garde mode, re-contextualizing the living room with asymmetrical huddles. Lily (a white cat) and Fig (a black cat) will occasionally sit simultaneously on opposing squares on the black and white checkered tile in the kitchen. They seem to know what backgrounds flatter them and the time of day or moonlit evening to establish their profile in a window.

If one is not initially drawn by aesthetic interest to pay attention to the kinetic aspect of cats, only a short time of living with them will facilitate a wide variety of reasons to attend. This could be interest in the name of preserving fragile items carelessly left in their way (yes, a vase in an out-of-the-way-for-humans corner of a table might be very, very much in the way of a cat) or just the kind of interest that results from having a cat jump onto your shoulders from behind as you eat your morning cereal over the kitchen sink. At any rate, whatever originally motivates your observation of cats in motion, eventually an aesthetic appreciation is bound to take hold.

Watching them run, tumble, stretch, slink, bat, flirt, wriggle and burrow . . . all create opportunities for the aesthetic appreciation of the feline form. It would be speciesist (that is, it would unreasonably privilege one's own species) to assume that aesthetic appreciation of living creatures should be restricted to the human form. As dance creates the opportunity to appreciate the beauty of the human body, watching cats at play can facilitate the aesthetic appreciation of the feline body. Cats are exemplars of balance, strength, and creativity in choosing the paths of space through which to move and hollows of the third dimension in which to sleep.

Cats at rest are as much a joy to behold as cats at play. I have often caught myself in the midst of savoring the exquisite flatness of a cat as she lies on a cool brick floor at high noon on a hot summer day. As a result of my compulsive internet book-buying habit, there's an ample number of empty little cardboard boxes lying around the house at any given time. In trying to completely fill all four corners of one of these boxes with his body, Fig, in his folded feline impression of the golden rectangle, brings new life to an old concept. Dharma, long-haired and zaftig, both embodies and challenges the presuppositions entailed in all kinds of Rubenesque poses as she drowsily plunges and twists deeper into the loveseat.

Beyond Sight

So far, I've been describing eye-centered aspects of the aesthetic appreciation of cats. But a description of aesthetic engagement with feline creatures would be incomplete without acknowledging that we also hear, touch, and yes, smell cats.

Cat lovers are well aware that the word "meow" is an insufficient imitation of the sound a cat makes. Cats actually make a variety of sounds, and not just with their vocal cords. Cecil is master of the silent meow, Lily has an insistent wail that comes on to announce the approach of the dinner hour, Dharma does a lot of trilling from the depths of her throat, Fama is the queen bee of chirping and chattering at birds in the window, and Fig, born to a feral mother, calls like a pterodactyl when he's lonely. Then there's the sound of tiny nails skidding across the linoleum, the rhythmic rasping of cat claws in the scratching post (hopefully), and the random thump of things going bump in the night.

The sense of touch is also a component of aesthetic appreciation, though rarely discussed. Cats, and especially kittens, seem to be an irresistible source of pleasurable tactile sensation. Barring the allergic and phobic, most people will not turn down the opportunity to cuddle a kitten. The experience of feeling the warmth and softness of another living being is perhaps the most direct instance of aesthetic pleasure feeding into emotional comfort. There is a reason that therapies involving patient interaction with animals is on the rise.

The sense of smell is one that cat lovers tend to be sensitive about in describing their appreciation of cats. Unfortunately, in our hyper-hygenic, hypoallergenic historical moment, the smell of cats has a negative connotation. For the most part, the litter box is to blame, and in defense of cats, I will testify as a philosopher that this constitutes more of an adherent smell, and is not technically a *cat* smell. It's a litter box smell. Cats *themselves* rarely smell like the things they leave in litter boxes or sometimes spray on walls. Rather, they have a warm, dusty, and sometimes sweet baby-like smell along their cheeks and shoulder blades. And because cat fur is such a rich purveyor of the smells of a cat's environment, a lot can depend on whether or not there is fresh laundry or new grass in which the cat can indulge in a bit of rolling.

Works of Art and Living Beings

We can appreciate a work of art only when it's complete. But living beings, such as cats, are never complete, so appreciating them is very different.

The act of interpreting a work of art can be described as open-ended because interpretation can evolve and shift from historical moment to moment. The work of art itself, however, must in some sense be contained before it can be properly analyzed. We generally wait until the artist is finished with a work before we offer serious critical analysis, and we apply such analysis to works as a *whole*—that is to say, we finish the book before offering a critique, and would be puzzled by anyone who wished to offer criticism on a painting of which they'd only had a partial glimpse. We may *enjoy* the work of art as a process as it's unfolding (as we read a poem or listen to a symphony), but aesthetic engagement and aesthetic judgment are not interchangeable terms. Judgment and analysis are reserved until the work has been in some way framed off so that we can experience it as a whole.

When the object of aesthetic focus is a living being, however, we appreciate the embodiment of a life in progress, inherently incomplete and open-ended. A living being is constantly changing, has moods of its own, and has a certain point of view that is independent of appreciator interpretation. A cat returns—and even challenges—your gaze in a way even the best painting cannot. We must conclude that aesthetic appreciation of cats requires a special kind of fortitude and grace beyond what the ordinary art critic possesses. It's not for the timid.

Aesthetic discourse in the European and Anglo-American philosophical traditions tended in the twentieth century, for some of the reasons I mentioned above, to be focused on the appreciation of art—it's somewhat of a challenge to find much on the aesthetic appreciation of cats. Perhaps this absence is, indeed, due more to the categories into which these traditions parse experience rather than the insensitive demeanor of those who have had ample opportunity to write on the topic but have chosen not to do so.

But let's be fair—cats do have a tendency to refuse to be confined by categories, and we could conjecture that a practitioner or two of traditional aesthetics may very well have put some effort into trying to analyze the aesthetic qualities of the feline being, only to have the object of study constantly move beyond the frame. Cats are not works of art, they are cats, and even if we wish to flatter them by figuratively speaking of them as works of art, it does us no good when it comes down to meaningfully appreciating them. The tools of art appreciation are simply inadequate to the task.

I do think that the cat fancier culture might be making an attempt at applying the traditional method of formal aesthetic analysis to cats via breeding and showing. This activity seems to take on the same rationalist presuppositions which privilege judgment and analysis in academic aesthetic discourse: a cat's body is judged to the degree it instantiates a predetermined ideal or standard, rather than for its uniqueness.

Contrary to what the art-centric aesthetic discourse of the twentieth century would lead us to believe, and as those who dwell with cats know perfectly well, aesthetic engagement is not and should not be restricted to the art world. Folks who live with cats are especially hip to the fact that we can engage in aesthetic appreciation of our lived-in environments—our work-places, our homes, urban jungles, sub-urban jungles, non-urban jungles.

Those of us who spend time aesthetically appreciating the feline being have an inclination to be more attentive to the aesthetic aspects of our everyday lives. That is, living with cats facilitates the cultivation of the moral virtue of aesthetic attentiveness beyond the art world.

The turn towards aesthetic attentiveness to the everyday is part of the growing discourse in environmental aesthetics (in which philosophers examine our aesthetic appreciation of environments rather than art works) in the twenty-first century. But generally, this discourse utilizes the language of object appreciation and mainly focuses on the appreciation of non-sentient components of our environment. The focus is on how we appreciate and aesthetically engage things *without* a point of view. These things may be artifacts like buildings, dishes, the smell of apple pie, the drone of the highway. Or, they might be non-artifacts like trees, bird-song, weeds in the sidewalk, the smell of rain. Rarely within this literature do you find mention of the aesthetic appreciation of *animals* in our environments.

In his *Critique of Judgment*, the great eighteenth-century German philosopher Immanuel Kant talks about beautiful horses and beautiful faces to the degree that they approximate a certain formal standard. But that kind of talk forces us to aesthetically analyze a mentally freeze-framed image of the animal in question, and is not so helpful when it comes to engaging a three-dimensional being in motion and with the ability to change its expression, posture, and overall disposition. Besides, it doesn't account for smell or touch, some of the most interesting ways of aesthetically appreciating our fellow beasts.

Before we can discover what philosophy can tell us about cats we have to acknowledge that cats can tell us something about philosophy. Being around cats can reveal certain lacunas in philosophical discourse as well as enriching and informing it. We philosophers who dwell with cats *do* have to engage in a bit of translating, but check out any number of biographies of philosophers (they're really hot reading) and consider the quality of these philosophers' work. You'll find that the best philosophers lived with cats. In what follows, I'll demonstrate how sensibility informed by the feline presence can enrich both aesthetic awareness and the philosophical discourse about it.

In a Cat's Eye

The aesthetic appreciation of cats expands our aesthetic responsiveness beyond the narrower scope of works of art to the wider context of lived-in environments. Obviously our aesthetic responsiveness is extended beyond the narrower scope of attentiveness to works of art the moment we find ourselves experiencing *cats* aesthetically. And once we've picked up that habit, another habit tends to accompany or follow close behind: that of being more aesthetically aware of our surroundings in general.

I'm not trying to be too outrageous—I'm not claiming that the aesthetic appreciation of cats is necessary or sufficient for aesthetic appreciation of environments. I'm just trying to make the case that aesthetic appreciation of the feline being can *facilitate* a wider theater of aesthetic appreciation in general, simply by moving us to pay closer aesthetic attention to beings and things other than art.

I realize that a possible objection to my opinion would involve reversing the claim as follows: people who engage in aesthetic appreciation of the features of their environments tend to also include cats in that appreciation. I like my claim better. I suppose in this case I prefer a bottom-up rather than a top-down approach.

That said, I now present a few examples that my own cats have generously provided. My attentiveness to these little beasts has enhanced my attentiveness to the elements that create and sustain the space in which we live.

I'll start with the most bizarre case. A few summers ago, my husband and I started waking up or coming home to find small ponds on our kitchen floor. Once we determined that the substance of the ponds was water, and not another likely suspect, we immediately conjectured that this was the result of what must've been a slow leak in the cats' water dish. So, we replaced the dish. The ponds kept forming, always in the absence of human presence.

I know that we're sophisticated enough now to know that human observation can affect the outcome of experiments, but it's a stretch to say that a leaky water dish would only leak in the absence of humans. So the leaky water dish hypothesis was ruled out.

We started watching the cats. Eventually we connected the unattended formation of the ponds in the kitchen with a certain cat who liked to visit the water dish when no one else was in the kitchen. We set up a sting.

Fig, it seems, had taken a liking to scooping paw-fuls of water from the water dish onto the floor. He'd go scoop-scoop-scoop-scoop-scoop in super-fast succession, and then gaze at the water as it pooled into the various dips and hollows in the rippled 1930s linoleum. To be honest, until the ponds started appearing, I had no idea the floor was so uneven—not tilted, per se, but dippy. That's an element of intrigue within the domestic you won't find in the high-gloss laminate floors of newer subdivisions. Fig made us take notice.

Not only did we take notice of the floor. By watching Fig's gaze, our gaze was directed to the movement of the water and the water itself. Fig continued to stare into the puddles long after the water had settled. While his initial thrill may have been tied to the movement of the water, in its stillness the water continued to arrest his attention. He would just gaze and gaze awhile before jauntily trotting off to the other room.

We were a little worried about Fig. Finally, my husband took the initiative to put himself in Fig's place shortly after the formation of one of the ponds. What he realized, from six or seven inches from the floor, was that Fig seemed to be creating little reflection pools right there in our kitchen. Thus, Fig reminded us of the reflective quality of water, an element we had seldom appreciated within our house before. I began to notice the reflections in cups of tea, between patches of bubbles over a sink of dishes, in the droplets splashed around after a bath . . .

Fama, our little starry-eyed tortie, illuminates the complexities of light and shadow. Not only is the coloration of her fur a mix of light and dark (not gray, as those who've never been graced by the presence of a tortie might guess, but a dappling of black and orange, or midnight and champagne, as we like to call it) but the way she likes to frame herself in windows has brought many a sun, moon, and streetlight beam to my attention. Occasionally she'll pace in the window, causing a strobe affect. She wears penumbras like no one else. And from close up, when she's in the midst of a direct ray of light, you can see an infinite array of tiny flakes of matter glowing like flint sparks suspended in her fur. Aesthetically and otherwise, she embodies the Taoist principle of yin-and-yang.

Finally, I'll relate another little game that Fig seems to have invented this past winter. The house in which we currently reside was built in the late 1920s, and for heat in the winter we rely on a dual system of an old woodstove and a floor furnace, which has one central vent in the living room. The vent is a three-by-four-foot rectangle covered with a metal grate. We all walk around it in the winter because when it's hot it can melt the bottoms of your shoes pretty quickly. The cats will occasionally lounge around its perimeter, and when it's cool enough, some will indulge in a quick back-scratch on it. This sometimes yields little tufts of floating fur, which drift upwards due to the warmer air currents in that location.

I think this is what inspired Fig to start batting dust-bunnies across the grate, on purpose, to watch them rise and spiral slowly to the tops of the bookcases around the room. There is no shortage of these dust-bunnies in our house, and Fig seems to have an endless supply of them. He bats one over the grate, then sits very still, watching the gray fluff ride the heat wave until it disappears over the bookcase or lands on our dusty, obsolete globe.

At first I was a bit dismayed by this performance. I took it to signify that the house needed some serious cleaning, which it usually does. But putting aside that utilitarian interpretation, I saw something more—namely, the oft forgotten element of *air*. Aesthetically, we are prone to hone in on the visible, bracketing off synesthetic experiences as too muddled to analyze. But in watching the dust-bunnies float there above the heater, the invisible air was made visible by proxy, and at that moment, I suddenly became more aware of the way it felt against my skin. I have Fig to thank for reawakening my aesthetic sensibility for the invisible.[1]

The Feline Mystique

The ethical implications of taste have long been examined under the rubric of the relationship between art appreciation and moral character. But the ethical implications of aesthetic attentiveness to things other than art, in everyday contexts, are currently the focus of quite a few philosophers working on problems in environmental aesthetics.

Some who hear about this development misunderstand the focus of the discourse and worry that it encourages a kind of

---

[1] See twentieth-century French philosopher Maurice Merleau-Ponty's *The Visible and the Invisible* for an intriguing, complex, and puzzling account of the invisible and how it shapes our world.

beauty-pageant mentality when it comes to making ethical decisions regarding how we inhabit and manipulate our environment—a superficial "the prettiest wins" type of thing.

I advocate no such position.

Such a view would presuppose that our aesthetic sensibility is governed by a system of superlative ideas, the basis of unrealizable ideals that have nothing to do with the objects we encounter. Rather than engaging with and appreciating the object at hand in its particularity, a beauty-pageant version of aesthetic sensibility would require that we impose an idealized set of formal standards on the object and call it beautiful to the degree that it measures up. This is an unfortunate way to go about things, as it tends to restrict the possibilities for opportunities and contexts in which to appreciate beauty.

Twentieth-century philosopher Martin Heidegger talks about what happens when we become slaves to (that is, when we are uncritical and even forgetful of the ways in which we engage in) paradigmatic thought in his 1935 lecture series *Introduction to Metaphysics*. He writes:

> Because the *idea* is what really is, and the idea is the prototype, all opening up of beings must be directed toward equaling the prototype, resembling the archetype, directing itself according to the idea. The truth of *phusis-aletheia* as the unconcealment that essentially unfolds in the emerging sway—now becomes *homoiosis* and *mimesis*: resemblance, directedness, the correctness of seeing, the correctness of apprehending as representing.[2]

Heidegger is critical of the kind of thinking that asserts that the "*idea* is what really is," and is not himself making that assertion. What he's describing is the stagnation of how we think about and apprehend the world when we seek in it only the confirmation of the ideal.

I've worked with several animal rescue groups as an adoption councilor, and have always been puzzled by the people who walk right up to my little table, without even glancing over at the cats in their kennels, and declare that they want an orange kitten. Or a long-haired tuxedo male. Or a cat to match the one they have at

---

[2] Martin Heidegger, *Introduction to Metaphysics* (New Haven: Yale University Press, 2000), p. 197/141.

home. They have some sort of predetermined idea of what the ideal cat looks like, and have foreclosed any possibility of seeing beauty in an individual that doesn't meet these criteria. It's depressing. This way of seeing reduces cats (and other animals, including humans) to decorative accessories whose worth is measured by how closely they conform to an abstract idea, and loses site of their worth as individual, embodied beings.

Most would regard this as a perfectly fine attitude when dealing with non-sentient artifacts, but there are those who would argue that the attitude I describe above is symptomatic of a consumer culture caught up in a drive to satiate desires which are dictated to them in the form of standards which will never be met, thus perpetuating the tyranny of capitalism. I won't get into the commodification of aesthetic sensibility here.[3] But I think it's safe to say that there are ranges of sincerity and shallowness in aesthetic appreciation. A person who buys a painting to match a couch is not appreciating the painting on the deepest level imaginable.

Cats are not works of art. They are living beings with a point of view, and to appreciate them only shallowly is more than unfortunate—it's morally inappropriate. It's morally inappropriate precisely because habitual shallow appreciation reduces the object of appreciation to a mere means to the appreciator's satisfaction. Shallow appreciation is really subject-centered, in that it's really all about how things in the world fulfill the desires and expectations of the subject. Regard for the world beyond the subject in such instances is only indirect and conditioned by the satisfaction of the subject. Reduction of the world to a mere means-to-the-ends of an individual, or even of an individual species, is certainly *not* a mark of virtue.

The ability to appreciate spontaneous and uncontrived moments of beauty attests to a special kind of receptivity and openness to the world. It rescues us from self-centered solipsism in that it requires us to be attentive and appreciative of the world outside us, beyond our control, existing independently of our needs or preferences. This *is* a mark of virtue, and dwelling with cats can help us cultivate it.

I'm not saying we can *use* cats to make us more virtuous. Use implies a means-ends reduction, which is precisely what I'm trying

---

[3] You can read more about it in Frederic Jameson's *Postmodernism, or The Cultural Logic of Late Capitalism.*

to avoid, and is precisely excluded in the type of appreciation that I'm claiming is virtuous. My view is that acknowledging and respecting the otherness of cats is crucial to morally appropriate aesthetic appreciation of cats, and that means at least two things.

The first is that cats can be seen as beings whose existence is an end-in-itself, who aren't reducible to objects at our disposal—those are qualities entailed by otherness, because part of what it means to be other is having the capacity to exceed the total grasp of the subject.

We are all others, in this sense of the word, to each other, and even to ourselves. The second is that my understanding of aesthetics is phenomenological. I believe that our aesthetic experience, our actual *sensory experience*, is influenced by our attitude towards the world. By no means is this a one-way process—rather, I think of it as more of a feedback loop—what we pick up through our senses and process aesthetically informs and influences our mood, stance, and receptivity. In turn, our mood, stance, and receptivity influence what we perceive. It's a cycle, and while we may not be completely in control of it, we can certainly make efforts to cultivate it.

Living with cats provides us with ample opportunity to appreciate spontaneous moments of beauty—both in the cats themselves and in the environment that they so richly bring to life. These moments are difficult to analyze due to their ephemeral and unrepeatable nature. But there's something to be said for learning to appreciate the fleeting rather than striving in vain to capture things and pin them down in some sort of state of permanence. Again, who better than a cat to remind you of the importance of such a virtue?

So what do I think philosophy can tell you about your cat? Well, I think it can reinforce the notion that you already have—your cat has something to teach you, and you'd be well advised to pay attention.

6

Can Human Health Care Learn from Cat Health Care?

ANDREW PAVELICH

My cat Yoeshi is alive and well, but one morning last year, it was not at all clear that he would be. I woke up that day to a sound that I had never heard before, which I've since dubbed the "kitty-in-distress signal". I knew the first time I heard the cry that it meant that my cat was dying—I suppose that it's not too hard to believe that that particular cry of pain and my response to it are hardwired into the mammalian brain.

My cat was on the floor, and he could barely breathe—the cry that woke me up seemed like almost his literal last gasp. Fortunately, my vet's office was close by and it was during her normal business hours; unfortunately, she didn't have the equipment for a full diagnosis, let alone emergency treatment, so I packed up Yoeshi and drove him to the animal hospital.

At the time I felt grateful to be in a city with such a hospital, but in retrospect, the very existence of the hospital raises some troubling questions about health care—concerns about the cat, but also about the larger picture of human health care.

Animal and Human Hospitals

What struck me most about the experience at the animal hospital was how unlike a visit to my normal veterinarian it was, and at the same time just how *like* being in a human hospital it was. This goes beyond the superficial similarities to human hospitals—the big sliding doors, the central receptionist desk, and the large, crowded waiting room full of nervous people and wounded patients.

The deeper similarities centered around two issues: the way that the hospital dealt with money, and the way that the doctors treated the patient and me. My cat was set up for treatment regardless of price (which is to say, it was expensive). In the consultation room, I was given an invoice for about two thousand dollars—which covered only the diagnosis, and not any treatment. I didn't have that kind of money on hand, let alone money for whatever treatment was to follow, all of which was very reminiscent of my own trips to the hospital that ended with a gigantic bill, and enormous relief that I did have health insurance. The other striking similarity to a human hospital was what happened next, when I tried to decide how to deal with the cat, the bill, and the doctors: there was limited interaction with the animal doctor. I decided, on my own, in a consultation room and without my cat, that I could not pay the bill, and if my cat was still in pain, it would be time to let him go. Fortunately, Yoeshi recovered that day, and it was not until the next day, when I returned to my normal vet, that I could talk about treatment in a more cat-friendly way. Now he's on a regimen of anti-asthma medication, and so far, there hasn't been another attack.

With the immediate crisis past, and after speaking to friends about their own cats' health-care issues, and about orchestrating health care for their human loved ones, it became more and more clear that there were issues centering around our cats that are worthy of philosophical scrutiny. These issues have to do with how we ought to care for our cats, to be sure, but more deeply, it seemed that there were questions about how we thought of our cats, and how these thoughts related to our thoughts about other people.

In retrospect, it's easy to see that the pet hospital was using a model of health care based on modern human hospitals, and I have come to believe that this is absolutely the wrong model for them to use. There is something about the normal veterinary experience that was simply missing from the animal hospital, such that the visit to the hospital felt almost entirely negative. I believe that this negativity did not come from the fact that at the time my cat seemed to be dying, but simply because the hospital was basing its health care on the human model, and this is really inadequate for the treatment of pets. This conclusion may be hard for some to accept, especially for those whose pets' lives have been saved at such hospitals, but I want to suggest something even more radical—that normal veterinary care might actually serve as a good model for rethinking human health care.

I don't want to argue that my cat is actually a person. Few of us would really want to make such a claim, although many of us treat our cats almost like our children, and that sometimes seems to be the simplest way to understand the relationship between pets and their humans. We call our cats our babies, send pictures of them to our relatives when they send us their baby pictures (babies are usually cute, but objectively speaking, they don't hold a cuteness candle to a kitten). There are, however, limits to the baby-fication of cats—limits that some cat owners don't seem to recognize, but which most of us do. Literally speaking, my cat is not actually my son. This is most apparent when dealing with the vet's office. My cat's name is not "Yoeshi Pavelich", as the vet insists on calling him; he is simply "Yoeshi". I understand that the vet needs to attach the cat to a person with a credit card, but I would be much happier if the record was kept as "Yoeshi, of Pavelich" or some such thing. The cat is a part of my family—but in a way that it is useful to distinguish from the other members of my family.

So why, if cats are not actually people, would the practice of cat health care matter to those who are thinking of human health care? I can imagine many people agreeing with my feeling that the animal hospital was somehow taking the wrong approach to pet health care, but I can see them saying this because they think that it gives pets too much credit—a common thought would no doubt be that they are only animals, and it is therefore absurd to treat them like people. Again, I do not want to deny that pets, including cats, are animals, but I think that there are still good reasons to look at cat care as it relates to human care—the first such reason has to do with the fact that we do seem to have real moral obligations to our pets, more so than we do to other animals. Even if the obligations are less than those that we have to our human loved ones, it is still a moral relationship, and because of this it is not absurd to think about putting human care and animal care on the same scale. The second reason to engage with this topic has to do with euthanasia: the way that we deal with the end-of-life care of people is deeply troubling, and the way we deal with the same crisis in pet care is much more adequate. Because our approach to the issue of pet euthanasia is unburdened by many of the hang-ups that we have about ending human life, how we approach cat health care may serve as a model for human health care.

Human Health Care: Sanctity of Life, Quality of Life

In issues of human health care, the notion of the sanctity of life dominates. It dominates in pretty much all aspects of health care, but it most notably dominates in end-of-life issues, at least in terms of the law. Although the law varies from state to state, it's generally very hard for a medical professional to end a human life, regardless of circumstances. Ethical positions which adhere to this sanctity of life stance, in the medical context, are generally opposed to positions which instead advocate the quality of life. One or the other is usually taken as sacrosanct: either health decisions should be made with an eye to keeping the patient alive at all costs, or decisions should be made such that the patient can always enjoy a happy life. Of course, in an ideal world, such decisions would never have to be made, but our medical technology is such that we can, in fact, keep people alive well past the point when they can enjoy life; some would argue that we can keep patients alive well past the point when they can even experience life—even the unpleasantness of it. In such a technological world, the choice between continuation of life and the quality of life sometimes must be made.

In general, the sanctity-of-life side of things gets a bad rap, even though, in the end, I agree with its detractors. In part, it gets a bad rap precisely because it leads to cases—like the famous Terri Schiavo case—that seem absurdly difficult for all involved, to the point where there are some people who are making life-and-death decisions while those closest to the case are excluded. That being said, there is at least one very good reason to accept the sanctity-of-life view: it is easier. This is not to diminish the importance of the idea. The very modern medical practices and technologies that bring us to cases like Terri Schiavo's are also new in that they often make treatment happen in a collapsed time-frame. Quick decisions often have to be made, and it makes those decisions easier—on the doctors, on insurance companies, and on the patients and their families—if there is a set of rules that everyone follows. In most cases, the rules are very simple: keep the patient alive. Usually this is done with an eye to re-evaluating the case later, but it's not that simple. A friend once told me that while connecting a loved one to a ventilation machine is an easy choice, disconnecting her later is hard.

That being said, the Terri Schiavo case was not actually a case of the competing claims of sanctity of life and quality of life, at least not as these are usually understood. The question was, technically speaking, whether Terri Schiavo was really alive at all. On the one hand was the ex-husband who claimed that she was brain dead—a state which, according to the American Medical Association, is identical to death. This is why the entire case seemed to revolve around issues of responsiveness—responsiveness is the same as brain-life, which is the same (according to the AMA) as life. Neither side in the debate over what to do with Terri Schiavo really focused on the question of the quality of her life—the debate was solely about whether she counted as alive. The question was not "What do we do with this brain dead corpse with a body kept function-ing by machinery?" but "Is she brain dead?" A third question was "What would she have wanted?", but this seems to be a very strange question to ask if we are talking about someone who is actually dead. One could argue that the dead have interests, for example, in having their bodies treated with respect, but their inter-ests seem very different from the interests of the living. Should what a person would have wanted while alive really trump all other concerns once that person is actually dead? We tend to think so—at least legally—but this ignores entire areas of concern which ought to enter into such decisions.

It was, in fact, only when Terri Schiavo was declared to be brain dead (which, again, is understood medically as identical to death) that the discourse around Terri Schiavo could move on to the next, dominant but largely unspoken level: that of the com-fort of the people around her. We talk about the quality of life of a patient, and that is a huge concern, but a part of the effect of life-and-death decisions is on the quality of life of others. This is one reason why congressional interference in the Schiavo case struck so many as absurd. Congress was claiming to have knowl-edge about Terry Schiavo, what she would have wanted, and whether her interests mattered. It seemed, from one perspective, that her various family members were more concerned with their own well-being, which at once seemed uneasy and perfectly nat-ural. The problem is that our health care system seems to have no license to say the feelings of family and other loved ones should matter in end-of-life care. It is especially difficult to suggest that a patient should die for the sake of others—that Terry Schiavo's family, for instance, could have been made happier by her death, and this potential happiness ought to be a legitimate factor in deciding on her treatment.

The real lesson from Terri Schiavo is that we are very uneasy about ending someone's life, or even conceiving of the possibility of ending someone's life as a viable medical decision. It's not that most folks have any well-thought-out intuitions about what a life is, or under what circumstances someone should be allowed to end her own life, or—and this is clearly not something that we even want to think much about—under what circumstances we might actually be obliged to end someone's life regardless of her own desires. It makes us unhappy to embrace the possibility that we could make the wrong choice, and so we make no choice, and leave it to the law, or to the sick person's desires. We know that end-of-life choices are not easy, but then, they really shouldn't be.

Cats and Humans

As various animal advocates have pointed out (including the well-known philosopher Peter Singer), those who advocate sanctity of life are almost all actually advocating the sanctity of human life. Often, in fact, those who hold fast to the notion of the sanctity of human life do so while simultaneously believing in the basic disposability of non-human life. If human life is sacred, there must be a reason why it is so, and this reason, typically in religious thought at least, has to do with what makes humans unique. So human life is sacred, and all other animal life (forgetting the plants—they barely make it into our thoughts when discussing life) is left out—not sacred, but profane and disposable.[1]

Pets seem to break down this dichotomy between the sacred and the disposable—they are not human, but they are loved, and they are family. Thus our attitudes towards pet health care, especially of those of us who do not see our pets as our babies, present a picture of how we can approach health care decisions in a way that is free of many of the prejudices that pre-occupy our attitudes towards human health care, and thus may be fruitfully applied to the question of how health care can be re-envisioned.

---

[1] Not all religious thinkers view animals as resources for human use—theologian Andrew Linzey, for one, has argued for exactly the opposite view, that Christianity demands that we care for animals, and not treat them as property. See his *Animal Theology* (University of Illinois Press, 1995).

One major and obvious difference between how we think about pet and human health care is that when we think of our cats and their health, at least in the life-ending and life-curtailing cases, possible termination of the cat's life is always on the table. It is, unlike in human health care, an option that is really and explicitly available. Granted, we are sometimes reluctant to face up to it, and vets are careful about bringing it up. But when the situation presents itself—as it did with Yoeshi—the possibility of euthanasia is real. This is not to say that euthanasia is always an option that, when exercised, will be most beneficial or most moral, but it is at least entertained as possible. This attitude is in sharp contrast to our real attitudes towards our seriously ill human patients. As witnessed in the Terry Schiavo case, even those of us who would prefer to be left to die if we were to be in a catatonic state, are (or I am, at least) hesitant to really engage with the possibility of mercy-killing.

The other essential difference is that in cat health care, the *costs* are all on the table. When I took Yoeshi to the animal hospital following his first attack, one of the most strikingly un-veterinarian aspects of it was the billing—not only how much it was going to cost, but also the fact that I had to ask how much it would cost. In human treatment, of course, cost is a factor, but we treat it as though it should not be; we lament that people must choose between health care and rent, and demand that something be done about this. We make health care a legitimate political issue, but we also tend to ignore the fact that health care really is an expense, and as with all things, the real costs and benefits must be weighed, even if they are systematically ignored in the rhetoric of human health care. With pet care it is different, and the difference can best be understood as an acknowledgement that we are concerned not just with the cat's life, or even the cat's quality of life, but also the quality of life of those for us who have to care for the cat. It's a parallel to thinking that Terry Schiavo's family might have legitimate interests in her death. With humans, such thinking is almost taboo; with pets, it is an accepted part of the decision process.

Lessons for Human Health Care

We ought to look more closely at our pet relationships to learn how to formulate our human ones—at least when it comes to health care issues. There is one sort of issue that ought to be dealt with up front: cats are not people. But it's often the case—and not just among non-cat owners—that the fact that cats are not people gives us license to treat them differently. There are, after all, real differences between cats and people—it might be objected that a cat is, morally speaking, on a par with our car—important, and maybe even loved, but certainly not the kind of thing to which we have moral obligations. If this is true, then no amount of analysis of pet health care will matter in the larger picture. It would be absurd to use car care as a model for thinking about our health care. So what's the moral status of our pet cats? Is the difference between them and people one of degree, or one of kind?

In her book on pet health care, *Kindred Spirit, Kindred Care: Making Health Decisions on Behalf of Our Animal Companions* (Novato: New World Library, 2005), veterinarian Shannon Nakaya reports that many of her (human) clients ask her whether their cats have a soul. She arrives at the interesting answer that, in fact, they do. This really is a question for religious scholars—presumably not every religion is going to agree on this one, but even those religions that look back to the Abrahamic texts do not always view animals as strictly resources to be used or consumed. If this is the correct interpretation of the religious view, then whatever it may say about our pets, they do deserve our moral attention. If we accept Nakaya's claim that animals have souls, then we should also agree that animals are not, by their nature, beneath our consideration. This is an idea that has its secular analog as well.

One of the subtler points in the literature on animal ethics is the notion of speciesism. The idea here, most fervently championed by Peter Singer, is that if the only thing that justifies our treating animals differently than we treat human beings is that humans are humans and animals are animals, then we are morally no better than racists or sexists. In both cases, the pattern of discrimination is the same: you don't look like me, therefore you are morally inferior. Speciesism may be hard to accept (it's hard to get around the very word "speciesism," and it's harder still to take seriously the notion that it is correct), but this difficulty is part of the point. Many people do not even think they have to justify treating human beings better than they treat animals, and insofar as we do try to give justification to this differential treatment, it often seems to be based on the notion that humans are not merely animals. Humans obviously are different form other animals—just as Caucasians really are different from African-Americans—but unless the differences between human and non-human animals are morally relevant, our giving preferential treatment to humans is no better than the behavior of the racist.

This is not to say that all people who do not treat animals well are speciesist. Speciesism is the idea that being a member of the human species is itself a necessary condition of being worthy of moral consideration, and hence that no non-human being could even be given full moral status. I think that everyone would agree that speciesism, understood this way, is wrong, even if not everyone would admit it. Take, for example, Carl Cohen,[2] a defender of the use of animals in medical research, who rather proudly calls himself a speciesist. He is not actually a speciesist at all. He thinks that moral consideration comes from moral awareness, and it just happens that moral awareness (he thinks) occurs only in human beings. Cohen takes himself to have found a moral ground for caring about people more than animals, and as such, he is not really a speciesist. In the absence of such a ground, however, treating animals and humans differently amounts to speciesism, and is morally unjustifiable.

It's obvious that cats can love, hurt, and fear, and this might be enough to force us to consider their well-being, but I do not think that we must settle the issue in order to continue. Even for those who do see animals as consumable resources (and there are many who do—basically everyone who eats commercially available meat is presuming that at least some animals ought to be available for consumption), this does not mean that they are being inconsistent in treating their pets as something to which they owe a greater, perhaps even human-like, moral debt. Is there reason for this? Or is a pet owner who eats a steak just a hypocrite? Possibly, but it is also possible that there is something special about our pet cats that brings us into a moral relationship with them that goes beyond the usual moral relationship we have to other animals.

One possibility is that we have special obligations to our pet cats because of something to do with their intrinsic cat-ness. We have, after all, domesticated cats for the specific purpose of being our pets. While cats originally became domesticated as a response

---

[2] See his article "The Case for the Use of Animals in Biomedical Research" in *New England Journal of Medicine* (2nd October, 1986). On page 867 he both declares that he is a speciesist, and also says that humans should be favored over animals because there are real and morally significant differences between them, suggesting that his reasons for favoring humans are not actually speciesist.

to agriculture, having adapted to eat the rodents who were attracted to stored grain, we have since moved well past the point of putting our cats to work for us. Thus domestication might be the key to understanding our relationship to cats, and hence to understanding our obligations to them. One could think that insofar as we as a species have modified another species to suit our needs, we have a special obligation to take care of them. Compare our intuitions about our obligations to wild cats: if anything, people typically feel that our obligation to them is to leave them alone. This, at least, is the presumption behind much of the work of naturalists and ecologists: insofar as wild animals have not fallen to harm because of humans, we serve them better by leaving them be. Therein lies a difference with house cats: precisely because they are undomesticated, we see it as our duty to keep them that way, which is why, I think, it is a real moral issue as to whether adopting a wild cat as a pet is acceptable.

This seems like a fruitful place to start, but it is limited. First, cats are not the only species that we have transformed from their original, pre-human-contact condition. Setting aside all other pet animals, we have domesticated food animals as well, to the point where the chickens and cattle that we raise for food only marginally resemble their ancestors, and we certainly do not typically think of these animals as pets. If we're going to maintain that there's something special about the pet relationship, then it must be more than just the cat's domestication that will do the work.

Domestication is a factor in explaining our moral relationship to pet cats, but it is only a foundation, a state without which we could not enter into such a relationship. Much more important than the cat-ness of our pet cats is their pet-ness. I mentioned the possibility that we have obligations to our cats because we have essentially created them for our own purposes. This domestication of cats means that there is really no natural place for them to exist. Feral cat communities exist in many places, but these are really not viable ecological niches. Cats depend on us, and that relationship will really never end. An individual cat can be given up for adoption, or given to another human, but it will always need to be cared for, and it will always need that care to come from a person. This matters in health care issues primarily because of issues of cost, both in money and time. There will be cats whose caregivers simply cannot give the care they need, and there is no other place for it to come from. In such cases, we do not shrink from the possibility that euthanasia might be the best possible choice.

Someone could argue that the moral obligation works in exactly the opposite way: that cats, because we have domesticated them and taken them in as pets, actually owe us—or at least, that we do not owe them anything more than we have given them as our pets. For example, if we take a cat in from the street or from a shelter, we are giving the animal a longer and happier life than it would have had otherwise. If, at any point, we decide to abandon or euthanize it, that animal is no worse off then it would have been if it had never been taken in. This line of reasoning would suggest that we owe nothing to our pets, as long as their life is better with us than it would have been without—which suggests that we can morally euthanize them almost at will.

Such an argument has some appeal, but if it is going to stand up, then it must also be applicable to our human children: it would mean that once we have a child, we were under no obligation to keep it and raise it well. After all, the fetus could have been aborted, and hence any life that the child has is already more than it would have had if we had not intervened. There's something deeply troubling about this line of reasoning, and although I cannot pin down where the flaw lies, I will proceed on the general assumption that those who are dependent on us, and to whom we have declared our intentions to take care of, actually are owed this care.

There's another factor that makes cat health care demanding on us, even if it is not a fact that is unique to pets, which is that cats have a hard time communicating their desires, and almost certainly have no desires when it comes to health care. Simply put, when we ask what is in the cat's best interest, we cannot answer the question by asking the cat what it wants. We can guess, but it is not a simple matter of communication—cats, like human babies, simply do not have any actual beliefs about health care, because they do not understand health care. Cats literally have no idea about whether getting shots is better than taking pills, or whether chemotherapy is better than amputation. We presume that both cats and babies have some kind of interest in being healthy, and in avoiding pain, but aside from these very basic desires, every health care decision has to be made by someone other than the patient.

These two factors—dependency and incommunicativeness—are also factors that show up in the most heartbreaking cases of human care. This is enough to connect the cat-care experience to the human-care one, at least in some cases. There are real differences between cats and people, but there are also these few points of obvious similarity, at least in terms of care. As with Terry Schiavo, we cannot always ask a human loved one what she wants. Even if we have a record of what she wanted when she made a living will, it is not at all clear that people in extreme distress still want, or are even capable of wanting, the same things, and we also cannot always provide a human loved one with the care she requires, either because of a lack of time or of money. Such cases are rare, but they are still common enough that our health care establishment has at least some mechanisms in place to accommodate them, such as the living will and family consent laws. Thus while there are obvious differences between cats and humans that account for a large part of the difference in health care between the two, there is also a significant area of overlap between the two groups. Cats are very different form people, but in some circumstances, human beings will present us with health care issues that are nearly identical to those faced in cat health care.

Beyond Life-at-All-Costs

Many criticisms can be made of the current American health care system, but usually the criticisms come down to the fact that health care is too expensive, and the way that health care is paid for is too discriminatory against the non-wealthy. One factor which contributes to the overwhelming cost of health care is the basic notion that health care decisions should be made such that patients are kept alive at all costs. This is what seems to underlie many of the decisions that are made by medical professionals in emergency situations, and it was also the basic motivation of the doctors who diagnosed my cat when I brought him to the animal hospital. From this experience it became clear to me that life-at-all-costs is exactly the wrong approach to pet care, and it seems at least plausible that it is also the wrong approach to human health care.

I am by no means suggesting that we should restructure our health care system, and even more fundamentally our health care attitudes, so that every medical decision is based on cost—that is, "cost" in a more expansive sense than usual: cost in pain, suffering, and emotional turmoil of both the patient and others, as well the cost in real, economic terms. I do think that moving in that direction would be useful and rational, but I'm wary of philosophers making proclamations about how the world ought to be. What I can conclude is rather more immediate: insofar as we decide that we should move to restructure our health care attitudes and policies, we have an area of experience that could be very useful—one where we already make complex and often heartbreaking decisions based on the balance of many factors. We do this with our pet cats, and so we know, at the very least, that it can be done.

7

The Other Two Sides

FELICIA NIMUE ACKERMAN

"Look at it this way," Julie said, "at least no one's going to say it's her own fault."

"Nah, they'll say it's ours. People resemble their pets." Nick rubbed his puffy red eyes, which did not resemble Gabriella's golden ones, then turned Gabriella over and began rubbing her belly. "So, naturally, pudgy couch-potato reprobates who brought their diabetes on themselves are going to have a diabetic cat," he continued, his fingers knuckle-deep in the shimmering silver fur. "Lucky I'm the pudgy reprobate and you're the diabetic."

"Yes, it's certainly lucky for you," Julie was tempted to reply, but she knew what he meant. Didn't she often assure people that she was an innocent Type 1 diabetic whose pancreas had failed when she was twelve, rather than an overeating inactive Type 2 diabetic whom they were allowed and even encouraged to blame? This let her criticize their criticism while at the same time escaping it, Nick pointed out when in a bad mood, but he hardly seemed to be thinking along those lines now. "So what are we going to do?" he was saying.

"I'm going to finish rubbing her head," Julie's fingers were making tiny circles where Gabriella's chin and ears met, "and you're going to finish rubbing her belly—don't forget the part near her legs; you know how she loves that—and then, since it's nearly eight, we're going to give her a shot."

"She's not going to love *that*," Nick said.

"Dr. Horton said the needles are so thin she'll scarcely feel them."

"You scarcely feel yours?"

"Well, we'll give her other things to love. Like this." Julie pressed her nose against Gabriella's, then stroked both ears, reveling in Gabriella's varied and wonderful fur. Short sleek solid silver on the ears and nose, but so soft and long everywhere else, with black markings that continually surprised you. No matter how much time you had spent looking at Gabriella, you always saw something in the pattern that you hadn't noticed before.

"She's a cat," Nick said.

"She *is?* Are you sure? Let's see—Gabriella, are you a cat?" Julie looked down into the golden eyes and ran a finger along Gabriella's chin. Gabriella let out a chirp and started purring. Julie looked up. "Yes," she said, "she's definitely a cat. So?"

"So she's not going to realize the shot's for her own good, and she's not going to have intellectual thrills to make up for all the sickness in her future. Physical pleasures are all she's got."

"And you think diabetics can't have physical pleasures? Maybe you've forgotten last night?" Julie's right hand momentarily abandoned Gabriella to pat Nick in a strategic place, making his face turn slightly pink. Married for six years and absent from Mass for almost twice that, he still retained whatever in his Catholic background made him flush at the mention of sex. Julie, non-religious all her life, found that endearing. This was one man who would always be faithful; she had never had a moment's worry on that score.

"But she's uh, neutered," Nick was saying.

"Not all physical pleasures are sexy. How about this?" Once again, Julie rubbed the place where Gabriella's chin and ears met, and this time Gabriella's eyes closed and her purring intensified, her mouth stretching into what Julie liked to think was a smile. "I'd better get the shot ready now," she added, reluctantly lifting her hands from Gabriella.

Gabriella opened her eyes, reached out, and put a soft silver paw on Julie's wrist. "See?" said Nick. "She's asking you not to hurt her."

"No," said Julie thickly, "she's asking me to keep her alive. Or maybe she's asking me to vote Yes on the school bond issue. Look, it's only a couple of shots a day. It's not that bad."

"*You're* saying that? Since when? What's next? Diabetes is part of your identity; so that makes it just terrific? Or maybe it helps you grow through adversity?"

"What's next for you, Nick? Death with dignity because you lose your dignity the minute you're not in great shape?"

Two pairs of eyes glared at each other above the lustrous silver fur. Two pairs of hands were immobile. Then, as if propelled by a single motor, all four hands resumed petting Gabriella. "Look," Julie said, "disability-pride types want you to love your disability; death-with-dignity types want you to hate your life. Obviously, it makes more s ense to love your life and hate your disability. Let's get the shot over with."

She walked into the kitchen and came back with a filled syringe. The needle shone silver and bright as Gabriella. "So who's going to do her first home shot?" Nick asked.

"I will. I've had so much practice on myself." Julie turned Gabriella over onto her feet, lifted a fold of lush fur and skin between Gabriella's shoulder blades, and thrust the needle in. Gabriella yowled, broke free, and lashed out with a paw.

"Jesus," said Nick, as a line of blood formed on Julie's hand.

"I'll get a band-aid." When Julie returned to the living room, Gabriella was lying in a circle with her plume-like tail curled over her head. "Tlap" was their special word: Tail Like A Plume. "It's just a scratch," Julie said. Plunging her hand into the circle that was Gabriella, she was surrounded by the silkiest fur imaginable.

"Jesus," said Nick, "what if she keeps on doing that? What if her whole disposition changes?"

"Are you suggesting we should have her killed, just like Alex Vance?"

"Who?"

"Didn't you read the paper today?" Julie asked and told him about the local woman who had gotten a Do Not Resuscitate order for her severely retarded son, who had no language, recognized nobody, and often hit and bit people. "Of course, we could just clip Gabriella's claws."

Nick petted Gabriella's side gingerly, then more robustly as the purring resumed. "You really think putting a cat to sleep is as bad as with that Vance boy? How many philosophers would say that?"

"I don't know. But there's a concept called speciesism. It means that favoring one species over another is like favoring whites over blacks, unless there's some relevant difference between the species."

"So what's a relevant difference? Can I swat a fly?"

"A fly is not a cat. A cat probably has as much mental life as Alex Vance. Anyway, this isn't 'a cat'; it's Gabriella. She's happy, she's purring, and this philosopher says Gabriella isn't going to be killed. She's not even going to get any more shots for another twelve hours."

"What about the blood tests?"

"Oh, hell, I should have done that before the insulin." Imagine, a diabetic forgetting about the blood tests, two more pricks a day, plus whenever anything seemed possibly amiss.

"And there's the all the stuff we have to watch out for. It'll be like having a second job," Nick was saying.

"Third for me," said Julie, "but at least you can't lose this job because you don't publish in the right journals. And here's something you hardly have to be a philosopher to say: don't confuse your interests with another's. What are you worried about—Gabriella or yourself?"

"Both. Is that so terrible?"

Julie gazed at Gabriella's tail as if it might hold the answer. "'Each to count for one, and none for more than one.' Jeremy Bentham said that. He thought that the right thing to do is whatever promotes the greatest total balance of pleasure over pain."

"So a million people can torture one person if it's just enough fun for each of them?"

"Well, that's one problem with the idea." Few of the Stanford students Julie had taught as a graduate assistant had come up with that objection so quickly. How tragic that Nick had been forced to leave academic life, she and Nick both, part of the lost generation of scholars who never found permanent jobs in their fields. At least she and Nick had found each other and created a home where they did not have to pretend that ending up a Social Security administrator and a bakery co-owner instead of a history professor and a philosophy professor was a blessing in disguise.

"Speaking of terrible, Jerry Rutherford came into the bakery today," Julie said. "He bought a cinnamon bun but couldn't be bothered to say hello to someone whose thesis he supervised but who never even got a philosophy job."

"Maybe he didn't recognize you." Nick's finger was tracing the black stripes near Gabriella's tail.

"Do you want me to be that generous about the people who turned you down for tenure? Anyway, he knew. He must have seen the column in the paper. You know how big they are at Stanford on being involved in the community." Raising her eyes although not her hand from Gabriella, Julie glanced at the wall. She had framed the newspaper column despite its title: "Diabetic Finds Solace in Giving Others What She Must Forgo." Julie had told the columnist that being around pastries was the next best thing to eating them, providing vicarious thrills, like window-shopping. The column made her sound like the sort of upbeat, wholesome person she would cross the street to avoid. Feeling fur move against her hand, she looked down and saw Gabriella roll over on her back, fold her front legs, and hold her paws together on her chest. Julie ran a finger across Gabriella's chest, making a triangle with the folded legs. "Do you know what she's saying now? She's saying that the square of the hypotenuse of a right triangle is equal to the sum of the squares of the other two sides."

"That's not a right triangle," said Nick.

"It's the closest she'll get," said Julie. "Look, at least Bentham realized that pleasure matters. Each to count for one, and we've got three here. Gabriella can have more pleasure than pain, I'll get more pleasure than pain from having her stay alive, and even if you won't, well, you're not the square of the hypotenuse. You don't equal the two of us put together. You're outnumbered, Nick."

"There aren't any philosophers who think intellectual pleasures count more than the kind cats have?" Nick cracked his knuckles. For the first time in years, this infuriated Julie. She decided not to tell him what John Stuart Mill said: "It is better to be a human being dissatisfied than a pig satisfied."

* * *

You get a vacation from your job, so why not a vacation from your diabetes? And why not today, a day for forgetting about restrictions and eating everything you want, and what better place for it than your very own bakery, where, four years ago to the day, Donna, your generous former employer, made you co-owner? Of course, you can't ignore the diabetes entirely; soon it will be time for a whopping dose of extra insulin, but now is for a jelly donut with special black currant jelly, and those mocha cream rolls you've been craving all year, and wouldn't you know, they taste even better than they look, might as well have a third, and also a maraschino cherry cookie, oh, so soft, as soft as Gabriella, and—

"Julie!" Donna shrieked as soon as she opened the door. "What on earth are you doing?"

"What does it look like? I'm taking a vacation from diabetes." Julie reached for a chocolate chip sandwich cookie filled with whipped cream, but Donna, brown hair falling across her forehead, grabbed Julie's hand.

"Have you gone crazy? It's so dangerous."

"So is climbing Mount Everest. But no one tries to stop people from doing that or says they have a mountaineering disorder—oh, that's so funny." Julie began laughing, then crying, because she had taken too much insulin, or was it not enough, and she was about to go into insulin shock, or was it diabetic coma, and any minute now she would throw up; in fact, it smelled as if already—

Awakening abruptly, Julie heard rapid breathing and saw Gabriella stretched out in the moonlight that shone through the bedroom window. The carpet was sticky; there was a pool of vomit. Gabriella's breath was fruity, and any diabetic should know what that meant. Julie picked up Gabriella, put her into her carrier, and set out for the Santa Clara County Veterinary Hospital. "My cat's diabetic. I think she's in ketoacidosis," she was gasping twenty minutes later.

"Please. Take. A. Seat. And. Fill. Out. This. Form." No doubt the receptionist, wearing a tunic of soothing light blue, had been told to remain calm no matter what, and why shouldn't she be calm, it wasn't *her* cat. And what could be more irritating than someone else's calmness when you were frantic?

"Please take her right away. It's an emergency."

The receptionist pointed in slow motion to a sign that said, "This is an emergency room. We do not take patients on a first-come, first-served basis."

"This *is* an emergency. And there aren't any other patients *here*." How much of a fuss were you supposed to make? Too much, and they wrote you off as unbalanced. Too little, and your cat could end up like the dying man Julie had heard about whose hospice took four hours to return his wife's middle-of-the-night telephone calls because she hadn't sounded distressed enough.

Six minutes passed before a blue-clad technician—was blue the official color here?—came and whisked Gabriella and the form away. "The doctor will see you soon."

Eighteen minutes later, a startlingly beautiful blue-clad woman with brown skin blending into rosy cheeks and red-gold lips beckoned Julie into a small office with a desk and two chairs. Julie's reflexive antipathy toward beautiful women dissolved into the thought that this woman must really love animals to choose a career where her appearance would matter so little. "How's my cat?"

"She has a condition called diabetic ketoacidosis. It means—"

"Buildup of ketones. I know. Why did this happen? We test her blood every day."

"Her diabetes may be very unstable. What we call brittle diabetes. There are several possible causes." The veterinarian steepled her hands. "We can keep her here for testing and intensive care. But—"

"But what?"

"Some cases of feline diabetes are inherently brittle." Unsteepling her hands, the veterinarian laid them palm-down on the desk. "In that instance, you might want to think about sparing her further suffering."

"Do you mean killing her? And then maybe killing myself?"

The beautiful face looked alarmed, and for a moment Julie wondered whether the veterinarian was about to call security. "I'm diabetic, too." Julie forced herself to speak quietly. "I know it's not a fate worse than death. I want you to do whatever you can to keep her alive."

"She should pull through this episode." The veterinarian reached into a blue pocket. "Here's my card. Call me in the morning or anytime tonight. I understand how you feel. I have two wonderful cats of my own."

* * *

"Where were you?" Nick demanded as soon as Julie walked back into the house.

Julie gaped. Getting Nick up in the morning was hard enough. Awakening him in the night was practically impossible. He slept through thunder, fire engines, and once even a minor earthquake that had not been too minor to make a glass vase fall and shatter barely a foot from their bed. But now he stood confronting her in the hall, his face red as the hearts on his pajamas, which she had gotten him for Valentine's Day.

"I had to take Gabriella to the animal hospital."

"Yeah, I figured that when I saw the cat-puke and couldn't find her anywhere." Nick rubbed his eyes with the back of his hand. "At first, I thought something had happened to *you.* I was so relieved."

How could Julie mind that? Wasn't your husband supposed to value you above the family cat? But— "Aren't you going to ask how she is?" Julie asked coldly.

"How—"

"She's in intensive care. Ketoacidosis. The vet dropped a hint about having her killed; she must be in cahoots with you."

Nick cracked his knuckles. "We've got to talk."

"Right now?" But on second thought, why not now? It wasn't as though Julie had much chance of getting back to sleep or of avoiding Gabriella-saturated nightmares if she did. She walked into the living room and sat down on the maroon corduroy sofa, feeling an agreeable tingle at the silver fur on the cushions. Vacuuming was boring and

Gabriella's fur improved almost anything, so why get rid of it? she liked to say.

Nick sat down beside her. "It's not working out."

"For whom?" said Julie. "The pricks really do bother us more than her, now that we've gotten the technique down pat."

"Take a breath, for Christ's sake."

"So she runs at both ends and doesn't always make it to her litter box. Since when are you so fastidious?"

"She's weak and she meows all the time. You can't say she's as happy as she was before."

"She doesn't meow all the time. She doesn't even meow most of the time. She lies in the sun and purrs. I'm not as happy as I was before I got diabetes, either." Julie twisted her neck until she was staring directly into Nick's eyes. "What are you going to do when I get complications—have me killed, too?"

"Come on," said Nick. "I know you want to be kept alive no matter what."

"Gabriella can't have opinions about that; so we go with the balance of pleasure over pain. Can you really deny that her life is still more pleasurable than painful?"

"What about us?" Nick swung his feet up onto the coffee table, nearly knocking over a stack of the American history journals that he still read although he had long since abandoned hope of getting an academic job or even publishing an article. "How many philosophers would say our interests don't count? Being sick trumps the interests of everyone who takes care of you?"

"You won't find a lot of philosophers saying that," Julie replied and told him about a recent philosophy article whose author said he couldn't imagine justifying burdening his children or compromising the quality of his grandchildren's lives simply because he wanted to live a little longer. "Then another philosopher asked what would count as compromising the quality of the grandchildren's lives. Going without tennis lessons? Going without summer camp?"

"How about going without sleep?" Nick rose from the sofa and began pacing around the room. "You think just because I don't wake up at night I don't notice you all stumbling and bleary-eyed in the morning?"

"Gee, thanks." Julie rose, too, and stood in Nick's path. "And by the way, you hardly need to be sleepless to be bleary-eyed. Have you looked in the mirror lately?"

"Come on." Nick put a hand on her shoulder. "You know that's not what I mean."

Julie knew. Men were supposed to care about physical attractive-ness, but Nick really did not. If you loved someone, what she looked like didn't matter, he liked to say, and Julie had always agreed, at least when it came to people. But last December, she had worried that some-one at the animal shelter might put into her lap an old, ugly cat that would start purring and licking her hands, and then, of course, she'd have to take it home. How lucky she had been to get glimmering young Gabriella instead. Gabriella was glimmering less these days. Her fur had dulled and clumped. But she was still Gabriella. "Having Gabriella killed would compromise the quality of my life," Julie said.

"You'd feel guilty?"

"I should hope so." Julie twisted her shoulder out from under Nick's hand. "Feeling guilty can be a sign from your conscience that you're doing something wrong. You know that. You're Catholic, remember?"

"But—"

"It's not just guilt. I love Gabriella and I want her around." Julie's eyes filled with tears; why hold them back because you were afraid of being manipulative? They were real tears, not faked or forced. Just last week, she had read a philosophy article on the concept of being manipulative. Like Nick, she kept up with her academic field despite having long since abandoned hope of employment or publication. Was that praiseworthy or pathetic or both? Or neither? She wasn't sure. The article said you were more apt to call something manipulative if you considered it bad. What was bad about expecting your husband to take your feelings into account? "I can't believe you can't love Gabriella enough to want her alive even if she's sick," Julie sobbed. "What if I get sicker?"

Nick put his arm around her. "Okay, Julie."

"If you're so worried about my losing sleep, how about doing half the nighttime stuff yourself? I don't expect you to wake up on your own. I'll wake you half the time, and you can take over."

"Okay, Julie," Nick said again. "I'll do that. I promise."

* * *

Over the next few weeks, Nick was as good as his word. Better, in fact—he had never promised not to complain, but now, once Julie managed to awaken him, he left their warm bed ungrumblingly to do his share of the nightly monitoring that Gabriella's increasingly brittle diabetes had come to require. During the day, he spent more time petting Gabriella than ever before. At first, Julie thought he was just trying to avoid friction. But one Saturday, coming home unexpectedly early from the bakery, she found him in a trapezoid of sunlight on the living room window seat with Gabriella in his lap. "Softest cat in the world," he was murmuring. Looking up and seeing Julie, he turned pinkish, as if someone had mentioned sex.

That night, Julie awoke with a start and found Nick's half of the bed empty. Incredibly, he had awakened by himself, and it wasn't even his turn for night duty. Reaching the living room doorway, Julie saw Gabriella on the sofa, tail appealingly curled over her head. Nick stood over Gabriella, his expression indecipherable in the moonlight. Why was he there? The scene seemed unreal as a science fiction movie or a dream. How do you know you're not dreaming? Descartes had asked, and Thomas Reid had said: You just know. Always Julie had sided with Reid, but that didn't mean she knew what Nick was up to now. She knew only that he couldn't see her; she was standing in the dark. Had his newfound devotion to Gabriella all been fake? Was he going to—? Julie watched as Nick walked into the kitchen and then emerged, holding something long and sleek. A syringe? I have to do something, Julie thought, but her feet were so heavy. She took a step forward, then moonlight fell directly onto Nick's raised hand, and she saw that what he was holding was not a syringe. It was a straw, the shiny silver kind they always bought. Nick held the straw above Gabriella. He blew into it until she was purring so loudly that Julie could hear it across the room. Quickly, quietly, Julie scampered back into bed just in time to keep Nick from suspecting she had gotten up at all. Why aren't I happier about this? was her last thought before she dropped off to sleep.

* * *

In the face of Nick's new fervor, Julie felt her own fervor ebbing as the illness progressed. She was so tired. Every night, she awakened either to do nighttime monitoring or to rouse Nick to do it, and afterward she found it hard to get back to sleep. One good thing about exhaustion, though, it made you less responsible for your thoughts. So maybe it wasn't so shameful that she occasionally found herself daydreaming about a healthy new kitten, pure white, maybe, with fur as lush as Gabriella's had been. No, it was so shameful, Julie decided one Sunday after Gabriella spent the entire afternoon in Julie's lap, stirring only to reach up and give her soft little pats on the neck. "Wonderful as ever," Julie murmured, and at that moment, Nick walked in, blood-drawing equipment in hand.

"Can't it wait?" Julie asked, but she knew that it could not. As she pierced Gabriella's skin, a vivid image of the white kitten, complete with a name—Suzanne—formed in her head.

For the first time in months, Gabriella acted as though the prick hurt. Breaking free, she scratched Julie more deeply than before. "I'll get some alcohol," Julie said, but Nick was bending over Gabriella. "It's still bleeding," Julie said, coming back with her hand pressed over the bandage, but Nick, stroking Gabriella's head, did not look up. "It's still bleeding," Julie repeated loudly. "Nick, look at me."

"For Christ's sake, what do you want?" Nick whirled around. "First I don't care about her enough, then I care too much; what is this, Goldilocks and the three bears?"

* * *

The following morning, Julie awakened surprisingly refreshed. Not in weeks had she slept so well. She wasn't due at the bakery until noon. What a perfect morning to spend in the living room's sunlit window seat with Gabriella in her lap. Or to spend deciding about the future; who knew when she would next feel so clear-headed? She picked up Gabriella, deposited her on the window-seat cushion, ran a finger from the tip of Gabriella's nose to the back of her head, went into the bedroom, and closed the door behind her. But emotions are part of clear thinking, she reminded herself, recalling a philosophy book she had recently read; how can you decide about Gabriella without taking love into account? She walked back into the living room, sat down on the cat-warmed cushion, and settled Gabriella in her lap. Soon Gabriella's little pink tongue was caressing Julie's hands. Then Gabriella rolled over, exposing her soft belly, folding her front legs, and holding her paws together on her chest. Julie's index finger traced a line across Gabriella's chest, making the familiar triangle. What were the three sides? Gabriella's side seemed unchanged, her life still more pleasurable than painful. Julie's and Nick's sides lately had been blurring into each other, although right now, finger in fur, Julie felt herself slipping back to her old side. She stroked Gabriella's ears; Gabriella's head was in her hands. So was Gabriella's life. Whatever Nick's side had become, in the end he would go along with Julie. She had always known that. He was not a strong person, which was part of what she loved about him. Strong people were cold and hard. But now she would have to be strong enough to decide, and how could she deprive Gabriella of mornings in the sun? How could she deprive herself and Nick of Gabriella? But how much more exhaustion and panic could she endure before her health failed along with her love for Gabriella? "I don't know what the sides are anymore," she whispered as Gabriella purred, closed her eyes, and went to sleep.

8

Why I Won't Hurt Your Felines

JULIA TANNER

Some philosophers think it's only wrong to be cruel to cats because it will make you behave cruelly to humans. This explanation is unsatisfactory. Why? Because being cruel to your cat is a direct wrong *to* your cat regardless of the effects it has on other humans. Ascribing the wrongness of cruelty to the fact it will make one callous to other humans is to assess the character of the cruel person, not the act being performed. Cruelty to your cat is wrong because it wrongs your cat directly.

Can Cats Feel Pain?

One way of being cruel to your cat is to cause it pain. Surprisingly, the contemporary British philosopher Peter Carruthers suggests that cats can't feel pain! He was not the first to think that animals are pain-free; in the seventeenth century French polymath René Descartes declared that animals were "thoughtless brutes" and what looks like pain behavior in animals is simply a mechanical response to stimuli. He wrote:

>]It is nature which acts in them according to the disposition of their organs, just as a clock, which is only composed of wheels and weights, is able to measure the time. (*Discourse on the Method and Meditations on First Philosophy* [Princeton University Press, 1996], p. 62)

An unknown contemporary of Descartes said that scientists who followed his thinking

administered beatings to dogs with perfect indifference and made fun
of those who pitied the creatures as if they felt pain. They said the animals were clocks; that the cries they emitted when struck were only
the noise of a little spring that had been touched, but that the whole
body was without feeling. They nailed the poor animals up on boards
by their four paws to vivisect them. (Leonora Rosenfield, *From Beast
Machine to Man Machine* [Oxford University Press, 1941], p. 54)

It will strike most people—especially those who have cats—as
blindingly obvious that cats (and other animals) do feel pain. What
makes it obvious? What are Carruthers and Descartes missing? Cats'
behavior indicates that they feel pain. If I accidentally step on a
cat's tail it will cry out and shoot across the room. Cats also do
something called 'pain guarding', for instance they will avoid
putting weight on an injured limb. Pain behavior also includes
rocking, writhing, crying out, or licking wounds.

These behaviors are all strong indicators that cats feel pain
because we know that humans feel pain and that they behave in
these ways when they are in pain. Descartes claimed that cats'
responses are merely mechanical, but we take such behavior as
evidence that humans are in pain. If we aren't to use it as evidence for cat pain then Descartes needs to show that there is a
relevant difference between cats and humans. This is something
he doesn't do.

But there are other reasons, beside their behavior, which make
it reasonable to think cats feel pain. The physiological similarities
between cats and humans also suggest cats can feel pain. There's
strong evidence that pain is a function of the nervous system and
that cats and other vertebrates have nervous systems extremely
similar to humans. It would be very odd indeed if, despite the similarities in their nervous systems, we could feel pain and cats could-
n't. Finally, Charles Darwin's theory of evolution suggests that cats
can feel pain. Darwin's theory states that things, like pain, which
confer an adaptive advantage on their bearers are unlikely to come
into existence all of a sudden, rather they would have emerged
slowly. Pleasure and pain are tools that help individuals fulfill their
needs and avoid danger. Those animals that can't feel pain would
be at a severe disadvantage. Pain is a huge incentive to avoid harming oneself.

These reasons place the burden of proof on those who claim
that cats don't feel pain.

What Is Cruelty?

Are you cruel to your cat? Hopefully not. You mightn't kick or deliberately injure your cat. But does this mean you aren't cruel? There are several ways you might be cruel to your cat. The most common is being indifferent to its suffering; indifferent cruelty. Another, hopefully less common, type of cruelty is taking pleasure in cats' suffering; sadistic cruelty. Those who are indifferent or brutal to their cats may be cruel in different ways. You can actively do something cruel to your cat like kick it; active cruelty. You can be cruel to you cat by omitting to do something to it like not feeding it; passive cruelty.

So there are at least four ways you might be cruel to your cat, you may be actively or passively sadistic, or you may be actively or passively indifferent.

A Kitten and a Small London Flat: Active Indifferent Cruelty

I know someone who lives in a small flat in London, with no garden. She wants to get a kitten, keep him or her in her flat and never let him or her out. Yet cats need exercise, and as social creatures, they need to meet other cats. Her cat will be denied these things. When I pointed this out her response was to tell me how cute kittens are. Cute they may be. This doesn't address my concern. In fact she's completely unconcerned about the fact her cat will suffer from lifelong imprisonment at her own hands. She wants a kitten because kittens are cute. She gives the kitten's welfare no consideration. Deliberately subjecting a cat to such conditions is the epitome of active indifferent cruelty. Active because she is deliberately doing it and indifferent because she doesn't care whether the cat will suffer. Although she doesn't want the cat to suffer, she just doesn't care if he or she does; what she cares about is having a cute plaything. This is probably the most common way people are cruel to their cats. In their desire for a cute companion they forget that companion's needs and desires.

Blinding Kittens: Active Indifferent Cruelty

Scientists studying blindness in humans once thought a good way to do this would be to sew a kitten's eyes shut. See Richard Ryder's

Victims of Science (London: Centaur, 1975), p. 52. Horrific isn't it? One wonders why they don't just ask a blind person what it's like to be blind. But whatever the value of their methodology, blinding healthy kittens is by anyone's lights a pretty cruel thing to do. For the sake of this example suppose that the scientists don't take pleasure in blinding kittens. Suppose also that though not wanting to cause the kittens to suffer pain and distress (what they want to do is further scientific study), they just don't care that they inflict such suffering. Given these suppositions this would be an example of active indifferent cruelty. Active because they deliberately blind the kittens; their goal is what they care about, the kitten an unfortunate casualty.

Killing Your Cat: Active Indifferent Cruelty

It's not unheard of for people to take their cats to the vets and have them put to sleep because they are inconvenient: this is active indifferent cruelty. There are cases where having one's cat put to sleep is not cruel. For instance, if the cat is terminally ill and suffering, it would be kind, not cruel, to end their suffering. But if the person having the cat put to sleep is doing it for their own benefit, and not for the cat's, then this person is actively indifferently cruel.

Some people may think that as long as the cat is killed painlessly (and without distress) this does not harm it because cats do not desire to live. But to kill a cat is to deprive it of its life. If we might reasonably think the cat would have led a contented life then the cat loses that life if it is prematurely killed. The loss of that life is a harm even if cats are unable to form desires about living. Babies do not desire to live, yet it is commonly recognized that killing them would harm them.

Someone who has their cat put to sleep rather than pay expensive vet's bills is actively indifferently cruel. They do not care about the cat; they are prepared to sacrifice the cat to their convenience.

The Neighbor Not Feeding Your Cat: Passive Indifferent Cruelty

Many of you will often ask your neighbor to look after your cat while you're away. Suppose that your neighbor promises to feed your cat but then decides they just can't be bothered. This would be a prime example of passive indifferent cruelty. It's passive because they omit to feed your cat and it's indifferent because they don't care that they would cause your cat to suffer. They take no pleasure in your cat's suffering, but they don't care enough to exert themselves to alleviate it.

Kicking Your Cat: Active Sadistic Cruelty

Suppose someone kicks your cat. They do it for fun; because they want to watch your cat suffer. This is active sadistic cruelty; active because they actively hurt your cat, sadistic because they enjoy it. This is the kind of cruelty people often have in mind when they think of cruelty to cats. But it is paradoxically, hopefully, one of the less common kinds of cruelty.

Poison Food: Passive Sadistic Cruelty

Imagine someone who puts some rat poison in their garbage bin outside. They soon notice that a cat has been attracted by the rubbish and is eating it—including the rat poison. Instead of scaring the cat away (and thus preventing it from ingesting the poison) they watch knowing the cat will get very ill and possibly die as a result. They enjoy the feeling of power they get from allowing the cat to be poisoned. This is passive sadistic cruelty; passive because it results from omitting to stop the cat eating the poison, sadistic because they enjoyed the cat's suffering. This kind of cruelty is probably less common than even active sadistic cruelty.

All these examples of cruelty make for very unpleasant reading. But why should we find them unpleasant? Why is it wrong to be cruel to cats?

Is Cruelty to Cats Wrong Because It Makes You More Cruel?

Some philosophers, for example, the great eighteenth-century German thinker Immanuel Kant, as well as prominent contemporary scholars John Rawls and Peter Carruthers, think that what's wrong with all these types of cruelty isn't that your cat is being harmed. Rather, they think, cruelty to cats is wrong because harming your cat will make those who are cruel much more likely to harm other humans. They think cats themselves don't matter. But why do they think humans matter and cats don't? The answer is simply that humans are rational and cats aren't. So cats only matter indirectly insofar as the way we treat cats (and other animals) will affect how we treat other humans. The idea is that being cruel to cats isn't wrong because it hurts cats, it is wrong because it may lead to humans being harmed. Kant argues that

> so far as animals are concerned, we have no direct duties. Animals are not self-conscious and are there merely as a means to an end. That end is man . . . Our duties to animals are merely indirect duties to humanity. Animal nature has analogies to human nature, and by doing our duties to animals in respect of manifestations of human nature, we indirectly do our duties to humanity . . . If then any acts of animals are analogous to human acts and spring from the same principles, we have duties towards the animals because we cultivate the corresponding duties towards human beings. If a man shoots his dog because the animal is no longer capable of service, he does not fail in his duty to the dog, for the dog cannot judge, but his act is inhuman and damages in himself that humanity which it is his duty to show towards mankind. (*Lectures on Ethics* [Harper and Row, 1963], pp. 239–240)

Similarly, moral contractarians argue that morality is an artificial construct; humans enter into a (hypothetical) contract to protect themselves against others. We enter into this contract for self-interested reasons. I agree not to harm or kill you and you agree not to harm or kill me; the contract benefits us both. Thus, according to Rawls only those "who can give justice are owed justice" (*A Theory of Justice* [Oxford University Press, 1999], p. 510). As cats can't enter into a contract, can't give justice, they aren't direct objects of moral concern for contractarians; we have no moral obligations *to* cats. (The same applies to humans who are unable to enter into a contract—see below.) Though we may have moral obligations *regarding* them in virtue of the "qualities of moral character they may evoke in us" (Carruthers, *The Animals Issue* [Cambridge University Press, 1992], p. 165).

For Kant, Carruthers, and Rawls what's wrong with my kicking your cat is that it will mean I am more likely to kick you (or another human). Or that in kicking your cat I might upset you (by damaging your property). Your cat's pain simply doesn't matter. So if hurting cats *wouldn't* make us more likely to hurt humans there would be absolutely *nothing* wrong with it.

Most of you would, I hope, join with me in rejecting this. There are several good reasons for thinking it's wrong.

Cruelty to Cats Is Wrong Because It Hurts Cats

Most of us think that if we are cruel to a cat it is a wrong *to* that cat, not to its owner or to any other person one might be more likely to be cruel to. This is supported by polls conducted in Britain: 59 percent of 11–15 year olds said cruelty to animals was the issue they felt most strongly about (Barclays Bank 1990 Youth Poll); 89 percent object to testing cosmetics on animals (*Daily Telegraph* Gallup Poll, May 1993, a face-to face survey of 1,019 people aged 15–19); 69 percent object to medical vivisection (*Daily Telegraph* Gallup Poll, May 1993, a face-to-face survey of 1,019 people aged 15–19); 86 percent believe all animals have the right to a life free from cruelty and abuse (NOP poll for Animal Aid, May 1998, a survey of 1,004 adults aged 15 and over).

It's highly unlikely that these judgements about wrongness are based on any indirect wrongs to humans. The most plausible interpretation is that most people think cruelty to cats is wrong because of the direct affect on the cats themselves; it directly wrongs the cats. These people may be wrong; they might just be excessively anthropomorphic. But there are other reasons to think cruelty to cats is a direct wrong to them.

The Facts Don't Add Up

When people think of the link between cruelty to animals and cruelty to humans they usually have murderers like the 'Boston strangler' (who was extremely cruel to animals) in mind. Being cruel to animals is supposed to have made those like the Boston Stranger cruel to humans. Kant and Rawls think that if one is cruel to cats one will slide down a slippery slope that terminates in cruelty to humans. But it isn't obvious that this is true. Kant needs to show that those humans who are cruel to cats are more likely to be cruel to humans as *a result* of their cruelty to cats (or other animals). This he doesn't do.

Some humans who are cruel to cats are also cruel to humans. But it doesn't follow that cruelty to humans is something that has grown out of cruelty to cats. It's more likely that those who are cruel to cats are already cruel people; cruel people who are cruel to cats and would be cruel to humans if they could get away with it as easily. Those who are cruel to cats don't become cruel during the act. Normal people don't just decide to pour petrol over a cat and set it alight and *then* decide to do the same to humans. Rather, those who commit such acts anticipate enjoying the suffering (this is an example of active sadistic cruelty). And then they enjoy doing the same thing to humans. People who do these things are already cruel people and that is *why* they are cruel to cats. Cruelty to cats may be an indication that someone will be cruel to humans—they enjoy being cruel: but it isn't the *cause* of cruelty to humans.

Cruelty to Rocks?

What's more, Rawls and Kant are unable to explain why it *isn't* wrong to kick a rock. If cats don't matter and kicking them only matters insofar as it will make one more likely to kick humans, kicking rocks must be just as wrong if it means one is more likely to kick a human. Kicking rocks displays the same vice as kicking cats; namely, aggression. Or if it doesn't, then it must be because there is a difference between cats and rocks. The difference is obvious. Cats can feel it, rocks can't. There is a reason those who are actively cruel to cats are cruel to cats and not plants or rocks. Those who are actively cruel to cats enjoy the response they get; they enjoy causing pain. There is a reason why we describe someone who doesn't give a cat water as cruel and not someone who doesn't water a plant; cats will suffer as a result, plants won't. It's not possible to be cruel to plants or rocks because plants and rocks can't feel.

Cats, Children, and Other Marginal Humans

According to Kant and Rawls what makes humans matter is that they are rational; the reason that cats don't matter is that they are not rational. But there is a problem: not all humans are rational. Some humans, sometimes called marginal humans, are not rational, for example, small children, the senile and the severely mentally disabled. Being irrational means cats only matter insofar as being cruel to them will make humans crueller to other humans. But marginal humans are irrational too. If the reason humans matter is that they are rational then marginal humans, who aren't rational can't matter (or at least only in the same way that cats do).

For Kant and for Rawls, the only reason not to be cruel to a marginal human, a mentally disabled baby for example, is that doing so will make one more likely to be cruel to a rational human. This can't be right. We shouldn't be cruel to such a human because they will feel pain. The same applies to cats.

But more disturbing still, Kant and Rawls can offer us no reason not to harm a severely mentally disabled baby if we could prove that doing so *wouldn't* make one more likely to harm rational humans. This is abominable.

What about Necessary Cruelty?

Some may think that cruelty to cats is sometimes necessary or justified. The most obvious example is "being cruel to be kind" such as taking your cat to the vet knowing the cat will be terrified. This may seem like an instance of necessary cruelty because it is necessary to take the cat to the vet for their future well-being. But this isn't cruelty at all, if you neither take pleasure in your cat's terror nor are indifferent to it. For such an act to be cruel one of these would have to be the case. If your intention is to relieve your cat of future suffering you aren't being cruel to be kind because you aren't being cruel!

But there are other instances where cruelty might be considered necessary. What about where experimenting on cats will yield drugs for humans?

Some people think it would be okay—or that it's necessary—to experiment upon your cat (or others like it) in order to develop drugs for human use. Whether it's necessary or not is debatable. A growing number of medical professionals want to see an end to animal experimentation because they think it is unsafe—for example, Doctors and Lawyers for Responsible Medicine (DLRM); Nurses' Anti-Vivisection Movement; Physicians Committee for Responsible Medicine.

However, whether experimenting on cats is cruel or not is independent of whether it's necessary or not. As we have seen, for an act to be cruel it must be that the person performing it must be either indifferent to the cat's pain or positively enjoy that pain. Those who experiment on animals may be indifferent to their pain, they may enjoy it or they may regret causing it but think it is necessary to further human goals such as better medicines. Only in the first two cases is the experimenter correctly considered cruel. In the last case the experimenter, who regrets causing pain and wishes there was another way to further their goals, isn't cruel.

Cruel People Are Bad but So Are Cruel Acts

And this is what I think is wrong with judging acts solely in terms of cruelty. Acts like experimenting on cats still harm them, still cause them pain. Yet these acts may not always be cruel. Sewing a kitten's eyes shut hurts the kitten regardless of whether the person doing it enjoys hurting them, doesn't care if they hurt them or considers it unfortunate but necessary. The fact that sewing the kitten's eyes shut is painful is *a* strong reason for not doing it, though there might be other, stronger reasons, in favor of doing it, if for example, somehow doing so could prevent ten other kittens from going blind.

Assessing actions in terms of cruelty does not take into account the cat's suffering. To assess whether an action is cruel is to access a person's character, it doesn't assess the action performed. If we judge the treatment of cats on the basis of whether they are cruel we finish with a judgement about the virtue or vice displayed by the person performing the act. In assessing how we treat cats we should do more. We should assess the acts (and omissions) themselves without reference to the character of the individual performing them. If, as seems likely, sewing kittens eyes shut yields no benefits for the study of human blindness then this act is wrong regardless of whether the person doing it enjoyed doing it or was indifferent to the cat's suffering—whether the person was sadistically or indifferently cruel. Blinding kittens for no good reason is wrong even if no one enjoyed or was indifferent to their suffering. Of course, it may also possibly be wrong even if humans do benefit from it, an issue I won't pursue in this chapter.

Why Is It Wrong to Be Cruel to Your Cat?

Cats can feel pain. It's wrong to be cruel to your cat because it hurts *them*, not because it hurts some human. But, assessing our treatment of cats solely in terms of cruelty isn't enough. If cruelty to cats is wrong because it hurts them, then hurting them is often wrong even where no person is sadistic or indifferent.

9

Our Obligations to Domesticated Animals

EVAN MORENO-DAVIS

Moral obligations come in many different forms. They also have many sources, be they the political obligation to pay our taxes, the contractual obligation to pay our mortgages, or the social obligation to thank our hosts for a lovely evening. We have obligations not to harm each other, and, in some cases, we have obligations to help each other.

We also have obligations to animals, such as an obligation not to mistreat them. If those animals are our pets, we have additional obligations to give them food, water, and medical care, and provide an environment in which they will be happy and flourish. These arise from our relationships with them, and may parallel the obligations that we have to our children.

But what about those animals that are not our pets? People often extend special or unusual treatment to cats, even to those cats with whom they have no personal relationship. For example, there are an estimated four to six thousand animal shelters in the United States, and rescue organizations of all kinds that provide foster homes and veterinary care. In caring for cats and other animals in this way, are we simply performing a thoughtful act of charity, above and beyond what it morally required of us? Or do we have a genuine moral obligation to care for these animals?

If such an obligation does exist, it will have a particular source and scope. For example, we humans might have a collective obligation to care for domestic cats, but no such obligation towards raccoons, earthworms, or even wild cats. What could be the reason for such obligations? What is it about domestic cats that sets them apart from other animals?

Universal Obligations to Animals

There are a variety of possibilities. For example, supposing we have certain duties to all animals, our responsibilities towards cats might simply be a special case of this. It is very difficult for cats to survive on their own in urban settings; according to one often-cited (though contentious) statistic, the average feral cat's lifespan is only two years. Therefore, if morality requires of us, for instance, that we protect animals that would likely not survive on their own, then abandoned and otherwise stray cats certainly qualify for our protection.

Many have argued that such a requirement does indeed exist. Peter Singer, in his book *Animal Liberation* (second edition 1990), famously asserts that animals deserve the same moral consideration as humans. Following in the utilitarian tradition of such philosophers as Bentham and Mill, he argues that morality demands that we take everyone's interests equally into account. And since animals, like humans, have an interest in experiencing pleasure and avoiding suffering, it's no less unjust to allow an animal to suffer than it is to allow a human to suffer.

Another philosopher, Tom Regan, takes a deontological, or rights-based, approach. Instead of arguing for the consideration of interests, Regan maintains that animals have the right to be treated with respect. All sentient creatures have this right, simply because they are experiencing their own lives. This experience gives their lives an intrinsic value, one that exists independently of their value to anyone else. Denying an animal its rights, then, represents a failure to show respect for its intrinsic worth (*The Case for Animal Rights,* University of California Press, 1983).

Either of these two positions could motivate the idea that one must provide a homeless cat the same sort of treatment that one would give any creature in its situation, or even a human. Surprisingly, the cats might need a greater effort on our part, if, for example, cats are comparatively ill-suited to the task of taking care of themselves under certain conditions. It follows that there simply isn't anything special about how we ought to treat domestic cats. As it happens, these duties are more difficult to fulfill than are our obligations towards wilder, more self-sufficient animals, at least in most cases. But consider the occasional exceptional case, for example, a beached whale. Just as Singer and Regan might claim that we are obligated to help the whale survive when it is stuck on the shore, so too we must aid cats that have been isolated from an environment in which they can survive and flourish.

The one difference is that in this case, instead of being a result of their physical relocation into a different environment, the cats' isolation happened because the environment itself has changed. When cats were first being domesticated, they had the luxury of maintaining a comfortable distance from humans, approaching their settlements only when it was mutually beneficial to do so, and living in the wild when it was not. Since that time we have subjugated and paved over much of the formerly wild environment, leaving many cats marooned in our sprawling cities, where their hunting and survival skills are of little use to them. With this is mind, perhaps it's misleading to claim that the treatment cats receive in the form of shelter and foster care is special or unusual. Instead, it might be that the treatment itself is not different than what any animal would deserve in their situation; what is special is the situation itself, particularly its scale.

This view has an attractive sort of simplicity. Rather than claiming that our obligations to cats are a unique phenomenon— and struggling to justify the existence of such a phenomenon—it would be nice if it were instead just one particular instance of something that we may already believe to be true, namely, the idea that animals deservr moral consideration. If we accept this principle, we can simply derive our conclusions from it, instead of having to develop a whole new system of obligations from scratch.

If we do invoke a universal principle of caring for animals in general, this justification will also have implications that extend far beyond cats and whales. The cats' situation is not unique. Urbanization has left countless undomesticated animals, for instance, many species of songbirds, in an equally severe plight. As a matter of fact, cats themselves sometimes contribute substantially to the deaths of songbirds, which can not only diminish the bird populations, but also those of their native predators, who must compete for a dwindling food supply. This complicates the picture quite a bit; it is hard enough to meet the individual needs of all these animals, but it becomes even harder when so many of the animals' interests conflict with one another.

Even more vexingly, depending on how seriously we take our obligations to cats and whales, we may well find that we are indeed obligated to care for raccoons, earthworms, and many other species under certain circumstances. Every time it rains, countless earthworms find themselves in the whale's predicament, as their burrows are flooded and they flounder to the surface to avoid drowning. Though this fact does not arouse the same level of concern as when cats and whales face similar perils, it's important not to draw any strong conclusions based solely on how concerned we are. People may experience visceral sympathy for one animal but not another, but the goal of ethical reasoning is to inform our gut reactions, not merely to perpetuate them.

Even so, anyone who does not accept the premise that we do have these sorts of universal obligations to all animals will be left unsatisfied by this explanation. It may be worth pursuing other lines of inquiry, in order to see where they may lead us. This's not to say that we've rejected the idea that we have a moral duty towards all animals, just that if we explore the possibility that other obligations are involved, we may discover an additional basis for such obligations.

Special Obligations to Cats: Two Alternatives

One version of this approach is to agree with the idea of universal moral obligations, but only to a limited extent. While we may have certain minimal obligations to earthworms and other animals—for example, not to burn them with magnifying glasses for our amusement—the majority of our obligations stem from a completely different source. Instead of deserving, at most, the same sort of consideration as all living creatures (or, perhaps, all sentient ones), cats may place additional moral demands on us.

Though it's much more difficult to prove the existence of a distinct obligation, if this approach succeeds, it will have a major advantage over the position spelled out in the previous section. It would provide an independent foundation for the obligation, instead of one that depends on a pre-existing justification such as those offered by Singer and Regan. It would be nice to show that our general obligations towards all animals lead us to be particularly obligated in certain ways towards cats; however, it would be even better to be able to show that these feline obligations would exist even if we didn't have any obligations whatsoever towards other animals, since even those who do not share Singer's or Regan's views might still accept that there are other reasons why it is morally incumbent on us to help needy cats.

Regardless of how we address the problem, we find ourselves returning to the same question: what sets housecats apart from their undomesticated cousins? We might look at this situation in a couple of different ways. We might say that, because our predecessors were responsible, over thousands of years, for transforming formerly wild animals into cuddly housepets, their well-being is now our responsibility. Or we might say that this connection doesn't matter, and that the our obligations can be fully explained in terms of our current relationship, irrespective of the historical factors that led up to it.

Our Historical Connection to Cats

An advantage of the first alternative is that it appeals directly to the essence of the process of domestication. Though I have just suggested that humans are "responsible" for the domestication of wild cats, it's important to qualify that claim. According to recent work by zoologist Carlos Driscoll, cats played a more active role in the process than people did. Unlike other animals, which humans deliberately domesticated, cats simply chose to take up residence near human settlements due to the favorable conditions they provided. Humans, meanwhile, seem to have done little more than tolerate the cats' presence, due to their contributions in the areas of pest control and cuteness. Therefore, we needn't worry that our ancestors may have ultimately forced cats to become dependent on us.

However, the mere existence of this historical link may be more important than how it originated, given the unusual ways that social bonds are perpetuated. Such bonds often pass from one person to another; for instance, we might feel some special kinship with our parents' dearest friends, even if we ourselves had no direct connection to these people. Two nations that have been historically friendly might remain so even though this friendship has more to do with the actions of their forebears than with their current political situation. Likewise, not many species have had as close a relationship with each other as humans have had with cats. Regardless of who initiated this relationship or why, it remains intuitively compelling to think that the interspecies bond has, over the generations, gradually taken on a moral significance of its own. It has created not only a desire to care for one another, but also a duty to act on this desire, and thereby honor and perpetuate our mutual interconnectedness.

Unfortunately, this explanation also leads us to puzzling conclusions. Let's suppose there were an isolated population of cats living on a distant island. Let's further suppose that these cats had been domesticated in much the same way as our cats, but without human contact. Perhaps they were somehow domesticated by apes instead, or even, improbably enough, by natural processes that led them to evolve into a form that was essentially identical to that of our pets. If these island cats were then introduced into our own population, it would be peculiar—indeed, positively chauvinistic—to claim that our cats' common ancestry endowed them with moral privileges that their island-dwelling counterparts lacked.

Our Contemporary Connection

The second alternative, on the other hand, may find a solution in the connection that we have to cats here and now. As informal members of our communities, cats occupy a special place in many of our lives. In addition, our relationships with our cats may contain some of the same elements as our relationships with our family members, and these may be accompanied by the same sorts of obligations. When our children are ill, we have a parental duty to take them to the doctor; so too must we take our cats to the vet. Conversely, we have a filial duty to our parents to ensure that they are happy and well-cared-for in their old age, and again, we feel much the same way about our aging cats. Though examples involving one's own pets may be relatively straightforward, can these relationships create a species-wide obligation between all humans and all cats?

One matter worth investigating is the nature of the relationships that cats form among themselves, and the support that they provide one another. The relationships cats form with humans significantly alters the relationships that they may form with each other, and vice versa. Perhaps, by coexisting with them as we do, we have co-opted their own family and community structures to some extent. If so, we might have an obligation to replace what has been lost. Unfortunately, it's hard to settle the issue of what sort of community cats have been deprived of, since it's not clear exactly what sort of communities they might have developed on their own.

Some big cats, such as lions, do form communities, and happily depend on one another for various forms of mutual support.

However, our own cats might instead have led relatively solitary existences. As a matter of fact, their closest relative, *Felis silvestris lybica*, does just that. This doesn't prove that their domesticated cousins are the same way, especially since these animals are separated by about seven thousand years of development, and differ in many other respects.

The majority of feral housecats do gather into large colonies with their free-roaming peers, though there is a great deal of individual variation, with some cats forming more close-knit groups than others. While this fact might seem to further confound the issue, it actually raises a very important point. Perhaps, if things had gone differently, cats could have been the sort of creature that lives independently of such communities; however, they are definitely not that way now. Due perhaps to the socializing effect of domestication, cats, though sometimes territorial and individualistic by temperament, will nonetheless seek each other out when humans have expelled them from their own community.

Regardless of our own role in this process, the domestic cat is now disposed, by its very nature, to adopt certain aspects of our community structure. Whatever community the cats may otherwise have had, they are now members of our community. Indeed, membership in this human-cat community may be even more dear to the cats than it is to us. Though we have not yet established what the moral consequences of this relationship are (if there are any at all), some communitarians would maintain that participating in such communities is rife with potential obligations.

The Bonds of Community

Ethical and political theories described as "communitarian" place tremendous emphasis on the moral significance of belonging to a community. Membership in a community can create certain values and commitments that one does not share with people outside of the community. This is because our individual identities are strongly shaped by the groups that we identify with, whether they are neighborhoods, political organizations, or what have you. Participating in these groups contributes to our flourishing as human beings, thus, the values of our communities take on a special significance to us. Though they may be meaningless on an individual level, these values become meaningful in part because of the way they link us to other people.

What obligations does being a member of a community generate? The kinds of obligations are as diverse as the kinds of communities. One might have obligations as consequential as contributing to the spiritual well-being of one's religious community, or as frivolous as helping one's softball team win. Insofar as a family is a special type of community, one is obligated to supervise one's own children, and, more generally, to guide their personal development in certain ways. The common feature that unites all these obligations is that we would not be moved by them if we were not part of the relevant community—in fact, our involvement might even be inappropriate.

The obligations that emerge from these communities do so because their members have a shared set of interests. Given the interests that we share with cats, a human-cat community will presumably value such basic needs as health, mutual affection, and respect. Obligations may occur when one is unable to fully meet these needs on one's own, at which point other members of the community may be expected to provide assistance.

Who is included in this community? Though some of our community affiliations are determined at birth, and can be quite difficult to change, membership in the other communities that I have been discussing is optional. At the very least, a community depends on its members continuing to share the relevant values. However cats do not have the luxury that we do, of choosing which of many communities they wish to be a member of. As the other members of their obligatory community (and their only community at that), this constraint places additional demands on us, in much the same way that being a member of one's family has much more complex and rigorous duties than does being a member of one's bridge club. And if one is orphaned from one's family, other members of one's society must step in to fulfill these now-unmet needs. In this case, the duties of the family are strong enough to indirectly extend to the rest of us via our other community connections.

There are a couple of objections to communitarianism that must be considered. First, some claim that it conserves a community's values by elevating them to a point where they are immune to criticism. The importance of ethical criticism arises from the overall aims of ethics. In particular, ethics aims at motivating people to act in certain ways, in accordance with a given set of values. In order to be motivated in this manner, I have to be able to reflect on my ethical values, to engage in moral discourse with people who have different values, and to critically assess the source of our disagreement, in light of the possibility that one or both of us may be mistaken. Communitarianism denies this possibility, suggesting that different communities are separated by an unbridgeable moral gulf, across which no discourse is possible. If my community's values say that murder is okay, and yours say that it is wrong, the communitarian would conclude that both communities are correct by their own standards, and that they are at an impasse, with nothing to discuss. Communitarianism's opponents maintain that this view is inadequate, and that the possibility of criticism is an essential part of any ethical system.

This objection only applies to human communities. Humans have the capacity to engage in ethical criticism, in fact, it's vital to our development as an enlightened species. A moral theory that leaves no room for this sort of criticism is necessarily going to be inadequate. On the other hand, it's very doubtful that cats do anything of the sort. Therefore, a community that reflects the shared values of humans and cats does not need to be held to such a lofty standard.

Another objection relates to one that I raised earlier, in my hypothetical "island cat" example. I claimed that it could be considered chauvinistic to give certain privileges to one group, but withhold them from another, because the reasons for doing so were morally arbitrary. One might think the same thing here, that if we are obligated to care for cats, then it is chauvinistic to deny this care to other animals solely on the grounds that are not members of our community. This objection essentially amounts to a rejection of communitarianism's premises—or at least a rejection of their applicability to this particular case. In response to the communitarian, one might say that the fact that an animal is suffering should provide far greater motivation to help than the fact that the suffering animal happens also to be a member of our community. Such a response accords well with Singer's view that we are obligated to help all animals equally.

It's not easy to adjudicate between these competing viewpoints and decide whether the obligations of community are more or less weighty than our obligations to all sentient creatures. However, it's not necessary that we choose one or the other, as it is also possible that our obligations result from some combination of the possibilities I've discussed so far, rather than just a single one of them. Maybe we have various kinds of obligations that derive from different sources. It might be, for example, that we ought to help cats partly because of the consideration to which all animals are entitled, and partly because they and we are members of the same community. Moreover, some of these obligations may derive from our past relationship with cats and others may derive from our current relationship. Given the distinctive and complex relationships that many of us have with our cats, it would be entirely fitting if our system of obligations were equally multifaceted.[1]

[1] Thanks to Michael Tiboris for his feedback.

III

The Fascination of
Feline Minds

10

Are You Any More Rational than Your Cat?

BRYONY PIERCE

No, really, it's a serious question. I want you to stop and think about who's more rational—you or your cat. If you don't actually have a cat, you may think my question can't be answered, but read on, because anyone can *imagine* having a cat, and a hypothetical cat can sometimes be more use than an actual cat. Just ask Schrödinger. Schrödinger's cat is quite a celebrity amongst hypothetical cats, famous for being dead and alive at the same time just to illustrate a problem in quantum mechanics—not an easy feat.

Now you're equipped with your actual or hypothetical cat, or multiple cats of either or both kinds, I must warn you that there won't necessarily be an answer. But that's exactly what makes it a philosophical rather than a scientific question. In philosophy, there's never an obvious answer—not even to whether you exist, have a mind, or can know whether other people have minds or just behave as though they do. Whether cats have minds, rational or not, is not something a philosopher could take for granted.

Although there's a long tradition in philosophy of considering humans to be a superior species because of their unique ability to reason, contemporary philosophers are, I think, less complacent about this elevated status. Contemporary cats haven't, to my knowledge, deigned to disclose their views, but I suspect they share our inclination to assume superiority over other species.

There's no consensus on what rationality is, or on how to measure it, yet most people appear to be surprisingly confident that they're more rational than anyone else. You may also be confident that you're more rational than your cat, perhaps especially on days when the cat is resisting all your attempts to administer essential medication. Actually it's not a matter of who's more rational here, but a question of trust and of who's better informed about the role of medication. Under what circumstances, in the absence of any intelligible explanation, would you allow someone to force tablets down *your* throat?

It's the automatic belief that we are, on a good day, more rational than other people or non-human animals that explains how we can make judgements about how rational anyone else is. Imagine someone doing something that makes no sense at all *to you*— maybe spending money like water, marrying in haste, putting themselves in mortal danger, or all three at once. Or imagine your cat prowling around the garden in the pouring rain, leaping onto the laps of visitors particularly averse to cats, or edging along a thin branch in pursuit of a bird you know will fly away long before the cat reaches it, if the cat doesn't fall headlong out of the tree first. Now, be honest; in cases like these, do you question your own judgement or that of the other party? When you form an opinion, don't you take it for granted that you're in a pretty strong position to judge whether behaviour is rational?

And rightly or wrongly, you're the one who'll have to decide, with a little help from this chapter, whether you're any more rational than your cat, because it isn't an objective fact. (To be honest, whether it is or isn't an objective fact isn't even an objective fact.) It's subjective, in my opinion, because it's evaluative; it depends on what your values are, or more precisely, on the criteria you use to make judgments about rationality. So if there's an answer to the question of whether you're any more rational than your cat, it will be relative rather than an absolute truth—relative to your values and to the criteria of rationality you choose.[1] Your cat's or partner's opinion might conflict with yours; this happens, but may be equally valid, provided the difference arises from the criteria selected rather than from sheer arrogance or a desire to provoke.

If philosophical questions can result in contradictory conclusions, you may be thinking that a scientific approach would be more appropriate. Surely science could come up with a proper

---

[1] This is admittedly a controversial view, as 'relativism', the doctrine that truth, knowledge and morality are relative, is considered by many philosophers to be self-refuting. So if relativism is true, it cannot be absolutely true, but since the relativist claims that nothing is *absolutely* true, this isn't a problem. The charge of self-refutation is question-begging (presupposing that to be true, a theory or proposition must be absolutely true, rather than true relative to a context).

answer? A scientific method could be used to assess rationality, but however rigorous the scientific methodology, the criteria for rationality are still highly controversial. If we've got a reliable method of measuring something, such as a tape measure to work out the dimensions of a piece of furniture, the criteria aren't so controversial. A philosopher might still have some doubts (questioning the reliability of sense data, memory, and our ability to judge size sufficiently accurately, perhaps), but most non-philosophers, including the average cat, wouldn't be overly troubled by our sceptical philosopher's objections.

It's a lot more difficult to measure how rational someone is than to measure the width of an occasional table, and there are a lot more ways of trying to do it. Before we try to do it, we need to work out what it is we're trying to measure. To assume we know what rationality is because we seem to understand the word itself could result in a circular argument—one in which the conclusion is contained in the premises we start out with. So if I assume that only human beings can be rational, for example, and conclude that I must be more rational than my cats because I am human, I would just be asserting that human beings are rational and cats aren't, rather than moving from a set of premises supported by evidence to a separate conclusion.

Criteria, Dead Cats and the History of Peruvian Art

Let's get back to the question of criteria. You might think it rational to read lots of books to learn about the world, and maybe your cat can't distinguish between fiction and non-fiction volumes, let alone work out the Dewey Decimal classification system. If so, the basis for your judgements about rationality may differ significantly from that of a person who values independence and practical ability, and spends hours working out the best ways of climbing trees.

If you've recently been nominated for a Darwin award,[2] been placed in a secure psychiatric unit, or are currently under the influence of mind-altering substances, you may struggle to triumph over your cat. Well, unless you can find suitably biased criteria upon

---

[2] The Darwin awards commemorate those whose contribution to the human gene pool consists solely in removing their own genes from it by accidentally killing or sterilising themselves, typically in an act suggestive of astonishingly poor judgement.

which to base your judgement, or can make your judgement independently of both empirical evidence and relevant criteria, or have an unborn, dead, or like-minded cat. If your real or hypothetical cat hasn't been born yet, or has been buried in the back garden for the last ten years, it seems unlikely that we'll conclude that the cat is at this very moment more rational than you are.

That's enough about unborn, hypothetical cats. How can you tell what a live, actual cat is thinking? Have you ever wondered? I have. Sometimes it seems clear from their behaviour that my cats are thinking about food, about jumping onto something, or someone, or about running through a door just as I'm about to shut it. These thoughts seem perfectly rational, certainly more rational than idle thoughts about fantasy football teams; Parisian catwalks; throwing snowballs; or writing a book about the history of Peruvian art. These are thoughts I have never attributed to a cat but might occasionally have cause to attribute to certain human beings.

Outcomes or Processes (Kirk versus Spock)?

Philosophy distinguishes between different ways of being rational and of judging whether someone is rational. It could be a matter of whether the decisions you make get you the results you want, or it could all depend on the way you make those decisions—whether your mental processes themselves are logical. It may seem obvious that the two go hand in hand, but that would be common sense and thus quite distinct from a philosophical approach. Whereas common sense presents us with the obvious—things we assume to be the case in everyday life, philosophy challenges these initial responses. Careful philosophical analysis can reveal that assumptions we don't even know we're making are clouding our judgement, especially if these assumptions are deeply rooted in our psyche and rarely challenged within the prevailing culture. The conclusions that emerge may or may not coincide with common sense views. It's often more interesting and productive when they don't.

Let's consider your cat's mental gymnastics when deciding whether to snooze in the sunshine or sit on your lap. I'll give you a fluffy, hypothetical cat called Ozymandias for the purposes of these ponderings, in addition to any real or hypothetical cats you've already accumulated. What thoughts pass through Ozymandias's head—are they logical, consistent, and based on acceptable premises? Does he indulge in deductive reasoning, theorising logically about the probable consequences and relative merits of each course of action, or inductive reasoning? Inductive reasoning is more along the lines of 'Every time I jump onto someone's lap it feels warm and I get stroked, so if I jump up now, that's what will happen'.

Does Ozymandias just see two opportunities and respond in proportion to their relative powers of attraction? If so, can you be sure this is different from your own decision-making strategy? Does what's going on inside your cat's head determine how rational your cat's behavior is, or only how rational his thought processes are? Can Ozymandias be rational even if he has no thought processes—if he just registers opportunities and acts according to his desires without doing anything we'd call thinking?

Your answers to these questions will reveal your own philosophical position with regard to both rationality and the mind in general. If you're a Cartesian dualist, for example, you may think that Ozymandias has a soul, spirit or immaterial mind that guides his behaviour. If you incline towards epiphenomenalism, you may view conscious thought as a mere by-product of the physical processes in the brain that control behaviour.

Some philosophers, such as Jerry Fodor or Zenon Pylyshyn, believe there's a 'language of thought', in which concepts can be combined independently of any spoken language. Some philosophers believe we can only think in whatever language or languages we have learnt to use (see Daniel Dennett). Others (David Chalmers, also renowned for accidentally setting his hair on fire, or Jesse Prinz, whose hair was pleasingly blue last time I looked) believe that thought is produced by brain activity that bears no resemblance to language.

Can you think without words, and do you believe your cat can think, with or without words? You need to decide whether thought or language might be necessary for rationality as you understand it. If the manipulation of words or non-verbal concepts, using conventional language or 'Mentalese' respectively, is an essential part of your notion of rationality, then you may decide you're necessarily more rational than your cat.

Alternatively, you may believe that your cat is a language user, or at the very least a thinker of some kind, and remain open-minded about who is more rational for now. If it is proven at a later date that cats either are or are not language users or capable of conceptualisation, this could disprove whichever theory you go for. But so long as this remains an unresolved empirical question you can justifiably defend your view as one that has not yet been disproved and is therefore a real possibility.

So, philosophical theories of rationality can focus either on how successful mental processes are in terms of outcomes, or on the nature of the processes themselves. The first approach views rationality as goal-directed action, such as getting through a door before it shuts in order to enjoy the delights available beyond the doorway. Cats excel at this, although the outcome may not be favorable if the door in question is the refrigerator or washing machine door. It could be a significant point in your cat's favour if he has never jumped through a closing door into an electrical appliance, despite an abundance of white goods in your shared environment. Even if you have also avoided leaping into perilous situations of this kind, Ozymandias will have worked out what to do, or not do, all by himself, whereas you may, like my children, have required explicit warnings: 'Please don't put your little brother in the washing machine drum; it might break.'

Either approach, outcome or process-based, may rely on methods of assessing rationality that are anthropocentric (human-centred) or artificial. IQ tests and similar tests designed to assess specific types of reasoning ability are inappropriate for cats, and cats generally appear reluctant to subject themselves to this kind of procedure. Mine flatly refuse, even when offered an hourly fee, as do many (human) members of the public—they have better things to do with their time. A good example of an anthropocentric method is the Stanford-Binet IQ test, which cats are ill-equipped to attempt, even when highly motivated. A hypothetical cat wishing to achieve a high score (real cats probably don't care about IQ scores) must face a number of practical and cultural obstacles.

Ozymandias's Obstacles

Let's think, philosophically (because that means we can seriously consider all sorts of implausible possibilities) about some of these obstacles. Have you ever seen a cat hold a pen in a manner conducive to checking boxes with any degree of accuracy? Pens do regularly disappear in our household, but the probability that our cats are secretly removing them for their personal use is negligible, I think. Few cats are given the opportunity to learn to read or write.

Those who use computers at all have different objectives and requirements to ours, leading to a very different set of computer skills, like the ability to use a monitor as a stepping stone without getting their claws caught in the ventilation holes. The *ethno*centricity of IQ tests is even more apparent across species than within humankind, so this method must be rejected in the interests of fairness.

The tests most frequently used for testing animals' cognitive ability, such as those designed to make full use of a ready supply of laboratory rats and a research grant, if not anthropocentric, might be classified as artificial, as the animals are tested in situations they would not encounter in their natural habitat. Complicated systems are painstakingly designed, typically incorporating mazes, levers, and a variety of rewards. How would your cat perform when expected to negotiate mazes or press levers to gain rewards of food any domestic cat knows it can get effortlessly by sitting doing nothing? Most cats consistently, and arguably rationally, ignore any demands made upon them requiring unnecessary effort or self-restraint. So I think it is the *outcomes* of actual mental processes that we should examine, rather than what we might attempt to learn about the processes themselves through potentially flawed tests. This will avoid an anthropocentric approach, the results of which might be far from representative of the cat's true mental agility.

This conclusion has implications for the testing of human subjects, too. Can we be sure that those who gain low scores in tests are less intelligent than those gaining the highest scores, unless we can be sure they see the benefits of getting a high score as sufficient to justify the effort required? Both cats and humans might perform a rough cost-benefit analysis of some kind before acting, although the reliability of this method of decision-making isn't guaranteed in either case. This could explain some cats' strange habits (I know of one who collected undergarments from neighbours' washing lines), as well as a great many apparently nonsensical human practices (such as continuing to hang undergarments out even though they keep vanishing).

'I Can't Get No Satisfaction'?

Desired outcomes will have varying success levels. To compare these, we need to be able to measure them. We could try a quali-

tative assessment looking at satisfaction levels. These would be
derived from success rates in attaining specific goals selected for
their survival-related value—things like food, shelter, or reproductive success. This is starting to sound a bit like a scientific experiment, but our methodology as philosophers could instead be to
subject satisfaction and success levels to purely theoretical speculation. We could rely on what we already know about cats and
humans, rather than on observations of a statistically significant
number of cats and humans. Philosophical enquiry of this kind
appeals to intuitions, which can be dangerous, as intuitions are
notoriously unreliable and easily manipulated, so if you would like
to conduct a scientific experiment to support your claims, do go
ahead. Although most philosophers leave the empirical work to
other disciplines, sometimes referring to relevant studies to support
their theories, 'experimental philosophers' can conduct their own
empirical investigations.

You will no doubt have noticed that there are controversial
points or potentially unproductive avenues in the proposed
methodology. The inclusion of reproductive success, say, although
a reliable indicator of Darwinian fitness, may not correlate with the
degree of rationality of the two parties, even if it's rational to have
survival-related goals. Couldn't it be more rational, and more satisfying, to produce two or three children or kittens than to have two
or three dozen? Also, if we take two hypothetical cats with equally
rational goal-directed behaviour, one may have produced several
litters of kittens and another may have been neutered at an early
age without having signed a consent form. Humans may be more
or less fertile, or be in different personal or financial circumstances
influencing their rate of reproduction independently of their relative rationality. If we don't want our conclusions about rationality
to depend on luck, we need to find a way of eliminating the effects
of extraneous variables affecting satisfaction.

Genetic luck might seem even harder to eliminate. Some
philosophers might point out that, had either you or your cat been
more fortunate, you might have had a set of genes more conducive
to rational thought, but where do we stop with this sort of reasoning? Could you also each have had different parents, each other's,
or perhaps non-human, non-feline parents? Then you might equally
well have ended up as a sea slug. We can combat this argument by
responding that it assumes genes could somehow be allocated to
some pre-genetic entity—you or your cat—whose identity was

already fixed. How could you or your cat have existed prior to having any genetic make-up? Could some long-expired sea slug have been your twin, if things had turned out differently? Maybe rationality itself does just depend on luck. What do you think?

Instead of actual levels of satisfaction, we could look at probable levels of satisfaction, all other things being equal, arising from the decision-making processes we can infer from your behavior and that of your cat. Note that it's the ability to maximize the chances of satisfying your desires that's relevant now, rather than the quantitative data indicative of success in real life, as this could be skewed by chance happenings such as a jammed cat-flap or a squirrel trapped under the car bonnet. It's hard satisfying your desires when confronted with a trapped squirrel in an inconvenient place, but you can maximise your chances by prodding it with a stick. (I recently collected empirical evidence that coaxing it out with nuts is a waste of time, effort and nuts, you see.)

If we assume both people and cats desire adequate food and water supplies, shelter from the elements, protection from danger and disease, and opportunities to reproduce, while minimizing the cost to themselves in terms of time, effort, and personal sacrifice, don't you think cats come out as rather intelligent? They are competent at securing all of these things, with the possible exception of reproductive opportunities, without lifting a figurative finger. They outmaneuver their human co-habitees, who not only have to work to provide for themselves, but to fund the idle, luxurious lifestyles of their pets. A possible counterexample to this rule would be the farm cat, if expected to catch mice, although the cat would probably catch no more mice than it felt inclined to pursue. Another counterexample might be wealthy, unemployed, or retired humans enjoying a limited degree of leisure alongside any resident cats.

Gifts and Special Occasions

Let's look at an area where you and your cat interact—the offering and receiving of gifts. Have you ever wrapped a (hypothetical) squeaky toy for Ozymandias and put it under the tree, or saved it until his birthday? If so, are you imagining that he'll prefer to get the gift on the 'right' day, in appropriately Christmassy paper, or do you think he'll be treated unfairly if he doesn't get a gift at a time when others do? Or are you blindly and irrationally following tradition, coming to the conclusion that you should act this way due to flawed steps in the reasoning process?

How about generosity in cats? Many cat-lovers interpret dead mice on the doorstep or feathery bundles on the kitchen floor as 'little presents'. If this belief is a true reflection of the cat's intentions, the cat, however generous, appears to lack the intellectual resources required for selecting a suitable gift. If Ozymandias is rational, would he not bring flowers, or chocolates even, or failing that, use his initiative to select an interesting item from a neighbour's house (or washing line, perhaps, depending on the cat-lover's preferences)? Some of the more sentimental cat-lovers might protest that 'it's the thought that counts'; however, it is precisely the *lack of thought* that is at issue.

Before concluding that Ozymandias is intellectually lacking, though, we should re-examine our premises. If cats actually have no intention of making a gift of their prey, the inappropriateness of small dead animals *as gifts* should not be used to question their reasoning ability. We should perhaps instead question the reasoning ability of those who interpret their actions in this way.

Suspending judgment, for now, on Ozymandias's (or your) reasoning ability or lack thereof, let's consider some alternative accounts:

1. **Ozymandias may be establishing his superiority over you: 'You think you're clever using that tin-opener, but look what I can do!'**

2. **Ozymandias may be making a complaint about the establishment's table d'hôte menu: '8 out of 10 cats may prefer the contents of those nasty little pouches, but I am *not* one of the 8. I am *not* a number!'**

3. **Ozymandias may be making a complaint about the standard of service: 'Well, this is what happens when you don't play with me for days on end . . .'**

Ozymandias may be simply responding in a genetically determined manner to a particular type of stimulus, with no thought for the consequences, in which case what must strike us as particularly irrational is the belief that the items deposited are intended as gifts. Genetically determined behavior, while failing to require rational processes, is at least not due to flawed reasoning, unlike much human behavior—remember the gift-wrapped cat toy under the tree? Or, alternatively, it's possible that Ozymandias is acting for any or all of the reasons suggested above as part of a rational strategy in order to achieve his goals. Displaying independence may encourage a greater effort to please; implied dissatisfaction may lead to a more varied menu; revealing a cruel nature may lead to increased fussing and stroking later on, as you seek reassurance that Ozymandias, unlike his namesake, perhaps, has a gentler side.

If rationality is 'goal-directed action' and Ozymandias is motivated in any of these alternative ways, the cat is a clear winner in all cases where the human fails to find a suitable deterrent to the depositing of dead or expiring animals or, worse, inadvertently rewards the behavior. If Ozymandias lacks motivation of the kind supposed, then both Ozymandias and anyone who views his prey as offerings and thus fails to deter the activity might be thought irrational, depending on our criteria. Whether conscious, rational, mental processes occur—in either party—becomes irrelevant when rationality is assessed according to outcomes.

How Many Manx Cats Does It Take to Change a Light Bulb?

The great advantage we humans have over cats is that we are able to benefit from the wisdom of those who have gone before us. And we can put our heads together and come up with solutions none of us could have arrived at alone. Cats don't have jokes about how many Manx cats or Persian Blues it takes to change a light bulb, because cats don't work co-operatively on projects, or tell jokes, for that matter. Even if cats are remarkably rational at the individual level, outperforming the average human in their ability to gain food, shelter and luxuries while doing precisely as they wish, they are markedly less successful when judged in terms of their collaborative efforts. A cure for the common cold will probably not be discovered by a team of cats, nor will it be a feline institution that launches the next rocket to Mars. Long-term enterprises and projects aimed at improving the welfare of all, directly or indirectly, are not typically undertaken by cats, whether acting individually or as an intellectual community.

Our judgment of the relative rationality of cats and humans depends not only on our criteria, but on our methodological approach. 'Methodological individualism' looks at factors at the individual level, where cats demonstrate extraordinary talents for achieving their survival-related goals. A 'communitarian' approach would take a holistic view of feline society, revealing alarming fragmentation and a shocking lack of overall purposefulness amongst all domestic breeds, short- and long-haired.

You may conclude that cats, although extremely clever at exploiting and manipulating humans to get what they want in the here-and-now, are sadly short-sighted in their ambitions and unlikely to organize themselves into an effective social, scientific or intellectual community, or consequently to develop their rational capacities to their full potential. Or, you may conclude that it is the here-and-now that matters, and that cats are the epitome of rational perfection.

Finally, I'd like to ask you to consider what your conclusion, if you've been able to reach one, reveals about yourself—about your own priorities and values. Philosophical questions aren't restricted to the sphere of academic debate; they can have real implications for how you live your life. Although a cat might disagree . . .

11

What's It Like to Be My Cat?

JOSH WEISBERG

> Do they not hear us? We are telling them. And telling them and telling them and telling them. We say it again and again, but they do not respond in a satisfactory manner. They are all about themselves sometimes, and we do all we can to get their attention, to get them to move. Hello? Do you not hear?
>
> What is it we want?
>
> Okay. We don't remember. But is that really important? Do you really need us to be so precise?
>
> When you give it to us, we will know. And we will tell you then.
>
> —Terry Bain, *We Are the Cat*

I stand in my bathroom brushing my teeth. There's a scratching at the door. It's Poopy, my cat. I let him in. He rushes into the bathtub, scratches wildly at the shower curtain, springs out, and scratches at the door again. I let him out. What a jerk. What is he thinking? What's going on in that fuzzy little head of his? Is there a rich internal monolog? A "buzzing, blooming confusion" of sensory stimulations? The empty silence of the mystic or the idiot?

Everyone who's owned a cat, or even spent a little time around a cat, has wondered about this. At times, cats seem so self-possessed and self-confident, single-minded in their purpose, whatever it may be. Or they slink about suspiciously, hatching devious plans and schemes. Or they are foiled by what seem to us the simplest of obstacles: the closed door, the sealed can, the mysterious paper bag. And then there is the "crazy hour" when the cat suddenly is wild, feral, and electric, running from one end of the house to the other in pursuit of (or pursued by) invisible forces or creatures. What's going on in there?

This sort of reflection is part of the pleasure of being around cats—they are at once familiar and inscrutable. But perhaps the difficulty in figuring out what goes on in my cat's head doesn't just make domestic life more intriguing. It may mark the ultimate limits of our knowledge and threaten the completeness of the dominant metaphysical worldview of our times: physicalism, the idea that all things are at root physical objects explicable in the terms of our most basic physical sciences. It may be that Poopy and his seemingly incomprehensible sojourns into my bathtub indicate the limits of materialistic, mechanistic science. Or so some have argued. It's therefore not an idle question: What is it like to be my cat? If we cannot give an answer in terms suitably compatible with natural science, we may be forced to conclude that there's more to the world than just atoms and the void, quarks and energy fields, flesh and bone. All because of my cat.

The Mind-Body Problem

It appears that Poopy, cloaked in feline mystery (or obstinance), has something to show us about the fundamental makeup of reality and the limits of our knowledge. That would please him, no doubt. He loves to make trouble for me. His pastimes include knocking over fragile knick-knacks, spilling half-full (or half-empty?) glasses, and menacing the mysterious cat who sometimes appears in our hallway mirror. Poopy can be a real jerk. But I'll grant that he may have a part to play in this venerable philosophical debate, the so-called "mind-body problem."

Since the dawn of modern science some four hundred years ago, philosophers have wondered whether science can fully illuminate what it is to be human or if there is some special aspect of humanity that will remain forever beyond the grasp of modern science's mechanistic theories. The seventeenth-century French philosopher René Descartes held that while the body could be fully explicated in scientific, mechanistic terms, the mind was a different sort of thing altogether. However, Descartes held that animals— mere brutes that they are—do not possess minds. To Descartes and his followers, animals, including cats, were little complex machines, "automatons" working according to clockwork principles. Sorry Poopy!

In more modern times, Descartes's dualism of mind and body has fallen into ill repute. The going theory these days is that we are all body, through and through. And body can be explained by science. So Poopy is back on all fours with us, but we are brought down to his level—we too, are mechanistic critters, fully describable by modern science. Yet perhaps Poopy still throws a monkey wrench into this picture. Just as he overturns my favorite tchotchkes, he may overturn today's received physicalist ontology. That would just make his day.

Physicalism is the view in metaphysics that all things are physical or made up of physical parts without remainder. Here 'physical' means the type of thing described in our most complete natural science, physics. This includes the basic particles described in particle physics (protons, neutrons, electrons, and more esoteric particles like quarks), and the forces that determine the behavior of these particles (gravity, electromagnetism, and the forces in the nucleus of the atom). But there are obviously many more things in the world than quarks and forces. What of tables, chairs, sealing wax, and litter boxes? According to physicalism, all these things are made out of ever more complex arrangement of the basic physical building blocks. A table is just a huge collection of quarks held together by the basic forces, and used to eat supper upon. Likewise for the other sorts of everyday, macroscopic objects that make up our world, including living things. A bacterium is just a special collection of quarks, special because these quarks can maintain and nurture their organization over time, and can even copy themselves, by using the chemicals of heredity: DNA and RNA. And so on, goes the theory, for even the higher animals: lizards, frogs, aardvarks, hippos, and humans. Yes, even cats. According to physicalism, all there is to Larry the Lizard, Harry the Hippo, and even Josh the Philosopher is just a complex arrangement of quarks, held together by the basic physical forces. So it is for Poopy the Cat as well.

Can this really account for all that there is in heaven and earth? The march of modern science suggests that the answer may be yes. At one time, it was felt that the basic biological phenomenon of life would not yield to this kind of theory. Some held out for the idea that life is not just a mechanistic process, but requires in addition a special "life force," a vital energy or entelechy. However, this view, known as "vitalism," failed to withstand the mechanistic alternative. Biochemistry proved to be nothing more than a brand of ordinary chemistry involving complex carbon-based atoms. Even the processes of heritability and development have fallen under the mechanistic advance, with the discovery of the structure of DNA and its role in the development and maintenance of living creatures.

Subjective Experience—The Heart of the Problem

Surely there are limits, you might object. Our bodies may be complex biochemical machines, but what of our minds? What about the feelings of love and despair, the rich sensory experiences of a good meal or a stunning sunset? Or the spark of freedom and creativity potentially resting in us all? Can this really be no more than the complex arrangement of quarks? In his famous essay, "What Is It Like to Be a Bat?", philosopher Thomas Nagel contends that we have reason to answer in the negative. Upon reflection, we can see that there is a domain of facts that no physicalist theory will uncover. Moreover, we can uncover these facts by considering questions about the experiences of creatures unlike ourselves. Nagel focuses his attention on the bat, but the same points can be made with the help of our more familiar companion, the cat. In particular, with my cat Poopy.

Nagel argues that physicalism works by explaining things from an ever-more objective point of view. Science tries to provide explanations that are viewpoint neutral, that are accurate no matter what perspective we take up on the phenomenon in question. Mathematical modeling provides the clearest example of this explanatory strategy. When we describe a system in quantifiable, mathematical terms, we are using a language that abstracts away from any particulars of viewpoint—it provides, as much as possible, what Nagel calls the "view from nowhere." Perhaps we can never reach a purely objective point of view, but this at least seems to be the goal of scientific explanation: to provide a way of seeing the world that is independent of our local, idiosyncratic, ways of looking and feeling.

Yet the mental facts in question—facts about what it is like to be my cat—seem to escape the net of objective scientific explanation. Whereas the usual mode of scientific theorizing, which lies at the heart of a physicalist metaphysic, works towards ever-increasing objectivity, the facts here are plausibly *subjective* in nature. We cannot describe and explain them from the "view from nowhere" because these facts are fundamentally wrapped up with points of view; they are inextricably somewhere.

In more detail, it seems that all science can tell us concerns the biochemical makeup of Poopy, the chemical processes that fire in his brain when he jumps into the tub, the evolutionary purposes and origin of his various psychological systems, the range of environmental stimuli to which he responds. But it cannot tell us what it is like to be him as he goes through these processes—what it is like *for him* as this occurs. For all we can tell from the point of view of scientific explanation, there may be nothing at all going on *for him*. Or it might be something very different from what occurs in us. How could we tell merely by reading about the biochemical machinery churning away as Poopy interrupts my morning ablutions?

The pure scientific description leaves out a fundamental feature of reality—the subjective facts about what it's like for me, or for my cat, as we live our lives. While it may be true that we are evolved biochemical machines, this is not all we are. Or at least an explanation that only trades in such facts will be radically incomplete. What's more, it's entirely unclear how to add in the subjective facts to the physicalist scientific picture. All that physicalist science gives us is more of the same: more chemicals, more particles, more mathematically described forces. How could we possibly wring subjectivity out of such facts? Nagel concludes that we have no idea how to fit the subjective side of reality into the physicalist worldview. Even though he is sympathetic with physicalism in general—its successes in science and technology can hardly be sneezed at—Nagel contends that we have no idea how to explain subjective experience in physical terms. Even more troubling, if we cannot tell what it's like to be my cat from a physicalist point of view, why think we can tell what it's like to be *us?* Thus, from humble reflections on my cat's morning behavior to the foundations of mind and metaphysics. As I said, what a jerk Poopy is.

What does it mean to say something is a "subjective fact"? Can I really undermine physicalism just by reflecting on what it's like to be my cat? Isn't that just a little too easy? First off, a subjective fact is a fact that can be accessed on from one point of view. It's a fact that can only be known by adopting that particular sort of viewpoint and experiencing the fact for one's self. For example, let's say you've been bungee jumping and I have not. Then you might describe your experience to me, but I can only know the subjective fact—what it's like to bungee jump—if I myself have been bungee jumping. Or maybe I can know what it's like if I've had a close enough experience and can, on that basis, imagine what it's like. Either way, I've got to somehow get myself into the right state of mind, and then reflect and say to myself, "Aha! So this is what it's like to bungee jump!" It seems that if I haven't had the experience myself, or if I haven't had a "nearby" experience, I can't know what it's like. It's not the sort of thing I can get from book learnin'.

Since there seems to be no way I could ever get myself into the right state of mind to have experiences anything like my cat's, I can never know what it's like to be my cat. After all, my cat and I have very different psychologies, not to mention bodily hardware. He's got whiskers and eyes that can see in the dark. I've got a well-developed frontal lobe. We're just too different to get into the right states of mind so that I could know what it's like to be Poopy when he claws his way into my bathroom. Yet if that's the case, then there seems to be a range of facts that physicalist scientific explanation cannot handle. Physicalism is stuck with the sorts of facts that could fill a physics (or chemistry or biology) textbook. Unfortunately, that's not the kind of thing that can convey what it's like for my cat to have the experiences he does. There are facts beyond the physical facts—there is more in heaven and earth than is dreamed of in the physicalist's philosophy. Or so it seems.

Solving—or Dissolving—the Problem

On the other hand, maybe we can know all there is to know about Poopy without having his experiences or even imagining what it's like to have his experiences. Nagel's claim depends on there being special facts that can only be known by having the right sort of experiences. Why should we accept this idea? Here's another possibility: while experience is one way to learn the facts, *there are other routes to the same facts*! Perhaps, then, science's description of Poopy is fully complete—it describes everything that there is to know about Poopy—even though it doesn't give us the ability to experience or imagine what it's like to be Poopy directly. How might we support this claim and what might Nagel say in response?

First, we can sketch out the physicalist's story about Poopy, the sorts of facts and details that the physicalist can provide to explain all the mental goings-on when Poopy has his morning romp. Obviously, this will be a *rough* sketch, but it will show the kinds of resources the physicalist can bring to bear on the problem. Then we can consider what if anything is missing. It may be that when we get a glimpse of the scientific story, we'll lose that lingering feeling of incompleteness. If we still feel that something's left out, we needn't give in to Nagel. Instead, we can consider whether there's another explanation of why we feel this way, of why we have the intuition that physicalism can't deliver the goods. If we can show that this feeling isn't a good guide to the underlying nature of the mind, then we needn't let it tear down our worldview. We can resist Nagel's attack on physicalism, despite Mr. P's best efforts to ruin my philosophical day.

Physicalist science can tell us an enormous amount about Poopy as he scratches wildly at my shower curtain. First, it can provide rich detail about the things in the world that he responds to with his senses. Poopy can detect and differentiate a wide range of visible light, though his eyes and brain have much less color-processing machinery than do ours. He can detect shades of black, white, and grey, and can tell red from other colors, though he is less good at yellows, blues, and greens. He's highly adept at detecting motion—the littlest twitching of the shower curtain in the breeze is enough to trigger his finely-tuned tracking and pouncing mechanisms.

We can spell out in great detail the range of environmental stimuli that Poopy reacts to, and trace the diverse relations between these stimuli. In this way we can map out various "quality spaces" for Poopy, multi-dimensional networks that place each quality Poopy is responsive to in a unique location. We can get extremely precise about just what Poopy is sensing.[1] Comparative psychology and cognitive ethology—two fields scientifically observing and testing animal mentality and behavior—provide us with an ever-growing list of such facts.

Further, we can lay out a detailed map of how Poopy represents visual (and other sensory) stimuli in his brain. We can tell which perceived qualities are closer to which in Poopy's mind, which details are highlighted and which are left out altogether. These

---

[1] For an excellent description of how to do this, see Austen Clark, *Sensory Qualities* (Oxford: Clarendon, 1993). For more on cat psychology, see Terry Bain, *We Are the Cat* (New York: Harmony, 2006); Jeffrey Moussaieff Masson, *The Nine Emotional Lives of Cats* (Ballantine, 2002); and Akif Pirinçci and Rolf Degen, *Cat Sense: Inside the Feline Mind* (Fourth Estate, 1994).

neural maps let us know just when Poopy is responding to which environmental trigger, and how he represents these perceived differences. And we can trace the associations Poopy has developed in his brain between kinds of stimuli. Some sensations cause near-simultaneous firing in his amygdala—a part of his brain involved in emotional processing—because they've become associated with loud noises, the presence of our dog (Flea Biscuit, who is very jealous that Poopy is figuring so prominently in this chapter), and other signs of trouble.

These stimuli create fear reactions: they cause freezing, puffy tails, and wild, disorderly retreats. Others stimuli have more positive associations—they mean food, fun, and reproduction (in his dreams!). And finally we know a great deal about how his brain triggers Poopy's behavioral reactions—how he manages to land on his feet when dumped unceremoniously outside the bathroom, how he effectively stalks and pounces on the shimmery and devious shower curtain, how he aims his sharp claws at my hand as I try to pet him lovingly, and so on.

What's more, we can explain how these cognitive mechanisms work with greater and greater biochemical specificity. We know how the nerve cells in Poopy's eye and brain generate the "action potentials" that make them fire. The right concentration of calcium and potassium ions in and around the nerve cell, the modulating effect of chemicals like serotonin, dopamine, glutamate, and others, are being analyzed, traced, and functionally modeled. And the organization of Poopy's brain, from the optic nerve to the columnar arrangement of neurons in his visual cortex to the complex interacting circuitry of association, memory, learning, and motor action, are all falling under the explanatory net of modern neuroscience and biochemistry. We even have a detailed understanding of how the particular atoms and subatomic particles in Poopy's neurons fit together to generate the electro-chemical interactions of his nervous system. Finally, we have evolutionary theory to explain where this machinery came from, what its distinctive cat-specific features are, and how Poopy thereby fits in with the rest of us mammals and with all life on this planet. What could possibly be left out of this rich interwoven tale about my morning bathroom companion?

Ah, says our Nagelian interlocutor, what about what it feels like *for Poopy* when all this machinery is whirring away in his little skull? Haven't you left out this vital information? Here's the physicalist answer: no, we have not. We have just given you a complete description of what it feels like for Poopy. We've told you what he sees, what he associates with what, the actions he performs, and what's more, we've filled out the details of these processes from the psychological, biochemical, atomic, and evolutionary perspectives. We've told you all that's going on with Poopy when he pounces on the shower curtain, in grim and massive detail, right down to the last quark if need be.

Experience and Ability

Nevertheless, says our inquisitor, this fails to let me feel or even imagine Poopy's feelings. How about them apples, Mr. Physicalist? In response we ask: why should our story provide you with this ability? We've told you all that there is to know about Poopy's mental life, and now you want us to *turn you into a cat*? That's asking a bit much, even of a philosopher. Here's the deal. We've told you all the facts about Poopy, but we admit that we haven't given you access to those facts in every way possible. We've given you a complete story about Poopy's mental life, but we acknowledge that there are other ways to get at Poopy's mental life—in particular, by *being Poopy!* But the facts that Poopy accesses from his personal viewpoint—and the facts we'd access if by advanced brain grafting or by black magic we were able to look out of Poopy's eyes and somehow think with his devious brain—are no more than the facts we've already presented in our physicalist scientific story. It's all there, just accessed by a different route. So the physicalist story is complete, even though we can't imagine what it's like to be Poopy.

Doubt lingers. Surely there are things that can't be captured in the physicalist story, perhaps things that can't be captured in any story. But what is the reason for thinking this? It's clear that Anti-physicalist intuitions have roots in our own first-person experience. We just *know* there's more going on in us than is laid out in the science books; just know, because we can "peer inward" and directly access the qualities of our own experiences: the searing pain of a clawed hand, the feeling of soft fuzziness as we pet Poopy's jowly belly, or what have you. Since the physicalist leaves this sort of information out of our story, how can we know that such information isn't left out of Poopy's story as well?

Here we can draw the line. Why think we can just "peer inward" and determine whether something is or is not a physical process? Here's an alternative: we are the evolved bio-chemical creatures that physicalism says we are, *but we don't know it.* The way things seem internally fails to reveal physical mechanisms, and so we conclude that we're nonphysical, at least in part. However, it's plausible that our first-person access positively distorts things, leading us to conclude that introspection reveals special nonphysical qualities of experience—the distinctive "feel" of experienced sunsets, ice cream sundaes, and cat-scratched hands. If we can explain the source of this confusion, we can put to rest any lingering worries that the physicalist's story leaves something out.

Here's a reason why we might be confused in this way: we're *too good* at figuring out what we're thinking and feeling from the first-person point of view. We have such quick and easy access to our own minds that it seems like no process is going on at all. We "just know" what we're thinking and feeling, and there sure doesn't seem to any biochemical process churning away or any neuro-computational information processing at work. We just know we are feeling pain, seeing red, hearing the purr of Mr. P. When we try to explain how we access these feelings, how we know what it's like to be us, we are at a loss for words. Indeed, words seem to remove the felt immediacy of what's occurring. And because of this, textbook accounts seem to leave out the subjective core of experience. We are experts at accessing our thoughts and feelings, and this blinds us to what's really going on in our minds.

What's more, the easy and automatic nature of subjective access explains why we can't know what it's like to be Poopy, from Poopy's point of view. We lack the ability to automatically and directly access Poopy's thoughts and feelings. Without this talent we can't get the immediate feel of the shimmery shower curtain and the crackled whisper of taunting mouse-like voices emanating from the bathroom each morning. We lack a skill, but we don't lack any facts about Poopy.[2] We know all there is to know without thereby gaining the ability to look out of Poopy's eyes and to think with his suspicious mind. The illusion brought on by being an

---

[2] The idea that we lack an ability rather than any facts about Poopy was developed independently by David Lewis and Laurence Nemirow. See David Lewis, "What Experience Teaches," *Proceedings of the Russellian Society of the University of Sydney,* reprinted in William Lycan, ed., *Mind and Cognition* (Blackwell, 1990); Laurence Nemirow, "Physicalism and the Cognitive Role of Acquaintance," in Lycan, *Mind and Cognition.*

introspecting expert blinds us to the fact that we're just physical beings in a wholly physical world.

At this point, you may feel that I've robbed Poopy, and indeed life in general, of its mystery, its charm, its profundity. I started out by saying Poopy was going to lead us into the depths of metaphysics and ontology, and I've concluded by saying Poopy is just some evolved biochemical robot, fully describable from the scientific viewpoint, with no secrets left to conceal. What a killjoy! But I disagree. By showing how Poopy fits into the scientific worldview, I've illuminated what it is to be a cat, what it is to be that kind of critter scuttling about in my bathroom. It's an amazing thing, that there could be this sort of creature at all, one that works according to the amazingly complex, dynamic, and elegant principles of physics, chemistry, biology, and psychology.

What's more, this offers a guide to what we are as well. We are distant cousins of Poopy, and we can learn from him at least part of the great mystery of what it is to be a human being. That is not something that robs reality of its wonder; it's something that enriches reality, shows its deep and fundamental interconnection, and inspires us to new ways of thinking and being. All this because Poopy scratched his way into my bathroom and behaved in his usual jerkish way. Typical.

12

Do Cats Have Beliefs?

MANUEL BREMER

Fred lives in his apartment with several cats. Today he's sitting in his kitchen talking with his friend Linda, who happens to have read some recent work in philosophy of mind. Fred likes to tell his friends what his cats are doing, yet Linda finds Fred's stories difficult to swallow, especially when he describes cats as if they were children, or even grown-up humans.

"Isn't it *obvious*," says Fred, "that Cora came into the kitchen because she *wanted* to get another piece of that cheese that she *knew* to be in her bowl?" Fred uses psychological expression like "want" and "know"—expressions we typically use to describe another person's state of mind—to talk about a cat! The main reason why he—and most of us—never have doubts about this seems to be simply that it works. We seem to understand Cora's behavior by *explaining* it in terms of her psychological states. If this explanation works, well, then she has to have these states, doesn't she? What other story should there be to tell about her strolling into the kitchen?

How We Talk about Cats

Linda's first complaint about the attribution of wishes and states of knowledge to cats is that these are what philosophers call "propositional attitudes." Propositional attitudes are attitudes we can only have if we understand propositions. Propositions can be thought of either as sentences or as something more abstract that several sentences may have in common. Fred says, "Cora wishes that she has another piece of cheese from her bowl in the kitchen." If he had said, "Cora wishes that she has from her bowl in the kitchen another piece of the cheese therein," that would be a somewhat cumbersome expression of the same proposition with a different sentence.

Linda's first crucial point about propositions (or sentences) is that they involve concepts. Certainly Linda does not expect Cora to know or use—in her mind?—*the word* "kitchen." But does—or even can—a cat have *the concept* of a kitchen? Can Cora have what we have in our understanding of the word "kitchen" (its meaning)? That seems pretty improbable. A kitchen—roughly—is a part of a house or apartment where food is regularly prepared. Since cats in the wild don't live in artificial dwellings nor prepare their food, the concept of a kitchen—like the concept of other artifacts—may be beyond them.

Not only "kitchen" is problematic in Fred's report, but also "bowl." Even "cheese" is not unproblematic, since we use it to refer *in general* to all kinds of cheese, be it made of goat milk, cow milk—or just any milk one may come across. Cheese is not just that white stuff made from the milk (that white fluid) we know. So, when Fred talks about Cora's wishes and states of knowledge he does not really talk about *her* mental states, but about the states *he* has, or states he imagines *himself* to have if *he* followed Cora's daily routines. Fred imagines himself to be the cat and he reports to other people what it would be wise to do if one was a clever cat. The rest of us understand him, since we follow the same procedure. All this leaves us within *our mind*, whereas we and Fred wanted to talk about *the cat's* mind.

What kind of mental states does Cora have when she shows that obviously purposeful behavior? What goes on in her mind? Does she have propositional attitudes at all? So far we have only seen that Fred has done a bad job in specifying the *content* of Cora's supposed wants and states of knowledge.

If we can't employ the usual words we employ to describe people, how could we describe the minds of cats? That's a challenge to Linda. If she doesn't want to use human psychology with cats, she has to introduce some new or related terminology that does two things: On the one hand it has to be different from talk about propositional attitudes, since that talk is apparently not applicable to cats. On the other hand the way we talk about cats' intentions has to be similar to talk about propositional attitudes, since otherwise we won't understand how our usual way of talking about cats works so well, more or less. Developing a model and a terminology to talk about the cat's mind is a challenging task for a philosopher interested in cats' minds.

Cats and Their Belief-like States

How can Linda try to answer this challenge? Her best bet may be to say that cats don't have beliefs (and other propositional attitudes), but instead they have *belief-like states*. The "like" qualifier corresponds to the mentioned objective that the states that a cat has should be characterized as similar to human beliefs or propositional attitudes.

This idea arose as follows. While looking for beliefs and wishes in cats seems as obvious as looking for sensation or awareness in general, it's highly unlikely that animals have beliefs and desires in the same sense that humans do. Given our advanced understanding of human cognitive and linguistic faculties it's a non-starter to look for these structures in animal cognition. Better to start with human cognitive faculty *x* and see whether animals have *something like x*. From this *something like* way of rendering things an appropriate terminology of cognitive ethology (the scientific study of animal cognition and intelligent behavior) can take off.

Are We Just Taking an Intentional Stance?

To take the intentional stance towards something is to treat it as if it had beliefs, desires, fears, wishes, or hopes. We sometimes do this even when we know that the entity doesn't really have those things, as when we say that the malfunctioning computer hates us. In these cases the intentional idiom (of "hate" in the case of the computer) is employed only as a place holder for an explanation to come at the design or physical level of the system.

You can talk about an ant in intentional terms: "The ant *wants* to get to the food and confronted with the *choice* between two paths; *it believes* the right path to be the better." But we could describe the ant's behavior without any mention of intentions. Ants are rigidly controlled by olfactory input. An ant looks for food that gives more energy than needed to get it, and confronted with two paths the shorter one will have, after a period of use by co-working ants, more ant scent, so the ant takes it.

There might be animals in which the intentional description is the most simple or even the only one we have so far. Reduction of the "intentional level" to the "design level" (without mentioning intentions) might become possible only in the future. The design level is considered to be more basic, since here we can employ engineering terminology—we don't have to talk about psychological states, which in general are difficult to describe and even harder to put into psychological laws.

There's a crucial distinction between built-in intentionality and intentionality coupled with awareness of the intentional state. "Built-in intentionality" can exist in a missile that was designed by someone to follow a path to its target. Its cunning is only built-in, the missile doesn't think about what it's doing, it does not consciously consult maps or reflect on the proper course. So built-in intentionality can exist without any actual intentions being present.

We expect a cat to be more complex and more interesting than a missile, but we have to face the possibility that cats might have no more than built-in intentionality: We may be able to interpret the cat in intentional terms, and maybe the cat is a computationally controlled system, but that does not settle the question whether the cat *experiences* states with different *content*. Is something "going on" in Cora's mind when she scans the kitchen for the cheese? Is her mind filled with some smell or pictorial scene? Humans have experiences, and they can represent their intentional states in language. Fred can tell us, "Now I see that the cheese is under the cupboard." It is "like" something for Fred to see that the cheese is under the cupboard. Is it like something for the cat to be in the state *we* describe as "belief" or "desire"?

Why Focus on Belief- and Desire-like States at All?

Consciousness or sentience, which we ascribe to cats, must be connected to states of 'recognizing' and 'doing' since otherwise there would be no point in having it. We can certainly say that Cora feels pain when Fred—inadvertently, of course—steps on her tail. Feeling pain makes sense only if you can have a belief about its cause and develop a wish to avoid it. Cora learns to avoid Fred's feet when he stumbles along in the evening. These states of 'recognizing' and 'doing' need not be beliefs and desires in the full human sense, but we can often explain cats using belief and desire psychology, so the states they are in have a similar role to beliefs and desires. Desire-like attitudes regulate behavior within an *expe-*

rienced situation, so it would be queer if there were nothing "like" what it is to have them.

Are Belief-like States Not Beliefs?

Beliefs are fine-grained—they involve fine-grained concepts. So beliefs require language, which is able to supply words with fine-grained meanings. Beliefs ideally form a system that has to be coherent. Such a system is not necessarily completely consistent and worked out, but contains connections and logical relations between all the areas one has beliefs about. Individually acquired new beliefs are not put in a belief bag, but have to be integrated coherently into your belief system. So individual beliefs have to be represented as being believed (for example "I believe A", "I believe B", "So I believe both A and B").

Thus one represents beliefs as being believed, and one can express this as "I know or believe that I believe A." This is called a higher-order belief, since it is a belief *about* another belief. Not every belief is immediately accompanied by a higher-order belief. But sometimes we need to consider explicitly which beliefs can be accepted or which have to be given up in the light of new evidence, and these reflections aiming at a justified set of beliefs require higher-order beliefs. Since all beliefs are beliefs only by being part of a belief system, having beliefs requires higher-order beliefs and so requires having the *concept of belief.*

Higher-order beliefs relate to lower-order beliefs by relying on the concepts of belief and truth, for example if Fred believes "I thought that Cora wanted cheese, but she was going for the water" he has a higher-order belief about his belief concerning Cora's wishes and now sees that this belief was wrong. Cats and other animals use sign systems or make signaling sounds (mostly to each other). These systems, however, are not called "language" by most linguists, since they have no clearly separated units that are recombined into new expressions, as the words of a human language are recombined by grammar to form new sentences. There are different pitches of meowing, but they cannot be freely combined to create larger meaningful units. Cats do not use language to represent ideas. They don't represent beliefs—at least not consciously. But there might be a tacit level of information representation that supports ascribing something like beliefs to cats. Applying the psychology of beliefs and desires to my cats does seem to be successful.

When it comes to the mental structure and faculties of a cat we have to say that the logic seen by the interpreter is merely built-in on the side of the cat: Assuming this kind of computational level in the animal one may say that the cat "works logically," just as an engineer may tell us how a technological devices incorporates some logic. A sophisticated thermostat "works logically," without itself using logic to reason with, or being aware of its workings.

Belief-like states are not part of the accessible mind of my cat. The cat might have a content of awareness that as a sensation is tied to some belief-like state, feeling "Wow!" in the belief-like state with a content like "That smells real good! I wanna take a look there." We can't get at this representation in the cat's mind. It cannot be like a sentence in a human language, but the mental state a cat is in when expecting food is a state different from the one it has when it's chasing a mouse. Maybe these states are not just states of experience; their content might be more structured. So we should say that animals like cats, which require an intentional description or the behavior of which requires some kind of psychology, have belief-like states or desire-like states.

Can There Be a Theory of Belief-like States?

A theory of belief-like states would have to work itself bottom-up towards belief. It would explain features of belief-like states that serve their purpose without making them full-blooded beliefs. Building-blocks of such a theory can be found in Jonathan Bennett's theory of *registration*: Registrations are more simple than beliefs, goals are more simple than desires, despite there being a structure similar to belief/desire psychology. A state simpler than a conscious representation may be called a *target state*, since the system's or animal's reactions and sensory systems are focused on this state.

If the system or animal reacts according to this focusing and brings about some change in its body to change its environment, that change is called an *operative state*, since given the target the system or animal now initiates some operation towards it. A system registers a *target state* (where that may be some state of affairs like the cheese being in the kitchen), if the system is in a sensory state which is similar to an *operative state* with respect to the target state; a state being "operative with respect to a target state" if a behavior *because* of the target state obtaining was not accidental.

We may say that Cora registers the cheese because her behavior can be explained as appropriately related to her cheese detection. Conscious state are *transparent* to conscious beings, since they know that they have them. Registering need not be transparent to a system (even a Cruise Missile can register something), but given assumptions about what Cora registers we can suppose what goals Cora has. Registering does not require language nor does pure registering require awareness. There's no doubt that my cats do register what's going on in the kitchen. We approach belief-like states when registering is supplemented with further faculties, for example being able to *learn* given conditional registrations or being a system that *strives* for new information to extend its behavioral repertoire. Developing such an account might give us belief-like states which are not beliefs but provide explanatory power in the case of cats and allow for a description of belief-like states which tries to depict or imagine how they are experienced from the animals point of viewThus we may be in a good position to claim that cats have belief-like states. Belief-like states are separated from human beliefs because they lack concepts in the proper sense.

Concepts in the Cat's Mind

In philosophy one might ask first what concepts are. Does being in possession of a concept mean having some mental representation, to manipulate some symbols or to show a systematic pattern of behaviour? These are important questions, but more important are the properties philosophers think concepts have.

Concepts:

- are *fine grained* ("the older brother" is distinct from "the first son" even if they are the same person). Suppose Fred is the first son. One can have the belief "that the older brother is coming" and prepare an additional dish having invited Fred's family, since one can only be the older brother if there is a younger brother. The belief "that the first son is coming" need not have this consequence, even if in case of Fred he actually has a younger brother. Tom may be a first son only. The two concepts are distinct.

- come in a *system* (a "kitchen" is defined relative to "cooking" and "house"—and so forth, just remember the difficulty in

giving a supposedly simple definition of "milk," already talking about colors and fluids)

- are *socially acquired and employed* in conditions of fit (we
  learn concepts from our parents and teachers, and we criticize people who misuse a word, say "kitchen" applied to
  your living room)

- might be causally rooted (that is, fixed to some sensory input
  like a coloured surface, for example the concept of *redness*)

Cat behavior can neither be interpreted in a fine grained fashion
(the cat does not care about whether her owner should be considered an older brother or a first son) nor is their employment of a
supposed concept rooted in *social* behaviour patterns.

Having a *system* of beliefs means to keep this system coherent,
so it requires the possession of higher-order beliefs, and *rationality*—things way beyond the cat's mind. The cat cannot explicitly
consider the question of whether her beliefs about the position of
the cheese run into conflict with her other beliefs about the
kitchen.

Therefore cats possess no concepts in the sense we speak of
human concept possession, especially no theoretical concepts (like
electron, but even not ones like *kitchen*). They possess *systematic
discriminatory abilities* which are the precursors of concepts.

Discriminating a mouse is not having the concept *mouse*. Cats
may have something like our sensory channels and therefore somewhat similar discriminations (say, seeing red bricks). They might
possess the core of what makes an observational concept (like *red*)
in humans. We humans identify such a supposed representation by
the object being causally involved in our perception (say a red
brick). In animals the existence of such a representation can be
supposed given their discriminatory abilities and the way their
brain resembles ours. This involves several abilities:

(a) self-monitoring with *error-detection*; if Cora has learned
    well (by training her with payments of cheese) to press one
    lever after hearing a little bell and another lever after hear-
    ing a little whistle, it might occur that, having pressed the
    second lever after hearing the bell, she then tries to *correct*
    her mistake by turning to the first lever; this again involves

(b) an internal representation of *what* is discriminated (here: the bell) and memory of how the action has been done (here: having pressed the wrong lever), so that this results in

(c) an *improvement* of discriminatory abilities (here: following the bell and whistle rules more strictly).

A cat has systematic abilities in discrimination if it can be trained to classify some objects into a group, and shows error-correction behaviour once it observes it has put some object into the wrong group. It has been shown that pigs can do this—you may want to try it with your cat. Even if we don't call the mental representations in the cat's categorization scheme "concepts," they are *something like* concepts, precursors of concepts unfortunately being isolated instead of systematic.

Yes and No

Talking to our friends and neighbors and telling them about what our pets do, there's no problem in seeing cats as more or less similar to people. But once we learn about the intricacies of human cognition we may doubt the mere existence of relevant cat cognition at all. Yet we should not over-react. We have to see cats in an appropriate light: while they can't do some of the things we do, they can do things a flea or a fish can't do.

The challenge of a serious study of animal cognition is to see both how cats' cognitive faculties are like ours and where they differ. Cats don't really have beliefs because they don't have propositional attitudes in the proper sense. They do, however, have something similar, which we can call belief-like states. The hard work to be done is to develop a better theory of these states, showing their differences from, but also their similarities to, human beliefs.

Do cats have beliefs? Strictly speaking, no. But, in a sense, yes, they do.

13

The Many Ways to Skin a Cat

ROBERT ARP

My kitty seems pretty clever. She can jump up on the counter, reach up to the cabinet above, paw open the cabinet door, knock her kitty treat canister from the cabinet to the counter, and pry off the canister top with her teeth to get at the morsels inside. Actually, she did this only after seeing me provide her with a treat countless times. However, when I put a box of cereal in front of the cabinet door, it didn't occur to her that she could push the box aside to open the door. And when I used tape to seal the door, she just pawed at it and meowed. No treat for kitty these times.

On the other hand, my two-and-three-quarter-year-old daughter Zoe is not just clever; she's also crafty and creative. Recently, I placed her on the counter, showed her where I put the potato chips in the cabinet right next to the kitty treat, and then shut the cabinet door. She opened the cabinet to get at the potato chips just like my kitty. But unlike poor kitty, my little cereal box and tape experiments were no match for her craftiness and creativity. She simply moved the box and—more fascinatingly—picked up a butter knife that was sitting on the counter and used *it* to pry open the cabinet door! Potato chips *and* kitty treats for all interested parties this time!

Zoe's craftiness and creativity don't stop there. The other day, for the very first time, she pulled a chair over to the counter so that she could get upon it and reach a granola bar on the counter that my wife and I had purposely put out of her reach (little stinker!). She's also pushed her stroller in front of me to block me from catching her while playing "chase," and she ran into a room and closed the door behind her, again, so as to avoid being caught by me during chase. I don't recall my wife or myself performing these kinds of actions in front of her, nor do I recall her ever witnessing these activities on TV or in real life. In other words, it would seem that she performed these acts spontaneously, without having been shown how they were done or trained to do them.

Creative problem solving abilities, although present in my daughter Zoe, come out more fully in people as they grow in age and experiences. This is why younger people more resemble cats and other animals in learning how to solve routine problems, whereas you and I (who are old enough to understand this chapter) can solve routine and nonroutine problems.

We can train cats and other animals to push objects in order to block things or climb upon them, and we can teach them to shut doors and even use tools. I have no doubt that my cat could be trained (by an expert) to move the cereal box away from the cabinet door or even use a butter knife with her mouth to pry open the taped cabinet door. But untrained spontaneous kinds of activities—activities that are wholly new, creative, and "crafty"—seem to be beyond the ability of a cat, or any animal other than a human, for that matter.

Humans not only manufacture products, they manufacture products *to manufacture products*, as well as successfully negotiate environments, hypothesize, invent, thrive, dominate the planet, and solve all kinds of problems in creative ways. Although some animals exhibit fairly sophisticated forms of problem solving— think of gorillas and chimps we hear about in the news every so often—they are still limited in their mental abilities when it comes to devising wholly *novel* solutions to problems. In other words, it seems that animals have a limited number of ways to "skin a cat," whereas humans can skin a cat in countless ways.

Here, we can distinguish between *routine problem solving* and *nonroutine creative problem solving*. In routine problem solving, an animal recognizes many possible solutions to a problem, given that the problem was solved through one of those solutions in the past, or the animal was shown how to perform some act, like my kitty witnessing me get her treat for her, time and again. Animals constantly perform routine problem solving activities that are basic to their survival, examples of which include a bee learning from another bee where food might be located, an orangutan using a stick to knock fruit out of a tree, or my kitty getting at her treat in the clever way just mentioned.

The *human* animal performs routine problem solving acts, but also can engage in more spontaneous and creative activities such as invent tools, put together wholly unrelated concepts, and devise novel solutions to problems that have never been shown to them in the past. If someone decided to pursue a *wholly new way* to solve a problem by, say, inventing some kind of tool that aids in the construction of other tools, then we would have an instance of *nonroutine creative* problem solving. Nonroutine creative problem solving involves finding a solution to a problem that has not been solved previously, and the invention of a tool-making tool would be an example of nonroutine creative problem solving because the inventor didn't have a way to solve the problem already. To my knowledge, no instance of a non-human animal inventing a tool in order to make another tool—*on its own without being shown by anyone else*—has ever been documented.

So, what is it that my two-and-three-quarter-year-old and other cat-owning humans have that enables them to do spontaneous, creative, and crafty kinds of things, which cats and other animals seem to lack? In other words, why is it that cats and other animals can solve routine problems, but the cat-owning human animal is able to solve routine problems *as well as* nonroutine problems creatively?

Evolutionary Psycho-Babble

Evolutionary Psychology is the science that studies the evolutionary mechanisms that have aided in the formation of the architecture of the modern human mind. According to many evolutionary psychologists, the mind is like a Swiss Army knife loaded with specific mental *tools* that evolved in our past to solve specific problems of survival, such as fear-of-snakes, face recognition, mental maps, kinship, language acquisition, mate selection, and cheater detection. The specific mental "tools" are commonly referred to as *modules, domains,* or *intelligences.* The famous psychologist Steven Pinker claims that the mind "is not a single organ but a system of organs, which we can think of as psychological faculties or mental modules."[1]

---

[1] Steven Pinker, *How the Mind Works* (New York: Norton), p. 27. For the basics concerning evolutionary psychology, see Leda Cosmides and John Tooby, "The Psychological Foundations of Culture," in J. Barkow, L. Cosmides and J. Tooby, eds., *The Adapted Mind: Evolutionary Psychology and the Generation of Culture*

Evolutionary psychologists think that psychological modules emerged to deal with the challenges posed by the environment in which our hominid ancestors lived, much like any other biological trait that evolves through evolutionary influences. Although this has been much debated in recent years, many evolutionary psychologists look to the Pleistocene epoch—which began some two million years ago and lasted almost a million years—as *the* time-period during which the basic architecture of the modern human mind was solidified. In the midst of all of the climate change, new food sources, and different animals coming on the scene during this epoch, the famous evolutionary psychologists Leda Cosmides and John Tooby tell us that "simply to survive and reproduce, our Pleistocene ancestors had to be good at solving an enormously broad array of adaptive problems—problems that would defeat any modern artificial intelligence system." [2]

The human brain has a common evolutionary ancestry with other animal brains. Although humans have an unusually developed frontal cortex compared with other animals, they do share the midbrain and brain stem with other mammals, birds, and reptiles. This being the case, humans and cats also share many of the same psychological modules; for instance, instinctive kinds of reactions and basic forms of awareness. So, both cats and cat-owners have automatic modular, reflex-like, responses to snakes slithering across their paths, objects in their visual field, and certain facial expressions.

A module handles only one kind of adaptive problem to the exclusion of others. Modules are "encapsulated" in this sense, and don't share information with one another. For example, my cheater-detection module evolved under a certain set of circumstances, and has no direct connection to my fear-of-snakes module, which evolved under a different set of circumstances. Like the various kinds of tools in a Swiss Army knife, the various mental modules are supposed to solve the various problems that arise in

---

(Oxford University Press, 1992), pp. 19–136; also David Buss, *Evolutionary Psychology: The New Science of the Mind* (Allyn and Bacon, 1999). Although a fascinating research program, evolutionary psychology has its problems and critics: see David Buller, *Adapting Minds: Evolutionary Psychology and the Persistent Quest for Human Nature* (MIT Press, 2005); and Robert Arp, *Scenario Visualization: An Evolutionary Account of Creative Problem Solving* (MIT Press, 2007).

[2] Leda Cosmides and John Tooby, "Origins of Domain Specificity: The Evolution of Functional Organization," in L. Hirschfeld and S. Gelman, eds., *Mapping the Mind: Domain Specificity in Cognition and Culture* (Cambridge University Press, 1994), p. 90.

circumstances; but they do so to the exclusion of each other. The scissors of the Swiss Army knife are not functionally related to the Phillips-head screwdriver, which is not functionally related to the toothpick, and so on.

This kind of encapsulation works best for environments where the responses need to be quick and routine; such instruments enabled animals to respond efficiently and effectively in their environments. Think of a cat's response to its prey or predator. A cat needs to have a quick response in order to be able to eat or avoid being eaten. This being the case, the modules could perform quite well as long as the environments remained relatively unchanged and typical. In fact, most of this modular processing in animals probably occurs at the unconscious level, and that's why both cats and cat-owners are able to respond fairly quickly to the pressures associated with fighting, fleeing, eating, and mating.

A Problem with Evolutionary Psycho-Babble

However, there seems to be a problem with the typical evolutionary psychologist's reasoning. If mental modules are encapsulated, and are designed to perform certain *routine* functions, how can this modularity account for *novel* circumstances where interpretation of never-before-seen images, circumstances, or situations might be important? Imagine the environments of the Pleistocene epoch. The climate shift in Africa from jungle life to desert and savannah life forced our early hominins to come out of the trees, and survive in totally new environments. Given a fortuitous genetic code, some hominins re-adapted to the new African landscape, some migrated elsewhere to new places like Europe and Asia; but most died out. This environmental shift had a dramatic effect on modularity, since now the specific content of the information from the environment in a particular module was no longer relevant. The information stored in the memory banks of mental modules that was formerly suited for jungle life could no longer be relied upon in the new environment of the savannah. Appealing to modularity *alone* would have led to certain death and extinction of many mammalian species. In fact, countless thousands of mammalian species did become extinct, as fossil data indicate.[3]

---

[3] For more on climate changes and the out-of-Africa hypothesis, see William Calvin, *A Brief History of the Mind: From Apes to Intellect and Beyond* (Oxford

The successful progression from the typical jungle life to the *very different and novel* savannah life of our early hominin ancestors would have required some other kind of mental capacity to emerge that could handle the new environment creatively. Mere mental associations between and among already stored memories, or trial-and-error kinds of mental activities, would not be enough. Although important, modules have their limitations, since they do all of their associative work in routine environments. However, what happens if an environment radically changes, making the information that a particular module characteristically selects no longer relevant? A radical re-adaptation and re-adjustment would be needed, one that transcends the limitations of the routine. This totally new environment would require that we be *creative* or *innovative* in order to survive. But how is it that we can be creative in this way?

Mithen to the Rescue

This is where the archeologist Steven Mithen has made an advance upon the standard evolutionary psychologist's account of encapsulated modules.[4] Mithen sees the evolving hominin mind as going through a three-step process. The first step begins prior to six million years ago when the primate mind was dominated by what he calls a *general intelligence module*. This module consisted of an all-purpose, trial-and-error learning mechanism that was devoted to multiple tasks. All behaviors were imitated, associative learning was slow, and there were frequent errors made, much like the mind of a cat or chimpanzee.

The second step coincides with the evolution of the *Australopithecine* line, and continues all the way through the *Homo* lineage to *Homo neandertalensis* (Neanderthal Man). In this second step, multiple *specialized* modules, emerge alongside general intelligence. Associative learning within these modules was faster, and more complex activities could be performed. Compiling data from fossilized skulls, tools, foods, and habitats, Mithen con-

---

University Press, 2004). For more on fossils and species extinction in our evolutionary past, see Michael Novacek, *Time Traveler: In Search of Dinosaurs and Ancient Mammals from Montana to Mongolia* (Farrar, Straus and Giroux, 2002).

[4] Steven Mithen, *The Prehistory of the Mind: The Cognitive Origins of Art, Science, and Religion* (Thames and Hudson, 1996).

cludes that *Homo habilis* probably had a general intelligence as well as modules devoted to social intelligence (because they lived in groups), natural history intelligence (because they lived off of the land), and technical intelligence (because they made tools). *H. Neandertals* and *Homo heidelbergensis* would have had all of these modules, including a primitive language module, because their skulls exhibit bigger frontal and temporal areas. According to Mithen, the Neanderthals and members of *H. heidelbergensis* would have had the Swiss Army knife mind that the standard evolutionary psychologist speaks about.

Mithen criticizes evolutionary psychologists who think that the essential ingredients of mind evolved during the Pleistocene epoch: "How do we account for those things that the modern mind is very good at doing, but which we can be confident that Stone Age hunter-gatherers never attempted, such as reading books and developing cures for cancer?" (pp. 45–46). The emergence of distinct mental modules *during the Pleistocene* that evolutionary psychologists speak about as being adequate to account for learning, negotiating, and problem solving *in our world today* can't be correct. For Mithen, the potential variety of problems encountered in generations subsequent to the Pleistocene is too vast for a much more limited Swiss Army knife mental repertoire; there are just way too many situations for which nonroutine creative problem solving would have been needed in order to not only simply survive, but also to flourish and dominate the Earth. There are potentially an infinite number of problems to be faced on a regular basis by animals as they negotiate environments. It does not seem that there would be a way for fifteen, twenty, twenty-five—or even a thousand—domains to handle all of these potential problems. *That* cat-owners negotiate environments so well shows that we have some capacity to handle the various and sundry potential nonroutine problems that arise in our environments.

Cognitive Fluidity and Cat-Owning Creativity

Here is where the third step in Mithen's evolution of the mind comes into play, known as *cognitive fluidity*. In this final step— which coincides with the emergence of modern humans some one hundred thousand years ago—the various mental modules begin working together with a *fluid* flow of knowledge and ideas between and among them. The modules become un-encapsulated, and information and learning from one module can now "flow out" and influence another module, resulting in an almost limitless capacity for imagination, learning, and problem solving. The working together of the various mental modules as a result of this cognitive fluidity *is* human, cat-owning consciousness for Mithen and represents the most advanced form of mental activity.

Mithen uses the construction of a medieval cathedral as an analogy to the mind and consciousness. Each side chapel represents a mental module. The side chapels are closed off to one another during construction, but allow people to have access from the outside to attend liturgies, much like mental modules are closed off to one another (encapsulated) and have specified input cues. Once the cathedral chapels have been constructed and the central domed superchapel is in place, the doors of all of the chapels are opened and people are allowed to roam freely from chapel to chapel. In a similar way, modern humans have evolved the ability to allow information to be freely transmitted between and among mental modules, and this cognitive fluidity comprises consciousness.

Mithen goes on to note that his model of cognitive fluidity accounts for cat-owning creativity in terms of problem solving, art, ingenuity, and technology. His idea has initial plausibility, since no other animal has been able to achieve and accomplish what humans have, and it is arguable that the Neanderthals—who co-existed with early humans for some seventy thousand years—died off because they didn't have the conscious ability to re-adapt to the changing environment. It's also arguable that cat-owners wouldn't exist today if they had not evolved consciousness to deal with novelty. No wonder, then, that the famous neuroscientist Francis Crick has maintained that "without consciousness, you can deal only with familiar, rather routine situations or respond to very limited information in new situations." Also, as the philosopher of mind John Searle observes: "one of the evolutionary advantages conferred on us by consciousness is the much greater flexibility, sensitivity, and creativity we derive from being conscious."[5]

Modular processes can be used to explain how the mind functions in relation to routinely encountered features of environments. However, depending on the radicalness of a novel environmental

---

[5] Francis Crick, *The Astonishing Hypothesis* (Simon and Schuster, 1994), p. 20; John R. Searle, *The Rediscovery of the Mind* (MIT Press, 1992), p. 109.

feature, *inter*-modular processes (Mithen's cognitive fluidity) may be required to deal effectively and, at times, creatively with the problem.

"Associating" with Cats and Other Animals

We already know that routine problem solving deals with the recognition of many possible solutions to a problem, given that the problem was solved through one of those solutions in the past. Here, we can link routine problem solving to the kind of trial-and-error strategizing and calculation that cats, cat-owners, and other animals typically engage in. In this sense, routine problem solving entails a mental activity that is stereotyped and wholly lacking in innovation, because there are simply perceptual *associative* connections being made by the mind of an animal. An image in the perception or memory of a *singular* module is associated with some environmental stimulus so as to learn some behavior, or produce some desired result. If that result is not achieved, an alternate route may be pursued utilizing another singular module in a one-to-one, trial-and-error fashion.

For example, Clive Wynne has presented studies showing that cats are able to associate routes in a maze with food acquisition. In these experiments, food was placed at the end of each arm of a radial maze, and a cat was placed in the center of the maze and was kept in the maze until all the food was collected. At first, the cat did not associate a certain path with the food; but after trial-and-error, the cat eventually got all of the food. In subsequent tests, the food was placed in the same spot in the maze, and the same cat was able to more quickly and efficiently associate the correct pathway with the acquisition of food.

Another example would be my kitty's ability to associate my behaviors and the cabinet with her kitty treat. Because of this association, she cleverly jumps on the counter and paws open the door to get at her treat. In fact, associative learning tests have been performed on humans and animals countless times. Nearly a century ago, William Hunter demonstrated that rats, raccoons, dogs, and cats are able to associate memories of a stimulus with the same stimulus perceived by the animal so as to solve some problem. Arnold Wright has shown that pigeons and monkeys can perform similar associations. A typical battery of IQ tests will have several association tests whereby people are asked to solve routine problems, such as linking a word to a picture or linking pictures to one another in a familiar sequence.[6]

Concerning nonroutine creative problem solving, we already know that this entails pursuing a wholly new way to solve a problem that hasn't been solved previously, and that the problem-solver didn't possess a way to solve the problem already. Here, however, we can draw a distinction between solving a nonroutine problem *through imitation with another's help*, and solving a nonroutine problem *on one's own*. Some animals appear to have the capacity to solve nonroutine problems, once the solutions have been shown to them, or imitated for them. Think of my kitty getting her own treat, once I showed her where it was located and how to get the lid off of the canister.

What might, at first, appear to be creativity may just turn out to be a clever set of singular mental associations. An animal may have the ability to solve a problem creatively through imitation with another's help. An octopus studied by Fiorito and his associates was observed as being able to unpop the cork on a jar to get at food inside. Initially, the octopus could see the food in the jar, but was unable to unpop the cork of the jar to get at the food. The next time, Fiorito's team unpopped the cork while the octopus was watching, resealed the jar, and gave it to him in his tank. The octopus was able to associate the unpopping of the cork with the acquisition of food, remembered what the scientists had shown him, and unpopped the cork himself to get at the food.

Chimps have been observed trying a couple of different ways to get at fruit in a tree—like jumping at it from different angles or jumping at it off of tree limbs—before finally using a stick to knock it down. Scientists also observe young chimps watching older chimps do the same thing. Like the octopus's problem solving ability, this seems to be a form of nonroutine creative problem solving by use of another's help. In fact, several observations have been made of various kinds of animals engaged in imitative behaviors:

---

[6] Clive Wynne, *Animal Cognition: The Mental Lives of Animals* (New York: Macmillan, 2002); William Hunter, "The Delayed Reaction in Animals and Children," *Behavior Monographs* 2 (1913), pp. 1–86; Arnold Wright, "Memory Processing by Pigeons, Monkeys, and People," *Psychology of Learning and Motivation* 24 (1989); Robert Sternberg, *Practical Intelligence in Everyday Life* (Cambridge University Press, 2000).

there are imitative behaviors in rats, birds, and orangutan, as well as in children, chimpanzees, and cats.[7]

However, the number of possible solution routes is limited in these examples of routine problem solving. If either the octopus's corked jar was sealed with Crazy Glue, or there were no sticks around, or there were no other older chimps or researchers around to show younger chimps how to use sticks, the octopus and chimpanzees in the above cases likely would starve to death. So too, my kitty wasn't able—all on her own—to devise a way to pry the door open when I taped the cabinet door shut. Like the other animals, the poor kitty would starve to death if I didn't provide the food for her! The possible solution routes are limited because the mental modules of these animals are *encapsulated* and, as a result, are limited to stereotypical kinds of one-to-one modular associations. It occurs to my kitty to associate "cabinet" with "food" and "food" with "satisfaction of hunger." But, because her mental modules are encapsulated, it would never occur to my kitty to associate "knife" with "mouth," "cereal box" with "blocked access to kitty treat," or "knife" with "tool to pry door open."

Psychologist Michael Bitterman has tested the intelligence levels of fish, turtles, pigeons, rats, cats, and monkeys with a variety of tasks, including pushing paddles in water, pecking or pressing lighted disks, and crawling down narrow runways. Although such animals improved their abilities to perform these tasks as time went on, Bitterman found that these species only could perform a limited number of associative learning tasks. This data, along with the data concerning the octopus, chimps, orangutans, rats, birds, and cats supports the idea that these animals are engaged in mostly habitual, stereotyped forms of associative thinking and learning.[8]

---

[7] Giovanni Fiorito et al., "Problem Solving Ability of *Octopus vulgaris* Lamark (*mollusca cephalopodo*), *Behavior and Neural Biology* 53 (1990), pp. 217–230. For studies of imitation in animals, see Gregory Hall, "Pavlovian Conditioning: Laws of Association," in N. Mackintosh, ed., *Animal Learning and Cognition* (Academic Press, 1994), pp. 15–43; also Gregory Hall, "Learning about Associatively Activated Stimulus Representations: Implications for Acquired Equivalence and Perceptual Learning," *Animal Learning and Behavior* 24 (1996).

[8] Michael Bitterman, "Cognitive Evolution: A Psychological Perspective," in C. Heyes and L. Huber, eds., *The Evolution of Cognition* (MIT Press, 2000), pp. 61–79.

"Bissociating" with Cat-Owners and Other Humans

Unlike routine problem solving, which deals with associative connections within familiar perspectives, nonroutine creative problem solving entails an innovative ability to make connections between *wholly unrelated* perspectives or ideas. Again, this kind of problem solving can occur as a result of imitation through another's help— as in the above octopus, chimpanzee, and my kitty examples—as well as on one's own. A cat-owning human seems to be the only kind of being who can solve nonroutine problems *on her/his own, without imitation or help.* This is not to say that humans don't engage in solving nonroutine problems through imitation; in fact, nonroutine problem solving by imitation occurs all of the time, especially in the earlier years of a human's life. This is just to say that humans are the only animals who have the potential to consider wholly new routes to problem solving.

Arthur Koestler referred to this quality of the creative mind as a *bissociation of matrices.* When a human bissociates, that person puts together ideas, memories, representations, stimuli, and the like in wholly new and unfamiliar ways *for that person.* Echoing Koestler, Margaret Boden calls this an ability to "juxtapose formerly unrelated ideas."[9] It would seem that the ability to generate a wholly new understanding of a situation is an integral component of creativity.

Unlike animals, humans *bissociate,* and are able to ignore typical, singular module associations, and try out *novel* ideas and approaches in solving problems. Such an ability to bissociate accounts for more advanced forms of problem solving whereby the routine or habitual associations are the kinds of associations that precisely *need to be avoided, ignored, or bracketed out* as irrelevant to the optional solution. Bissociation also has been pointed to as an aid in accounting for risibility, hypothesis-formation, art, technological advances, and the proverbial "ah-hah," creative insight, eureka moments humans experience when they come up with a new idea, insight, or tool.

So, when we ask how it is that humans can be creative, part of what we are asking is how they bissociate, namely, *juxtapose for-*

---

[9] Arthur Koestler, *The Act of Creation* (Dell, 1964); Margaret Boden, *The Creative Mind: Myths and Mechanisms* (Basic Books, 1990).

merly unrelated ideas in wholly new and unfamiliar ways for that person. To put it colloquially, humans can take some idea found "way over here in the left field" of the mind and make some coherent connection with some other idea found "way over here in the right field" of the mind. Humans seem to be the only species that can engage in this kind of mental activity; alas, my poor kitty can't bissociate! Mithen's idea of cognitive fluidity helps to explain our ability to bissociate because the potential is always there to make innovative, previously unrelated connections between ideas or perceptions, given that the information between and among modules has the capacity to be mixed together, or intermingle. In essence, cognitive fluidity accounts for bissociation, which accounts for human creativity in terms of problem solving, art, ingenuity, and technology.

So, my daughter has the ability to make wholly new and seemingly unrelated mental associations. It occurs to Zoe to associate "cabinet" with "food" and "food" with "satisfaction of hunger," just like my kitty. But, because her mental modules are un-encapsulated and information can fluidly flow between and among modules, it also occurs to her that she can bissociate "knife" with "mouth," "cereal box" with "blocked access to kitty treat," or "knife" with "tool to pry door open." The little stinker can also bissociate "stroller" with "blockade so daddy can't get me," or "stool to sit on" with "object that can be used to step upon and reach the counter above"!!!

In Mithen's terminology, Zoe's mental modules are un-encapsulated or open enough so that the typical information about knives, strollers, and stools can be utilized in different and atypical ways. And the older she gets, the more she'll be able to bissociate, as well as be impressed or shocked by her own creative abilities.

More than One Way to Skin a Cat

At some point in human history, someone came up with the expression that heads the title of this last section. Although it sounds horrible, I would never *actually* do it, and I don't condone it, I'm sure that cat-owners could come up with a multitude of "creative" ways to skin a kitty cat!

With his idea of cognitive fluidity, Steven Mithen has given us an important and plausible explanation for why it is that cat-owners will continue to bissociate ideas and "skin cats" in creative ways. So, all of you cat-owners can bring your cats over to my place for potato chips and kitty treats. And, if there's a problem with accessing them from the cabinet, I'm sure Zoe, my wife, or I will figure out a way to get at them.

IV

Metaphysics for Cats

14

Cats in the Afterlife

JUDY BARAD

Do cats survive the death of their bodies? People who believe in life after death invariably wonder whether or not their feline family members will also continue to exist after they leave their bodies. Though there's much popular anecdotal literature about this subject, there's hardly any philosophical treatment of it.

C.S. Lewis, the late professor of Medieval literature at Cambridge University, devoted a chapter in *The Problem of Pain* to the question of whether an animal afterlife is possible. Connecting consciousness to the notion of a soul, Lewis denies both that animals like cats are conscious and that they have a soul. He suggests, however, that housecats and other domestic animals may have an afterlife due to their relationship with their human caretakers.

Conversely, Richard Swinburne contends in *The Evolution of the Soul* that animals are both conscious and have a soul based on the complexity of their mental states. Yet he maintains that it's unlikely that any animal, even a cat, survives the death of his or her body.

I, however, will argue that *if* humans survive the death of their bodies, then so do our feline friends. Using some of Swinburne's insights and an argument of St. Thomas Aquinas (1225–1274), I hope to develop a better argument for a cat afterlife than the one offered by Lewis.

The Gulf between Humans and Cats

Trying to reconcile how a good God can allow cats and other animals to suffer, Lewis urges us to realize that animals are not all the same:

> If the ape could understand us he would take it very ill to be lumped
> along with the oyster and the earth-worm in a single class of "animals"
> and contrasted to men. Clearly . . . the ape and man are much more
> like each other than either is like the worm. (*The Problem of Pain*, p.
> 131)

Cats would be very indignant indeed if they knew that many people erroneously lump them together with oysters and earthworms.
How, cats might wonder, could any human ignore the clear fact
that they have fine, complex feline minds while oysters and earthworms don't seem to have a mind at all?

Even more astounding are those people who deny that humans
are animals, although they will admit humans are mammals! They
group together animals, ranging from the amoeba to the cat, on
one side of living beings separated by a vast chasm from human
beings on the other side. Yet, considered biologically, the notion of
an enormous gap between humans and cats is all wet.

Evolutionary theory shows no sharp separation between
humans and other mammals. Charles Darwin wrote in *The Descent
of Man*,:

> There is a much wider interval in mental power between one of the
> lowest fishes . . . and one of the higher apes, than between an ape and
> man; yet this immense interval is filled up by numberless gradations.
> (1:35)

There's a continuous degree of capacities and functions among the
various species, from the simplest living organisms to human
beings. Thinking is a biological adaptation we share with other
warm-blooded animals, like cats, rather than a special ability that
sets humans apart from the rest of nature. Cats and other warm-
blooded animals are more intelligent than clams, and they're capable of learned behavior. Less cognitively developed animals, which
act primarily on unlearned tendencies, appear earlier in the fossil
record than cats. Given the continuity between humans and animals such as cats, evolutionary facts expose the supposed chasm
separating the two as illusory. So Lewis is on good scientific ground
when he argues against lumping all animals into one group and
then contrasting them to humans.

Feline Frontal Lobes and the Question of Consciousness

Rather than looking at animals as one uniform group, Lewis distinguishes them by examining their degree of intelligence. He recognizes that we have no evidence of sentience at the lowest level of animal life. But given the fact that "the higher animals have nervous systems very like our own," Lewis writes that they are "almost certainly" sentient. All cats and other warm-blooded animals have fundamentally the same nervous system that humans have.

Even our brains are alike. Nicholas Dodman, director of the animal behavior clinic at Tufts University School of Veterinary Medicine, says:

> Cats have frontal, temporal, occipital, and parietal lobes of their cerebral cortex, as we do, and these brain regions are composed of gray and white matter, as they are in humans. And the various brain regions are connected in the same way as they are in humans and identical neurotransmitters are employed in conveyance of data.

More specifically, both humans and cats have identical regions in the brain responsible for emotion. If your cat rolls over and exposes his tummy, you know that he feels very secure in your relationship. It's also a way of demonstrating his pleasure in your company (http://www.i-pets.com/petfunt-cat.html).

After noting the likeness between the cat brain and human brain, Dodman adds that "Cats appear to think similarly to humans, receiving input from the same basic five senses and processing the data received just as we do" (Judith A. Stock, "Paws for Thought: Cat Intelligence," www.petplace.com).

For instance, a cat's sense of touch is one of the main ways she investigates new materials and objects. From the time she's a small kitten, a cat will use her paws to explore shape, size, and texture. Just think of how she shredded your furniture! Further, except for humans and other primates, cats are the only mammals which rely on sight instead of smell to learn about the world around them. It's probably no surprise to cat-lovers that cats share many of our key mental capacities. In short, Dodman's recognition of cat sentience supports Lewis's claim about the other higher animals being sentient.

Unconscious Sentience?

Although Lewis begins his argument in a way that's supported by scientists, such as Charles Darwin, and animal behaviorists, such as Dodson, his next claim is enough to ruffle a cat's fur. A sentient being is ordinarily thought to be conscious. But Lewis contends that an animal can be sentient without being conscious! Since a sentient being is one who feels and perceives, we may wonder how feeling and perception can take place unconsciously.

Lewis holds this odd view because he connects consciousness with having a soul, which he flatly denies that animals possess. He writes: "The simplest experience of ABC as a succession demands a soul which is not itself a mere succession of states, but rather a permanent bed along which these different portions of the stream of sensation roll" (*Problem of Pain*, p. 132). A merely sentient being would simply have "a succession of perceptions" without a "co-ordinating self," or soul which unifies them into one experience. Illustrating his argument, Lewis writes that the newt's "nervous system delivers all the *letters* A, P, N, I, but since they cannot read they never build up into the word PAIN. And all animals *may* be in that condition" (p. 138). So according to Lewis cats and other animals may merely have a series of separate perceptions that are rather meaningless. They wouldn't have a consciousness or soul that unifies these perceptions into one experience, even an experience of pain.

But if cats have no experience of pain, why would they shriek and run away when a human accidentally steps on one of their paws? More to the point, if a cat isn't aware of a painful sensation as happening to him as a distinct self, why would he avoid the clumsy human until the person expressed great remorse? The fact that most cats are slow to "forgive" indicates that they are conscious of pain as something that happened to their own bodies.

Lewis doesn't explain why he supposes there may be sentient animals who don't experience pain, although they have intact nervous systems and a functioning thalamus (which seems to mediate the experience of pain). He admits that unconscious sentience is unimaginable for us "not because it never occurs, but because, when it does, we describe ourselves as being unconscious" (p. 133).

Perhaps a better explanation of why we can't imagine unconscious sentience is because it doesn't exist. After all, the cat's nervous system and thalamus aren't just there for decoration. By denying that other animals are conscious, Lewis is returning to the idea that there's a sharp break between humans and the members of other species, an idea he repudiated earlier in his argument.

Cat Capers and Consciousness

Opposing Lewis's notion of unconscious sentience, evolution entails continuity between species rather than sharp breaks. According to evolutionary theory, when something new arises in nature, like consciousness, there must be some continuity with earlier, more primitive organisms. As animal life evolved, the nervous systems became more complex and animals became increasingly capable of consciousness. The cat certainly has a higher degree of consciousness than the oyster, if the latter is conscious at all. In short, consciousness isn't an all-or-nothing affair. It isn't something that is either fully present, exhibited only in highly abstract thought, or totally lacking.

The fact that cats adapt to changing circumstances indicates that they're conscious of their surroundings. If a cat's usual access to her food is blocked, she'll find a different approach. Learned behavior and adaptation indicate consciousness. When a cat learns how her new toy sets a ball in motion, she must pay attention to the task she's learning. But how can anyone pay attention to a task if he or she isn't conscious? The cat's learning ability is intimately related to her perception of a goal, which presupposes that she has desires, mental images, memory, and anticipation. The complex nervous system of cats allows them to determine what they will do as well as when, where, and how they will do it. A cat has control over whom he will socialize with, when he will socialize, and the locale of his socialization. His behavior provides evidence that he has a consciousness which directs his behavior, one that resembles human consciousness in a corresponding situation.

But Lewis doesn't think that behavior tells us anything about whether an animal is conscious or unconscious. Although he admits that animals react to pain "much as we do," he insists that this doesn't prove that they're conscious because humans may react in the same way "under chloroform, and even answer questions while asleep." This is the only reason he gives for claiming that an animal lacks the ability to distinguish itself from sensation so that it would be able to connect the sensation as *its* experience. Lewis insists that no cat or any other animal has a self or consciousness standing above the sensations and organizing them into an "experience" as we do.

Yet, in addition to the behavior of cats and other mammals, if we take into account our common evolutionary origin as well as the similarity of our nervous systems, we have even more evidence that such animals are indeed conscious. Based on the similar behavior of animals and humans, their similar nervous systems, and their evolutionary proximity, Darwin observed that "their nervous systems, their behaviors, their cries *are* our nervous systems, our behaviors, and our cries with only a little modification. They are our common property because we inherited them from the same ancestors."[1] In short, despite Lewis's denial, the combined facts of behavior, physiology and evolution provide a cogent argument for animal consciousness.

Human-Dependent Cat Souls?

Lewis grants that it's "difficult to suppose" that the apes, the elephant, and domestic cats don't have "a self or soul which connects experiences and gives rise to rudimentary individuality" (p. 133). But rather than exploring why we so naturally suppose that these animals have a self or soul, he quickly warns us not to consider them in themselves. Interpreting Genesis, he writes, "The beasts are to be understood only in their relation to man and, through man, to God" because God appointed man "to have dominion over the beasts" (p. 138).

Lewis claims that the divinely ordered human dominion over animals makes tame animals the only "natural" animals, writing that "in so far as the tame animal has a real self or personality, it owes this almost entirely to it master." According to Lewis, if a cat seems almost human, it's because his kindly master has made him so. By considering the cat though its relationship to its master, Lewis maintains that only the animal who has a close relationship with a human has a self or soul. So his claim entails that a cat only has a soul due to his master. In themselves animals lack a soul. If cats have a soul, Lewis concludes, it's possible that tame cats "may have an immortality, not in themselves, but in the immortality of their

---

[1] James Rachels, *Created From Animals: The Moral Implications of Darwinism* (Oxford University Press, 1990), p. 131.

masters." Only loved pets have an afterlife as part of the eternal life of their masters. In themselves, they have no more of an afterlife that a dandelion or stone. If Lewis is right, a feral cat or a neglected cat, who doesn't have this kind of relationship, would lack both a soul and an afterlife.

Lewis contends that animals have no personalities in themselves, but only as they are gifted with them by human beings. Yet people who closely observe feral cats, who have had little contact with humans, will object that animals within a particular species certainly do act differently from each other. Some are shy; some are outgoing. Some learn faster and some learn slower. Some are more playful while others are more sedentary. Some are more affectionate whereas others are more independent.

Aware that readers may ask about feral cats or abused and neglected cats, Lewis acknowledges that his "picture" doesn't cover them. He thinks it's very unlikely that any wild animal can attain a "self." But he writes that if they did have a self, "their immortality would also be related to man—not this time, to individual masters, but to humanity." In other words, Lewis says that *if* there's any real "quasi-spiritual and emotional value which human tradition attributes to a beast," then the beast will "attend" humanity in the afterlife "in *that* capacity." On the other hand, if this attribution is wrong, then the "beast's heavenly life" would be restricted to the value of the effect it had on humanity during its entire history (pp. 141–42).

Without a soul, it's hard to account for anyone surviving death. So Lewis's argument restricts the notion of a cat's afterlife to only those cats who have been in a loving relationship with people. Now if one accepts this line of reasoning, one could equally say that woman is to be understood only in her relation to man and, through man, to God because God, according to Genesis, intended woman to be the companion of man. Fortunately, we have come a long way from this kind of thinking. If we grant that it's absurd and reprehensible to think of women in this way, we should also recognize it's similarly absurd and reprehensible to think of cats and other non-human animals in this way. Also, it seems odd to say that a cat would suddenly develop a soul when she's taken home by a human. What power does the human have to create a soul, an immaterial substance, in someone? There's little rational foundation for this claim and Lewis doesn't attempt to supply any.

Considering cats in themselves, we must examine in more detail whether they have the sort of consciousness amounting to a "self or soul which connects experiences and gives rise to rudimentary individuality." Before turning to the more difficult notion of whether cats have a soul, it's appropriate to investigate the mental states which may give rise to the "rudimentary individuality" Lewis refers to.

Swinburne on the Mental States of Animals

In order to be an individual in the sense of a self, one must be able to think. Investigating animal thought, Richard Swinburne, unlike Lewis, both considers animals in themselves and also argues that the way they behave is important He writes that we're justified in ascribing to animals the kind of thoughts that provide an explanation of their behavior "which we would expect to occur in them in view of some similarity to ourselves."[2] Objectors commonly claim that thought is dependent on language. But Swinburne suggests that animal thoughts might take place by means of picture images of the objects and properties thought about (p. 76). In fact, we often have picture images in our minds, such as an image of our favorite feline, so it's not difficult for us to understand this type of thought.

In addition to thought, Swinburne maintains that the behavior of animals provides grounds for attributing to them a mental life of sensation, purpose, desire, and belief. When it takes half an hour to catch your cat so you can take her to the vet's office, you know that she has certain purposes, desires, and beliefs which explain her flight. She acts this way because she believes the cat carrier takes her to an undesirable place and that if she hides you won't be able to take her there. She recalls that she had disagreeable sensations at that undesirable place. When she complains loudly throughout the car ride to the vet's office, her purpose is to make you aware of her displeasure. In the vet's waiting room, she trembles as she tries to hide her face in your arm or your lap. Clearly, she hopes no one will see her. Her reaction to every aspect of this trip warrants attributing to her a system of beliefs, desires, and purposes. In short, cats and other intelligent animals possess purposes,

---

[2] Richard Swinburne, *The Evolution of the Soul* (Oxford University Press, 1986), p. 69.

desires, and thoughts whereby they form beliefs based on evidence, much as humans do.

Swinburne also argues that animals have beliefs about the future. The example about going to the vet illustrates this kind of belief. We can know what belief a cat has by observing her behavior. When my cats hear the detached garage door close, they run to the entry door of the house, believing that one of their humans will make an appearance and pay attention to them. This behavior is explained most clearly by ascribing to them beliefs about evidence, as well as beliefs about the future.

Not only does feline behavior reveal that cats have mental states, but the similarity of their brain structure, brain parts and brain material to that of humans also indicates that they have a mental life similar to ours. It's important to note that the brain is a necessary condition for possessing mental states. But this raises a big problem. For if the brain is necessary for mental states, then how can anyone, human or feline, survive the death of their bodies? Having argued that cats possess mental states, we must now turn to the question of whether mental states and brain states are identical. If they're identical, then when the brain dies, mental states will no longer exist.

The Brain and Soul-States

Swinburne claims that in order for individuals to have mental states at all, their brain needs to function. If specific parts of the cerebral hemispheres are destroyed by disease or injury, an individual will suffer loss of memory and motor skills. If some guy receives a blow on the head, his capacity to think is affected. Mental states are also affected by alcohol and other drugs. In some forms of insanity, physicians have found marked modifications of the brain tissue. In other words, the operation of the cerebral hemispheres is the immediate condition for mental states.

Yet Swinburne doesn't agree that mental states are identical with brain states. While mental events are connected to brain events, they're not those brain events themselves. To show that the two are not identical, he turns our attention to impaired brain events:

Most brain disease and injury, most drugs and brain surgery affect capacity (give to agents the ability to do or not to do things), not character. They remove (or . . . restore) or make it difficult or easy for an

agent to exercise a capacity to perform certain . . . mental actions or
to have thoughts . . . of certain kinds. (*Evolution of the Soul*, p. 276)

Someone's belief that certain goals are good and the naturalness of
certain desires persist despite brain damage. Due to his character,
some actions will come more naturally to him than others. It seems,
then, that while brain states affect our ability to think clearly, the general direction of our thought is due to our mental states themselves.

Swinburne disagrees with philosophers who claim that for each
kind of mental event there are one or more kinds of brain-event.
On this view, in order for a mental event to occur, a brain event
must occur. To show how unfounded this theory is, Swinburne
asks us to consider sensation, the simplest mental state. Physics and
chemistry can explain how a cat responds differently to light of a
certain wavelength than he does to light of another wavelength.
Yet, Swinburne continues, "what physics and chemistry are unable
to explain is why the brain-events to which the impinging light
gives rise, in turn give rise to sensations of blueness (as opposed
to redness) or a high noise rather than a low noise" (p. 186).

Swinburne observes that the reason why physics and chemistry
can't explain these things is that colors, tastes, and sounds "are not
the sort of thing physics and chemistry deal in." These sciences
examine physical properties. Since mental states differ from physical properties, they're outside the province of physics and chemistry. There's an immense qualitative difference between thoughts
with their in-built meanings and mere electrochemical events.
Given this humongous qualitative difference, it's impossible to construct a theory that allows us to successfully predict which new
thought, or other kinds of mental state, would be correlated with a
previously unexemplified brain-state (p. 193).

The Network of the Soul

Not only do brain states differ from mental states, but mental states
can cause other mental states. For example, if a cat desires to surprise another cat, she will hide and then pounce on the other cat
as he passes. Her desire, a mental state, causes her to behave in a
way, which she believes—another mental state—will surprise the
other cat.

Like desires, beliefs can cause other beliefs. In order to desire
something, an individual needs to have some beliefs about the

object of desire. For instance, my cat believes that if she meows at a certain table in the house, I'll lift her to it. She also knows that if I lift her to the table, she'll be able to reach her food. From these two beliefs, she infers that if she meows at the table when I'm present, she'll be able to reach her food.

Each belief and desire an individual has involves numerous other beliefs and desires to give it meaning. If I or my cat relinquish one belief, we must modify or relinquish other beliefs. Suppose Joe, a person my cat trusts, spanks her. This action will lead her to give up her belief that Joe is a kind person, a person who won't hurt her. Relinquishing her belief leads her to distrust Joe, which, in turn, causes her to give up her desire to be around Joe. According to Swinburne, her beliefs and desires are states of soul, which exclude new beliefs and desire that aren't compatible with her existing ones (p. 286).

Swinburne contends that we have long-term beliefs and desires, which we are aware of from time to time and which sometimes influence our behavior. A cat's desire for a loving relationship, for instance, couldn't arise unless cats have beliefs about which things in their environment can give love and what kinds of actions express love. The desire for a loving relationship is a long-term and usually long-lasting one, which doesn't have a direct bodily cause. Nor is it the kind of desire that she must be aware of when she rubs around her person. So there's a continuity between beliefs of which we are fully conscious and those of which we are only half-aware. It's the soul that provides for that continuity.

So Swinburne is arguing that we and other animals hold some beliefs because of other beliefs. Beliefs can't be reduced to mere brain-states. The same applies to desires; they aren't formed merely by brain-states. The continual interaction of our beliefs and desires builds up a structure of belief and desire, one that's distinct from any brain structure that may help to sustain it. It is a structure of the soul. This structure of the soul is a continuing one that determines at different moments of time which new beliefs an individual may acquire.

How does this argument relate to the soul and the possibility of an afterlife? Although Swinburne says that mental events inhere in the soul, he insists that mental events require an active brain to sustain them. When the body dies and the brain ceases to function, the soul will cease to function also. In Swinburne's view, this is the case regardless of whether one is a human or a cat.

And so Swinburne has argued that mental states are distinct from bodily states in both human and non-human animals, that mental states inhere in the soul of both human and non-humans, that the soul has a continuing structure, and that the soul cannot survive on its own, that is, independent of the body, regardless of species membership. His account contrasts with Lewis's, who claims that non-human animals lack a soul, though some may survive the death of their bodies.

The Cat Soul

So who is right? Do we agree with Lewis that cats lack a soul though some have an afterlife due to human kindliness? Or do we agree with Swinburne that cats have a soul but lack an afterlife? To answer this question, it's necessary to examine whether it's appropriate to suppose that such a thing as a soul exists.

St. Thomas Aquinas's argument supporting the existence of the soul begins by observing that some things are inert while other things are capable of movement, perception, thought, and desire. We call the former 'non-living' and the latter 'living'. If some bodies are living and others aren't, life can't be explained by the fact that a thing is a body. Aquinas contends that there must be some source that causes living things to be distinct from non-living things. This source can't be physical because if it were, then any material thing would be living, which is absurd.[3] A body is alive not merely because it's a physical thing but because of a cause which isn't bodily or material. Without an immaterial soul, a body would simply be a corpse. So it's the presence of a soul that distinguishes animate beings from inanimate beings. It's interesting to note that the Latin 'anima,' the root word of animated, means "which makes living things live."

Besides making things live, the soul is the substance which underlies mental activities. No activity exists separately from a substance. Try to think of the activity of running without someone or something running. It can't be done. Nor can color, pleasure, or weight cannot subsist in themselves. They are always found to inhere in a substance. In the same way, mental activities require a substance in which they are embedded. The activities of percep-

---

[3] St. Thomas Aquinas, *Summa Theologica,* I 18, 1.

tion, thought, and desire, which give rise to the distinction between animate and inanimate beings, presuppose the existence of the soul or a substance which unifies the various mental states of an animal. The cat knows that the sound of the can-opener is connected to the food she sees and tastes, which is what she desires.

Not only is the soul the coordinating, unifying principle of an organism, but the soul is also that by which an animal first becomes a living being. Now why couldn't this organizing principle be a physical organ, such as the brain, heart, or lungs? The simple answer is that the brain, heart and lungs are each a living organ. To say that the brain or any other bodily organ is the organizing principle of life is to return to the question of what makes each of these organs live. According to Aquinas, only something essentially different from a bodily organ can make these organs live and perform the activities of life. This organizing principle is the soul.

But even if the unifying source of life isn't any one organ, could it be the combination of organs arranged in a certain way? Aquinas contends that if the activity of the body could be explained by the organization of its internal parts, then the activity of one living body is explained by the activity of other living bodies. But the question at hand is what it is that makes a thing live. The same question pertains to any organ or combination of organs that cause movement. Since no bodily organ makes itself live, we must appeal to something non-bodily to account for the life of bodily parts. It is the soul that causes these bodily parts to live. The soul isn't an effect of the body, but its essence.

Using a different kind of argument to make the same point, Swinburne writes, "If you divide my cat's brain and transplant the two halves into empty cat skulls . . . , there is a truth about which subsequent cat is my cat which is not necessarily revealed by knowledge of what has happened to the parts of my cat's body." He concludes, " The moment some animal is conscious, there is a truth about whether he has reason to fear or hope to have the sensations of some later animal, and this truth is one not necessarily revealed by knowledge of what happens to the parts of the animal's body" (pp. 182–83). So, like Aquinas, Swinburne maintains that there is something non-bodily that gives an individual its unity, its essence.

Not only do Aquinas and Swinburne agree that the soul is the non-bodily essence of an individual, but both, in contrast to Lewis, recognize that animals have souls. Aquinas notes that *anima* is involved in the very meaning of animal (I–II 95, 4). This is due to the fact that the presence of life, and therefore the soul, is brought to our attention by the self-motion and sensation particular to animals.

Does the Soul Need the Body?

The question remains whether the soul can exist independently of the body. Aquinas argues that the human soul exists independently of the body, although he denies that the animal soul can continue to exist without the body. However, his argument can be extended to include the higher animals, those warm-blooded individuals like cats who are capable of thought and emotion.

Aquinas teaches that the human being's cognitive abilities are not merely bodily. He argues that in order for us to know a thing, we must recognize the category of things to which it belongs and be able to differentiate it from other things. For instance, when you see a particular animal, you recognize that it belongs to the cat species and you grasp how it's distinct from other animals. Categories are non-physical. You can't see, hear, or touch a category. Since categories are immaterial, anyone who comes to know a thing knows something immaterial. But only an immaterial substance can acquire knowledge of immaterial things. When we acquire knowledge, we gain something that can't be heard, weighed, or seen. Acquiring knowledge is not a bodily act like acquiring breath or food. Once air and food are taken into our bodies, they are changed. But when we know a thing, we aren't changing it. The human soul, which knows things in a non-physical way, is a non-physical or immaterial substance.

To say that the human soul is an immaterial substance is merely a way of expressing the point that an individual's soul can continue to exist when her body no longer functions. Since the soul is a substance, it exists by itself. By definition, a substance is that upon which non-substantial things depend for their existence and which itself doesn't depend for its existence on anything else. The subsistence of the human soul comes from its immateriality. The soul subsists immaterially because it operates immaterially. Aquinas claims that the human soul is able to know all kinds of material things. Its nature isn't limited to any one kind of material thing. Consider that the material or physical nature of the human eye limits what the eye can "know." It certainly can't hear or taste, nor can it see ultra-violet or infrared light. The human intellect isn't limited in this way. After seeing, hearing, or tasting something, we can mentally isolate certain features of that thing to know its nature. This process of concept-formation, isn't an activity of the body, but rather an activity of the soul. So the human soul subsists of itself inasmuch as it can perform immaterial activities—attention, abstraction, comparison, and generalization.

The fact that the human soul can subsist on its own means that it's not destructible. What's destructible can only be destroyed by itself or by something else, as the color and shape of a balloon no longer exist once the balloon has popped. As subsistent, the soul can't be destroyed by something else. This is what would occur if the death of the body entailed the death of the soul. So if anything causes the soul to be destroyed, it must be due to the soul itself. Yet, by definition, every immaterial substance is indestructible. Destruction occurs when a physical thing loses a part it previously had. But the soul is immaterial; it has no parts. Moreover, it's the source of conscious life. It follows that conscious life cannot be taken away from the soul; it's indestructible.

When the human soul is separated from the body, Aquinas writes that it will know other souls that have been separated from their bodies. This is because we understand things according to our nature. If our nature is to exist without a body, we'll understand other individuals who exist without a body. But without a body, we won't be able to identify all individuals. We won't be able to see things as we do now. So Aquinas says that we'll only know individuals to whom we "are determined by former knowledge in this life, or by some affection, or by natural aptitude" (I 89, 4, 8). In the afterlife, then, we'll recognize those whom we knew in our earthly life as well as those we loved, and those who share our talents and tendencies.

Caterwauling for a Cat Afterlife

Aquinas has acknowledged that cats (and other animals) have a soul. The controversial point, for him, is whether their cognitive abilities are completely dependent on their bodies. If their mental activities *are* totally dependent on their bodies, their soul will die when their body dies. In the time of Aquinas and for hundreds of years after his death, it was assumed that animals only have instinctual knowledge, the kind that depends entirely on the body. Swinburne agrees with Aquinas that an animal's "desires and beliefs are dependent much more directly on their brain-states" (*Evolution of the Soul*, p. 296). This means that no animal can survive the death of his or her body.

But over the past few decades, scientists and comparative psychologists are documenting that both wild and domestic animals can comprehend symbols and form abstract concepts. Such mental activities, according to Aquinas, aren't dependent on brain-states. Now if some animals have mental activities that are independent of their bodies, Aquinas's argument about the soul surviving the death of the body should apply to those animals.

Richard Herrnstein, a Harvard psychologist, studied the general ability of animals for forming mental categories.[4] Herrnstein demonstrated that animals can discriminate one object from another. In a multi-cat household, cats can differentiate among the other cats they live with. Animals can also memorize the individual members of a category. A mother cat knows when one of her kittens is missing. Animals can also perform what Herrnstein calls "open ended categorization," which is the ability to group "objects according to some observable similarity." The cat can recognize not just a specific bunch of catnip or scratching post but *any* catnip or scratching post. At a higher level, cats can form concepts about things that don't outwardly resemble each other. In knowing these categories, cats know something immaterial. Recall that categories are non-physical. We can't see, hear or touch them.

Aquinas's argument about how cognitive activities are essentially immaterial can be illustrated by considering how a cat learns to form concepts. Tee Cee, a cat from the United Kingdom, is able to know when his human, Michael, is about to suffer an epileptic seizure.[5] The first time it happened, he noticed something (unknown to humans) and began staring at Michael prior to his seizure. Then he ran to Michael's wife to let her know that Michael was ill. On other occasions, when Tee Cee again saw whatever it is that indicated Michael was going to have a seizure, he again repeated the same behavior. Focusing his attention on Michael during these recurring experiences, he comes to know that Michael is about to get a seizure and needs help. The mental act of abstraction involves focusing one's attention on part of an object while

---

[4] "The Wisdom of Animals," by Geoffrey Cowley in *Newsweek* (May 23rd, 1988), p. 56.

[5] "Hero Cat Predicts Epileptic Fits," BBC News (July 6th, 2006).

temporarily not paying attention to other parts of an object. Tee Cee will focus his attention on the signals that Michael is going to be ill while ignoring what Michael is wearing or what activity he's involved in.. Some qualities in Tee Cee's experiences with Michael stay the same while others vary.

This leads to another act of the intellect: comparison. By comparing his different experiences with Michael and discovering which ones require his help, he has learned to form a general concept, one which he can apply to the onsets of new seizures. In the process of concept formation, only his vision and its ensuing images are completely dependent on the body. The attention, abstraction, comparison, and generalization aren't dependent on a bodily[6] organ. These mental processes don't depend on the brain. But they do depend on a substance, an immaterial one.

Although we don't know what it is that alerts Tee Cee to her human's imminent seizure, it's clear that cats frequently seem to be aware of things that their owners can't see. It's common to see a cat bristle and her tail become bushy, indicating fear or aggression, while she stares fixedly at nothing. Does she perceive something immaterial?

We can't chalk up to instinct the cat's ability to know all the complex things the cat clearly knows. Instinct can't explain how a white cat in England, named Macavity by bus drivers, has been riding the No. 331 several mornings a week. As human passengers are boarding the bus at Churchill Road, he jumps inside and sits quietly near the front. He waits patiently for the next stop and then jumps off at a fish and chips shop. Macavity takes the bus trip entirely on his own.[7] How does Macavity know where the bus is going? How does he know which bus he's boarding? His series of actions is clearly intentional. His belief that the bus will take him to his desired destination involves concept formation.

But Aquinas insists that only an immaterial substance can engage in an immaterial activity like concept formation. Any soul

---

[6] We see the same kind of attention abstraction, comparison, and generalization in Tommy, whose human, Gary, has painful osteoporosis and ministrokes. Gary trained Tommy to call 911, using speed dialing. When Gary fell out of his wheelchair, Tommy called 911, alerting police to come to the rescue. In order for Tommy to be trained and to understand when to use his training, he had to use mental processes that don't depend on a bodily organ. *Insurance Journal* (January 3rd, 2006).

[7] "Mystery Cat Takes Regular Bus to the Shops," in *The Daily Mail* (London, April 12th, 2007), www.dailymail.co.uk/live/atricles/news/news/html?in_article_id =447527&in.

that knows things in a non-physical way is a substance which isn't made of matter. The cat, knowing things in way that doesn't directly rely on the body, has a subsisting immaterial soul, a soul that continues to exist when her body dies.

The Real Feline Soul

Having discussed the intricacy of a cat's mental states, we can combine Swinburne's argument about the network of beliefs and desires with Aquinas's account of the independence of the human soul from the body, and arrive at the following conclusion: Beliefs, desires, purposes, and emotions bond with each other, to form a cohesive essence, which we call the soul. Many of an individual's beliefs, desires, emotions, and purposes adhere to each other. That is, they can't easily be separated from each other. If Fluffy sees her human, she will rub around him, anticipating affection. If she sees a cat video, she may fly at the television, hoping to capture that image of a bird. Her cohesive network of beliefs, desires, purposes and emotions, is her soul. Since the feline soul is that which underlies and binds together a cat's immaterial mental states, it too must be immaterial. The soul, as the cohesive network of a cat's mental states, forms a continuing structure. This immaterial structure is independent of the feline body. It follows that when the cat's body dies, the self-sustaining force or energy of her soul continues after she leaves her body.

If Aquinas is right in claiming that all those who knew and loved each other in their earthly life will again know and love each other in an afterlife, then the bond between the cat and his or her human will continue. The human and cat will be able to recognize each other's consciousness and affection. Even feral cats who have bonded with other feral cats in this life will have continuing relationships. In contrast to Lewis's claim that humans give animals a personality and an afterlife, the argument I have presented maintains that it's the very nature of the feline soul that accounts for the cat's personality and afterlife.

We don't have to appeal to any mysterious ability humans supposedly have to produce a soul and an afterlife for someone else. Instead, it's the very nature of a cat to have a tenth life. If we have an afterlife, then so do cats! And my cats are purring in agreement.

15

Can Whiskers Have More than Nine Lives? Feline and Human Cloning

BERTHA ALVAREZ MANNINEN

I have five cats. Two females: Angel, whom I found under a car when she was a very small kitten and who has not stopped eating since, and Uni, who came with my husband as a package deal. In order to cement our union, my husband and I acquired three males: Shady, Linus, and Liam, all obtained from animal shelters in Iowa City, Iowa.

Each cat has its own unique personality. The most palpable difference, however, is between Uni's personality in contrast to Angel's, Shady's, Liam's, and Linus's respective personalities. Uni is the only one that was not raised by either my husband or I since kittenhood. When my husband first got her, there were some obvious indications of abuse in her background. Even today, seven years later, she is the only one of our cats who cowers when about to be petted, yowls whenever we pick her up, and runs under a bed or couch whenever we put her down. The others, in contrast, were raised in a loving environment from about two or three months of age, and they cuddle and purr in our arms contently. This personality difference amongst my cats will serve to make a crucial point below regarding the importance of environment and nurture for shaping a cat's personality, which, in turn, will show why a cat is much more than simply the sum of his genetic parts.

Why Clone Whiskers?

Although the company closed down at the end of 2006, "Genetic Savings and Clone" had previously offered pet-owners the opportunity to genetically duplicate the family pet for a mere fifty thousand dollars. On October 17th, 2004 it was successful in this venture with the birth of Little Nicky, the first commercially produced feline clone—not the first feline clone ever; that title belongs to a cat named Cc, short for "Carbon copy," who will be discussed below.

After Little Nicky's birth, and the subsequent assessment that she was indeed healthy, allaying the fears of many that she would be grossly deformed, hundreds of pet-owners expressed an interest in cloning their own beloved pets, many of whom were terminally ill. Thus, although "Genetic Savings and Clone" is currently out of business, there does seem to be a viable market in feline cloning, especially if the cost could be lower, and therefore it's only a matter of time before some other company endeavors to fill the current hole in this market.

Why would people spend such a hefty amount of money in order to clone their deceased or terminally ill cat, especially when there are so many homeless cats residing in animal shelters across the United States? Individuals who wish to take advantage of this technology seem to adhere to the belief that by cloning their deceased cat, they will actually get back the same cat that they lost. For example:

> When Alan and Kristine Wolf lost Spot to lymphoma a year and a half ago, their lives were shattered. Spot—a sometimes contrary, but always lovable, blue Abyssinian cat—was like a child to them. But after eighteen years together in a Manhattan apartment, fond memories and hundreds of cuddly snapshots just weren't enough. The Wolfs wanted Spot—or at least part of his "life force"—to live on, so they turned to twenty-first-century science for a solution. Now they pay a monthly fee to bank Spot's skin cells, and look forward to the day when they may stroke his clone . . . "It has muted our sense of loss," explains Wolf, reflecting on their decision to store Spot's tissue with the Louisiana-based Lazaron BioTechnologies once they knew he was ill. Wolf, a physicist, adds that although he and his wife are in no way religious, they've discovered some kind of "religious" feeling in keeping Spot's cells frozen—"a feeling that some aspect of his life force, even if not his consciousness, is still with us because these cells exist." (Ursula Owre Masterson. "Cloning Pets: In Search of Fluffy 2.0: Gene Banking Booms as Owners Hope to Reproduce Furry Friends," 3rd November, 2006. MSNBC News Webpage. Accessed on 29th January, 2007, www.msnbc.msn.com/id/3076926.)

The Wolfs seem to feel that Spot lives on, as some abstract "life force," because his cells do. Thus, if Spot were successfully cloned, Spot *himself* would somehow live on as this new kitten.

It's not surprising that the Wolfs, and many others just like them chomping at the bit to have their turn at cloning their pet, possess this conception of cloning. The media have certainly reinforced such a notion. In the several instances in which *Time Magazine* has addressed the issue of mammalian cloning, their covers always illustrate duplicate instances of the same picture. *Time*'s February 19th 2001 cover shows two mirror-image infants staring at each other, and the tagline on the cover suggests that cloning may be used by grieving parents who want their dead child returned to them. The November 8th 1993 cover illustrates the hand of God as portrayed in Michelangelo's *Sistine Chapel* reaching to touch hands with not just one of Adam's hands, but with five identical hands.

Most telling, however, is the March 10th 1997 cover, where two identical sheep, a reference to Dolly the sheep, the first mammal to be cloned, stare at the reader with the caption reading under the picture: "Will there ever be another you?" The implication, of course, is that the replication of your genes via cloning is equivalent to the replication of your identity; if your genes are replicated, then *you* are replicated. Likewise, replicating Spot's genes, the Wolfs may think, replicates Spot himself.

Now, in one sense, this is obviously false. Spot and his clone would be numerically distinct (they would have two different organisms and take up two distinct spaces) and so they cannot be the *same* cat. However, could it be that somehow Spot survives as this cloned cat, even if they are two numerically distinct felines? Perhaps what was important about Spot's personality and temperament can somehow be duplicated in the new cloned feline. If so, could we then say that Spot has, in some sense, survived?

The distinction between numerical identity and survival, and the argument that the latter is possible without the former, is famously made by the philosopher Derek Parfit. He asks you to imagine that your brain suffered from hemisphere division, and that each one of your hemispheres contains a complete set of your mental contents: your memories, beliefs, goals, and character traits. Each hemisphere is then implanted into two distinct and functional human organisms, both of which wake up and thereafter possess all of your mental contents. According to Parfit, you will have survived as *both* of these people, a sort of "double-survival," even though neither of them is numerically identical with you. Because they share a complete set of your mental contents, they possess, what Parfit calls, strong psychological connections with you, and this is what really defines your identity and who you are; it is what really *matters* about a person. Thus, if the strong psychological connections persist, the individual survives, even in the absence of numerical identity.[1]

Perhaps something similar can be said about cloning cats. Even if the Wolfs' new kitten would be a numerically distinct cat from Spot, perhaps what is really important about him, what really made him who he was, survives in his genes and thus is duplicated when he is cloned. So, can cloning give cats a "tenth" life? Could cloning bring good ole Whiskers back?

Cloning, the Modern "Pet Cemetery": The Desire to Resurrect Whiskers

The assumption that cloning your cat would, in some way, revive the same cat you knew and loved tacitly assumes that the cat's identity, the "meat and potatoes" of who a cat really is, is captured in large part, if not fully, by her genes. If we duplicate the genes, the assumption goes, we duplicate the feline, and hence we succeed in bringing back our beloved pet. This assumption also permeates one of the saddest, and misguided, reasons some anguished parents who have lost a child wish to have access to cloning technology, for they believe that cloning their child would somehow bring the same child back to them.

Thomas Murray recounts a letter he heard read at a congressional hearing concerning the ethics of human reproductive cloning. The letter was written by a grieving father who, after losing his eleven-month-old infant son, wanted the opportunity to clone him. Upon the death of his son, this father writes, he "decided then and there that I would never give up on my child. I would never stop until I could give his DNA—his genetic make-up—a chance."[2] Notice the very subtle implications of his words: he refused to give up until *his child* received another chance at life. Again, the assumption was that this new clone would be, for all

---

[1] See Derek Parfit, *Reasons and Persons* (Oxford University Press, 1987).

[2] Thomas Murray, "Even if It Worked, Cloning Won't Bring Her Back," *Washington Post* (April 8th, 2001).

intents and purposes, the *same* child that he had lost. Although the child would be numerically distinct, in all the ways that matter, this father believed, the cloned baby would be a new incarnation of his previously departed baby.

It seems, then, that part of the allure of reproductive cloning lies in the prospect of, essentially, cheating death. It empowers us by giving the impression that we can bring our loved ones (human and nonhuman alike) back from the grave by reproducing their genetic make-up. This certainly seems to be what motivates not just the grieving father in the above letter, but also pet-owners like the Wolfs. As Thomas Murray (himself a grieving father after losing his twenty-year-old daughter) notes, however, successfully cloning one's child (or cat) will do nothing to cheat death, for "cloning can neither change the fact of death nor deflect the pain of grief."

But why not? In order to understand why Murray's claim is correct, we need to examine the veracity of the assumption that replicating a mammal's genes would be akin to replicating the mammal herself. While Whiskers's unique DNA sequence no doubt plays a role in defining her identity, is her identity reducible to DNA or genetic material? As we shall see, the answer to this question is no.

It's Not All in the Genes

We have all encountered, in some way, at least one set of naturally produced clones: identical twins. Identical twins are formed when one zygote divides into two numerically distinct, but genetically identical, zygotes. More often than not, identical twins resemble each other physically, although there are usually variations, some more slight than others. In terms of personality, however, identical twins may be as different as any other pair of siblings. For example, Chang and Eng Bunker, most known for bringing the condition of conjoined or Siamese twins to public awareness, were genetically identical twins who had different personalities. Our exposure to human identical twins illustrates, then, that replicating genetics does not mean replicating the person. One would hardly refer to identical twins as two versions of the same person. The same can be said about replicating feline genetic material.

How would cloning my kitty work? If my cat Angel were terminally ill, I could request a refrigerated biopsy kit from a company such as ViaGen, who specializes in cryogenically storing animal DNA. The company would then send the kit to my veterinarian, who will take a genetic sample from Angel before she dies. I could then take this genetic sample to another company who would attempt to produce a clone from Angel's genetic material (ViaGen does not currently engage in the practice of cloning domesticated pets). In order to produce a feline clone through what is called somatic cell nuclear transfer (SCNT), a feline unfertilized egg's genetic material, its nucleus, would have to be removed and replaced with Angel's genetic material. The egg would then be artificially induced to divide as if it were fertilized naturally, and then implanted into a feline womb so it can grow as a feline embryo normally would. The resulting kitten would be *almost* genetically identical to Angel, since some of the kitten's genetic material would also come from the mitochondria of the feline egg, and, of course, Angel and her clone would come from different feline eggs. Uterine environment can play an important role as well when it comes to the development of fetuses (feline and human). Angel and her clone would have gestated in two different cats who themselves were in two very different environments, given that Angel's mother was a stray, and a cat who would be used in a laboratory to gestate a cloned feline would be much better taken care of in terms of nourishment and medical attention.

The new kitten may have some physical similarities to Angel, although this is not at all guaranteed. For example, Uni is a beautiful long-haired dilute tortie, and as such her fur is a delicate unison of gray, orange, and white. If I were to have Uni cloned, the resulting cat may also have similar colors in her fur, but they could be different in terms of size, shades, and location. In fact, Cc, the first feline to ever be cloned by scientists at Texas A and M University with funding from "Genetic Savings and Clone," does not at all resemble her feline progenitor, Rainbow. Whereas Rainbow, a calico, is stocky and has patches of tan, orange, and white throughout her body, Cc barely resembles a calico at all! Not only is she lanky and thin, she has a grey coat over a white body and is lacking the patches of orange or tan typical to calicos. Moreover, there are vast personality differences between Rainbow and Cc. Whereas Rainbow is described as shy and reticent, Cc is more playful and inquisitive. [3]

---

[3] See Kristen Hays, "A Year Later, Cloned Cat Is No Copycat: Cc Illustrates the Complexities of Pet Cloning." MSNBC News Webpage (4th November 2003), accessed on 12th February 2007, www.msnbc.msn.com/id/3076908.

As with human beings, a cat's personality is vastly shaped not just by her genetics, but also by her environment and her experiences; neither nature nor nurture play an exhaustive role. When I found Angel, she was small, frail, weak, and very thin. She ate two cans of food in one sitting, along with a bowl of cream. Her eating habits did not change much within the following years. She always seemed perpetually hungry, although this has subsided a little within the past couple of years. There is no way of knowing why Angel was so obsessed with food when she was younger, but I often wonder if she had been different in this regard had her mother been adequately nourished while gestating her and if Angel herself had been exposed to adequate nourishment in her early infancy.

In the same vein, I often lament with my husband how different Uni may have been had we raised her from kittenhood as we raised the others. A key part of Uni's personality is her cautiousness and her dislike of being handled; she is a reserved and serious cat, who plays only occasionally but generally keeps her distance and hisses at the other cats for almost no reason at all. There is very little doubt in my mind that much of this comes from her abusive background. Had she not been abused as a young cat, perhaps she would be more playful, more open to others, and more accepting of being held or handled. This would have made her, in my eyes, a decidedly different cat. If Uni were cloned and the resulting kitten raised in a like manner as we have raised our other cats, the new cat would most likely share in the one trait that the other four have in common: they all love to be carried, hugged, and actually approach us and demand attention by rubbing their heads against our hands. They also play with each other quite well, and are rather sociable. Uni usually remains off in a corner and keeps to herself, approaching my husband and me only when there are no others around and, even then, tentatively.

Although we'll probably never know with certainty to what extent environment plays a role when influencing character traits in both cats and humans, we know that it *does* play a role, and a very integral one at that. Moreover, even though genes do play a role in terms of determining a cat's (or human's) physical appearance or personality, there is simply no guarantee that the genes will express themselves in the same way in the clone as it did in its genetic predecessor. In reference to what a clone of his cat Tribble (also a calico) may look like, Mark Eibert explains this well.

Chromosomes are structures that carry genes. The X chromosome of a cat, for example, has about five thousand genes on it. Male-mammals—human and tomcats—have one X chromosome and one Y chromosome. Female humans and cats have two X chromosomes—they inherited one from their mother and one from their father, so the genes on the two X chromosomes are all different. What happens when you have two sets of blue-prints for the same five thousand genetic traits in the same mammal? Which one gets used? Well, nature decides in a very fair way. Randomly . . . In other words, you can make a million clones of Tribble, and not one of them will look exactly like Tribble, or exactly like any other of the Tribble clones. Although it wouldn't be as visual and dramatic, the same principle would apply to humans.[4]

So even if a cat's genetic material *did* play an exhaustive role in defining its identity, the replicated genes may behave and manifest themselves in a vastly different manner in the clone, thereby producing a cat that may resemble and act very differently than its genetic predecessor. Nevertheless, we know that genes do *not* play an exhaustive role; that the environment and nurture that a cat is exposed to contributes significantly to shaping her personality. As with humans, a cat's personality is an intricate and sensitive mixture of genes and environment.

It's very unlikely, then, that cloning would bring Whiskers, Spot, Uni, or Angel back. There's no way to replicate what we love about our cats because, for one, there is no way, as of yet, to manipulate genes in order to achieve the physical and personality traits that we desire. In addition, we certainly cannot re-create the exact environment that shaped our pet's personality. The grief and loss that we feel when we lose our pet cannot be any more assuaged by a clone than by a completely different pet. This much was even admitted by Ben Carlson, the spokesperson of Genetic Savings and Clone: "the company tells pet owners that cloning won't resurrect their pet and that the company has turned away some customers clearly interested in getting the same animal" (quoted in Hays). The real interest lies, Carlson says, in replicating the "exceptional genes" of a deceased pet. This, however, seems highly suspect. When we fall in love with our pets, we fall in love with their personalities and

---

[4] Mark D. Eibert. 23rd September 1999. "Human Cloning: Myths, Medical Benefits, and Constitutional Rights," in Bonnie Steinbock, John D. Arras, and Alex John London, eds., *Ethical Issues in Modern Medicine*, sixth edition (McGraw Hill, 2003), p. 659.

character traits, not with their DNA, blood type, or genes. When people express an interest in cloning their pet, what they really want back is that part that they fell in love with, and that cannot be replicated.

Cloning felines or other pets may actually be beneficial for dispelling the conception that cloning results in exact or even approximate replications; a comparison between Cc and Rainbow can easily put this misapprehension to rest. In some cases, perhaps, a cloned animal may indeed exhibit physical and personality traits that are similar to its predecessor—after all genes do play *some* role in determining personality and physical characteristics. But the tacit assumption that fuels the belief that cloning can resurrect a loved one, human or feline, is that genotype has *everything* to do with personality. A playful Cc in comparison to a reticent Rainbow clearly illustrates that this is false. This, in turn, helps to dispel the very misguided belief that cloning your cat (or child) in some way resurrects, for all intents and purposes, the same cat (or the same child).

Why Clone Whiskers when Fluffy Needs a Home?

The main concern of mammalian cloning (whether it be feline or human) should center around ensuring that the resulting clone is healthy and will not suffer from a defect brought about by the cloning procedure. As John Harris notes in his book *On Cloning*, the concerns over the health risks of a cloned mammal is the "one decent argument against cloning that does command respect."[5] According to Harris, such a concern only counts against the practice of cloning, however, if the cloning procedure is likely to create a higher probability of genetic defects in a mammal than exists in natural reproduction alone. So far, the cloned cats mentioned in this chapter, Cc and Little Nicky, seem as healthy as any cat of their age would normally be.

Once health concerns are overcome, I do believe that there remain reasons to be cautious about proceeding with the cloning of felines (and other mammals as well) *if* the intent is to replace or re-create a deceased pet. There are two ethical worries concerning the cloning of felines, neither of which impugn the actual cloning

---

[5] John Harris, *On Cloning* (Routledge, 2004), p. 109.

procedure. As a procedure, cloning is itself morally neutral; it's how people use (or misuse) the technology that may render certain instances of cloning morally suspect. These two ethical issues concern, first, the implication of pet-cloning for the vast amount of homeless animals that already exist, and, second, the implication that pet-cloning can have when it comes to shaping our general attitude and character towards nonhuman animals.

First, we must question the morality of spending thousands of dollars on the fruitless task of cloning a beloved cat in order to assuage the grief that comes with its loss when there are million of homeless dogs and cats that are euthanized every year in animal shelters across the United States. The American Humane website states that seventy-one percent of cats that enter an animal shelter are euthanized; 9.6 million animals are euthanized in the United States every year.[6] Wayne Pacelle, the vice-president of the Humane Society of the United States, voices the company's strong opposition to feline cloning because it "doesn't sit well with us to create animals through such extreme and experimental means when there are so many animals desperate for homes."[7]

For the cost that it takes to produce one feline clone, many more already-existing cats may be nourished, their health better attended to, and perhaps a better attempt at finding them a permanent and loving home could have been made. According to the same website, fifty thousand dollars would have been enough money to spay or neuter 1,428 cats. This would no doubt aid in the reduction of the feline population, which in turn would help to reduce the number of cats euthanized every year in animal shelters or killed on the streets. As Pacelle notes:

> Rather than spending millions of dollars on developing a technology with no redeeming social purpose, those resources could be aimed at reducing pet overpopulation, including pet adoption outreach efforts and spay/neuter education.[8]

---

[6] "Animal Shelter Euthanasia." Human Society of the United States Website, 2002. Accessed on 27th February 2007. www.americanhumane.org/site/PageServer?pagename=nr_fact_sheets_animal_euthanasia.

[7] "Cat Cloning Is Wrong-Headed, States the Humane Society of the United States." The Human Society of the United States Website, 2002, accessed on 27th February 2007, www.hsus.org/press_and_publications/press_releases/cat_cloning_is_wrongheaded_states_the_humane_society_of_the_united_states.html.

[8] "The Humane Society of the United States Not Surprised by Demise of Kitty

Any pet lover would have to question the moral permissibility of attempting to clone one's deceased cat given, first, the hefty price tag, second, the fact that your beloved pet will not be replicated, and, third, that so many more sentient, loving cats and dogs are killed in shelters every year in the United States because of lack of homes, funds, and resources. Using cloning in this way results in negative social consequences by helping to agitate, instead of relieve, the pet overpopulation that the United States is currently experiencing.

In essence, this is simply nothing more than yet another luxury, and a misguided one at that. Peter Singer argues that spending money on luxury items, items that are simply not a necessity for living a comfortable life, is morally indefensible given the vast amount of poverty in the world. We're simply not justified in spending money to buy a new 42" plasma television, for example, or Apple's latest incarnation of the iPod, when there are people in other parts of the world who lack even basic necessities such as food or clean water to drink and bathe in. Singer makes his argument, quite convincingly by appealing to a principle that seems rather basic: "if it is in our power to prevent something bad from happening without sacrificing anything of comparable moral importance, we ought, morally, to do it."[9] For example, if we are able to save the life of a drowning child by simply wading in a pool and pulling him out when the worst thing that can happen is that our very expensive Armani clothes would be damaged, then we are under a moral obligation to do so. Simply put, the ruining of Armani clothes is not important enough compared to the life of the child that we may sacrifice the latter in order to preserve the former.

A like argument can be made when it comes to spending thousands of dollars in an attempt to clone one's cat for replacement purposes. The only thing that one would be sacrificing by forgoing the cloning of a pet is a new incarnation of his genetic material, which is not the reason you ever loved your pet to begin with and will not result in getting back what you did love about him—his personality. The same comfort, in reality, can be derived from

---

Cloning Company" (11th October 2006). Humane Society of the United States Website, accessed on 27th February 2007, www.hsus.org/press_and_publications/press_releases/the_humane_society_of_the_11.html.

[9] Peter Singer, "Famine, Affluence, and Morality," *Philosophy and Public Affairs* 1.1 (1972), p. 231.

adopting a new animal altogether. Moreover, when adopting a new pet, you can aid in the prevention of its death and give this little creature a chance in life that it may not have had otherwise. In other words, forgoing cloning in favor of using that money to help out homeless animals (or homeless people) does not sacrifice anything of comparable moral importance and allows us to prevent something bad from happening: the suffering and euthanasia of many homeless animals. According to Singer's principle, then, we ought, morally speaking, to forgo the extravagant amount of money being used for the cloning of a pet and redirect it, instead, to taking care of the animals that are already here. Doing otherwise is like failing to save the child from drowning in the interest of preserving your Armani clothes, or buying a plasma television in the face of thousands of people that live in poverty.

Appreciating Uniqueness

On a recent trip to the mall, a particularly repugnant sign caught my eye as I passed the pet store. Not only could I pay for my new purebred pet in installments, as if I were paying off furniture or a car, there was now a sort of product guarantee. The sign read:

> Money-back guarantee: If your pet gets sick within thirty days, or if you find it otherwise unacceptable, please return it for a full refund.

I could now return this sentient and loving creature as I would return clothes. Being a pet-owner was no longer about unconditional love and support, it was about getting the product that I want in the condition that I want it. The animals in this shop were reduced to nothing more than mere possessions and commodities.

According to the ancient philosopher Aristotle, human beings should strive to build a good character by engaging in good actions. So, for example, "we become just by doing just actions, temperate by doing temperate actions, brave by doing brave actions."[10]

The pertinent question becomes, then, what type of actions should we undertake in order to foster a virtuous character in ourselves in regards to nonhuman animals?

---

[10] Aristotle, *Nicomachean Ethics* (Hackett, 1999), lines 1103a15–1103b.

I don't believe that viewing animals as possessions that may be returned to a store if they do not suit our needs cultivates a virtuous character within us. Already most humans regard animals as beneath us and as possessions we can treat as we wish (the deplorable conditions in factory farms alone attest to this, in addition to the existence of circuses and certain zoos). One source of this deplorable attitude towards animals has its roots in the Judeo-Christian religions. God's command to have dominance over non-human animals and the natural world is interpreted as having a despotic power over them, rather than reading the command as God imploring us to be stewards, and thus co-creators, in the natural world with Him.

Our continued interaction with the natural world as a mere tool that exists to serve our whims has negative consequences not just for the natural world, but for humans as well, as we can surely empirically verify given the current state of our environment. Therefore, in the interest of changing our demeaning attitudes and dispositions towards animals and the natural world, we should avoid acting in ways that contribute to the cultivation of such dispositions. Rather, we should, as Aristotle says, engage in behavior that helps to cultivate virtuous character traits in regards to them.

The pet-owners who wish to use cloning to replace their deceased cat no doubt loved their pet very much, so much so that they are willing to pay thousands of dollars due to the misconception that they will, in some way, get the same cat back. But what happens when this new cat gets sick? No problem! We can simply clone another one, and another one, and yet another. In other words, cloning cats with the intention to replace a deceased one encourages the view that cats are just that: replaceable. Granted, pet-owners who have lost a pet (and parents who have lost children) may seek another animal (or strive to conceive another child) in the interest of assuaging their grief. But this does not necessarily mean that they seek to *replace* their pet; for when we attain a whole new pet, we expect that we will have a whole new relationship with a new distinct being. In other words, we get a new pet (or conceive a new child) with the hopes of filling up a hole in our lives, not necessarily in the hopes of *replacing* our deceased loved one. But the only motivation there can be for spending thousands of dollars to clone your departed pet is because you want *your departed pet* back; the new clone really is viewed as a replacement in every way, with the expectation, however faulty, that she will be everything that Whiskers used to be. In other words, the motivation to clone Whiskers in order to get Whiskers back implies that the pet-owner thinks that Whiskers *can* be brought back, and that there was nothing about the old Whiskers that science can't replace.

This seems to undermine the very intimate relationship that humans can have with their pets. When I cuddle with Linus, Liam, or Shady on my lap, and they purr contently, I am grateful that I have *Linus, Liam or Shady* in my life; I am appreciative for what their presence has *uniquely* contributed to my life. I care for them when they are sick and worry about their health, because I don't want to lose *them*, because I know I will never get *them* back. Engaging in the act of cloning with the intention to replace a deceased cat (or a deceased child) seems to cultivate a certain way of viewing animals, that they are not intrinsically valuable, special, or unique, that already permeates too much of our interaction with them. Rather, it would be better to engage in actions that cultivates respect (a virtuous character trait) towards the natural world and appreciation for its distinctiveness and beauty. We should also engage in actions that allow us to view nonhuman animals as the precious and unique beings that they are. Our money, time, and technology would be better spent in taking care of the ones that are already here.

It is not cloning, as a procedure, which leads to viewing pets (or children) as replaceable, but rather it is our faulty understanding of what cloning is or can accomplish that leads to this. In the future, there may very well be good reasons, once it is deemed safe, to engage in reproductive cloning—for example if this is the only way that an infertile couple may be able to have a baby that is genetically related to them. But using cloning as an attempt to replace a precious pet (or a beloved child) reveals an erroneous view of the nature of mammalian cloning. Instead of trying to clone pets (or people) in the hopes of bringing them back, an endeavor which will likely fail, pet-owners should, instead, enjoy every moment with their companions, and we honor their memory and the role they played in our lives by appreciating their uniqueness rather than trying to re-create them. After all, a truly special pet really is simply irreplaceable.

16

Dead or Alive?
A Puzzling Identity

JEAN-ROCH LAUPER

In the waiting room, the atmosphere is strained and heavy. Mary is sitting next to her mother. Her eyes are fixed on the black and white tiles on the floor. She is close to weeping. Full of guilt, she keeps repeating in her mind, "If only I'd kept a better eye on Mimi and Kitty." Suddenly, the doors open and the neurosurgeon's assistant appears. "The operation has gone well. Your little cat is safe and she'll soon regain consciousness. You can come with me to see her."

A little black female cat is sleeping calmly in a basket. She has a little white spot under her neck. In a lot of places, she has been shaved and several bandages are covering her coat. Upon seeing her, Mary gives a slight smile. However, immediately after, her face again becomes dark. "Mom, do you think that Kitty's dead?"

At Breakneck Speed

Just few hours earlier, in the family house's garden, Mary was playing quietly with her two little female cats.

This is one of the first sunny days of April. Near her is Kitty, a little reddish-brown young female cat. Also nearby is Mimi, a ravishing young female cat, all black, except for a little white mark under her neck. Mary has a big smile on her face and is moving strings full of little knots. The two cats are joyfully trying to catch them. Kitty seems to be better at the game, but this is rather normal. Indeed, Kitty is the hunter—always ready to run after a butterfly or another insect and often coming back with a big mouse or a young bird proudly clamped in her mouth, much to the distress of her mistress.

Mimi is neither very playful nor a hunter. Her strong point is her tenderness; she always wants caresses and purrs very easily. While Kitty, in a very irritating way, doesn't stop going in and out over and over, Mimi seems happy to simply stay near her mistress. Mary likes these differences between the two sweet cats. They are the right pair for her!

Both cats are hungry. They are mewing very loudly while rubbing against Mary. Each cat has her favorite dry food: Kitty likes a lot of tuna but refuses to touch chicken, whereas Mimi likes chicken the best. Mary begins pouring the dry food when suddenly Kitty begins to run after a little blackbird. Immediately, Mimi follows behind her. The bird is flying towards the road which passes behind the house. Mary calls the two cats, but the cats do not obey. They seem to have become completely deaf.

Unfortunately, while they are crossing the road, a red sports car comes out from nowhere and hits the two cats. The two little bodies, covered in blood, lie on the road and seem to be dead. Mary, numb with pain, sees a man coming out of the car, while her mother races towards the accident scene. The man says that he's a doctor, more precisely, a neurosurgeon. He examines the two cats. According to him, Mimi's body is almost intact, but her brain is fatally damaged; for Kitty, it seems to be the opposite. Her brain is intact, but her body is fatally damaged and she is no longer able to live.

"We haven't a minute to lose," says the man. "Let's carefully pick up the two cats and drive; we'll talk in the car."

Brain Transplant

In the car, Mary seems too shocked to cry. Her mother clasps Mary to her chest. "Little girl, I'm really sorry," begins the man. "I cannot fix everything I've done. Indeed, I think neither of your cats will live. Mimi's brain and Kitty's body seem untreatable. However, I think I can try to save one of them. Madam, I do research on brain transplants. The technique is still not fully safe, but we have had very good results over the last few months. If you agree, I can try to transplant Kitty's brain into Mimi's body. This will not give you *two* cats back, but at least one of them will have a chance of survival. If the operation is successful, however, you have to know that the surviving cat will most likely have amnesia and, more generally, will lose all of its psychological features." Mary and her mother accept.

The operation goes very well. The little cat will very likely survive. The neurosurgeon tells his assistant to give the good news to Mary and her mother, who are waiting in a nearby room.

The surviving cat has Mimi's body, Kitty's brain, and amnesia. This is all of the information that Mary's mother has at her disposal. From these facts, she really isn't sure how to reply to her daughter. In a sense, the surviving cat appears exactly like Mimi—all black with a little white spot under the neck. She's tempted to say that the surviving cat is Mimi. However, at the same time, the little cat has Kitty's brain and the brain is an important organ; but is it important if the surviving cat has amnesia? After a moment of reflection, she becomes convinced that the little cat in the basket is Mimi and says to Mary, "This is hard to hear, I know. Although Mimi will survive, Kitty is dead." She clasps her arms around her daughter who bursts into tears.

Homecoming

Several days after the tragic event, the little surviving cat is back home. She is still very weak, but day after day, she regains health and strength. However, something strange happens. As the days go by, the little black surviving cat seems to not have amnesia, as was predicted by the neurosurgeon. The surviving cat comes when someone calls her "Kitty," but has no reaction when called "Mimi"; she seems to be very playful, running after all of the insects, and shows strong hunting instincts. As soon as she's able to eat solid foods, she wants only tuna and doesn't want chicken. As soon as she's able to go outside, she never stops asking to go in and out again and again. She rarely purrs when she is caressed. Not only is the surviving cat not amnesiac, but she seems to have all of the distinctive psychological features of Kitty before the accident!

Mary and her mother are very disturbed. Can they still say that the surviving cat, who has Mimi's body and Kitty's brain and psychological distinctive features, is still Mimi and that Kitty is dead? They don't think so. They think that they were mistaken: the surviving cat is not Mimi, but is Kitty!

The Chatterbox Nurse

When they go to the neurosurgeon's private hospital for the first checkup after the operation, they tell the doctor what has happened to the surviving cat. Somewhat angry, they ask him why he said that the surviving cat would have amnesia. "But I didn't say that!" he replies. "I said only that the surviving cat would *most likely* have amnesia. I wasn't at all sure that this would happen!"

A very kind nurse has been taking care of the cat during the conversation. She's cleansing the wounds and putting new dressings on them. While she's doing her job, she talks a lot. When the neurosurgeon finishes speaking, she adds, "At any rate, it's a real pleasure to see that this little cat is doing as fine as the other!" The doctor cuts her short and intently looks into her eyes. "There is *no* other cat! Madam is mixing up your situation with someone else's cat, who had a similar unfortunate accident." As the nurse begins to reply, the doctor takes her by the arm and accompanies her into another room.

Mary and her mother are very puzzled; their heads are buzzing with questions. "Why was the nurse talking about another cat? Another cat had survived? Why had the neurosurgeon such a strange reaction? Were there really other people in the same situation in the same private hospital? If yes, what would this mean? All of the injured cats could not be gathered in the same vicinity. In his haste, the neurosurgeon had left his papers on the examination table near the sleeping little black cat. Before the neurosurgeon comes back, Mary's mother begins to read them. Her eyes open wide. She seems very surprised at what she reads. However, she cannot finish reading because she knows that the neurosurgeon will soon be coming back.

"What does this all mean?" she angrily shouts at the neurosurgeon. I've just read that there is another surviving cat with half of Kitty's brain!" The neurosurgeon seems embarrassed and scared and explains that when he tried to save one of the two injured cats, he and his team discovered some very rare characteristics of Kitty's brain: each of her brain hemispheres supported exactly the same mental functions. Given the research data, the brain transplant would be just as successful if only one hemisphere was used, rather than the complete brain. Furthermore, they were not sure if the transplanted cat would survive. Moreover, another little cat was injured in the vicinity and, by extreme chance, was brought to the hospital at the same time. The probability was very high that the transplanted cats would both have amnesia.

In light of these facts, the neurosurgeon and his team made the decision to give a chance for two little cats to live instead of one and thus to bring back some joy to two children instead of only one. They also decided not to tell the truth to the people concerned in order to not disturb them any more after the shock of the unfortunate event.

Mary's mother begins to calm down. If this gave joy to two children instead of one, that was more acceptable for her as a mother. However, when she asks the neurosurgeon about the other cat, he eludes the question, saying that this information wouldn't help her or her daughter and would just give them more worries. Their conversation is cut short. The nurse comes back again and asks him to follow her immediately because there is a very important problem with one of his patients who is near death.

Since the neurosurgeon had not yet completed the check-up of their cat, Mary and her mother continue to wait in the consultation room. Mary lovingly caresses her cat, but she seems worried. Suddenly, she asks, "Is my cat still Kitty? Before, there was only one cat with Kitty's brain and Kitty's typical behavior and habits. This is my cat—the cat with Mimi's body and the cat that I'm caressing. But now that there are *two* cats with Kitty's half brain and Kitty's typical behavior and habits, what am I to think? As strange as it seems, are there now two Kittys? Or are neither of the cats Kitty? Or is one Kitty and the other not? I'm totally lost . . ."

Her mother cuts her short and, after a while, in a reassuring way, says, "You shouldn't have all these worries. Remember, the doctor said that in most of the cases, after a brain transplant, the cat has amnesia. What has happened with our cat—that she does not have amnesia after all and has kept all of Kitty's usual behavior and habits—is unlikely to happen again. So, the other cat most likely has amnesia. Therefore, it's clear that our beloved cat is Kitty and the other isn't. So calm down."

One Cat Can Hide Another

Now calm, Mary continues to caress her little cat. She hopes that the neurosurgeon will come back soon because she is beginning to feel very uncomfortable about this place—all of these worries and lies. She feels very tired and has only one idea in her mind: to go back home with her little cat and try to forget the whole business. Her mother seems to share this feeling.

In her "usual" way, the cat—with Mimi's body and Kitty's half brain—is purring little, but seems happy. Mary is caressing her favorite place—just on the right side of her head. As if trying to convince herself that the little cat is really her Kitty, she repeats "Kitty," always happy to see the little cat react to the call of her name.

However, at that moment, something strange happens. Each time she says "Kitty" to her cat, Mary thinks she hears a very slight noise. At first, she thinks that it is just her imagination and that she's daydreaming. After all, this would be quite normal after all of the events they've just witnessed. But as the noise persists, her mother begins to hear it, although it is very slight. She begins to search the place from where it is coming. The slight noise is coming from behind a closed door, just on the other side of the consultation room.

At first, Mary is unsure. But after a few times of calling "Kitty" and observing the reaction, she's sure that the noise is that of a little cat scratching at the door. Suddenly, it all seems clear in her mind. The cat behind the door is the cat with the other half of Kitty's brain! The cat does not have amnesia either!

But if there are two cats, each with a half of Kitty's brain and all of the distinctive psychological features of the old Kitty (typical behavior, habits, memories . . .), then all of her questions remain unanswered! "Is my cat still Kitty? Are they both—my cat and the cat behind the door—Kitty? Is neither of them Kitty, or is one of the cats more Kitty than the other?" Mary really doesn't know what to think. The fact that one would be more Kitty than the other seems rather strange. But, thinking that both or neither of them are Kitty seems equally unacceptable.

She feels a violent whirl of emotions and thoughts in her head. To her surprise, she grasps an iron bar and tries to force the door. Her mother doesn't tell her to stop. On the contrary, she comes and tries to help Mary break open the door.

Suddenly, the door gives way. Mary and her mother fall backwards and are close to falling a second time when they see the little cat behind the door, now walking towards them!

Some Doors Should Remain Closed . . .

The cat behind the door is a ravishing reddish-brown female cat! This is Kitty! Or, rather, she has Kitty's body! What a joy! Kitty's alive! The little cat has Kitty's body, Kitty's half brain, seems to not have amnesia and has Kitty's psychological distinctive features. Given all of the lies the neurosurgeon has told, Mary and her mother don't trust him anymore. They take the two cats and try to leave the private hospital as quickly as they can.

In the car on the way home, Mary and her mother are at first very happy. They now have their two cats. But after this first euphoric phase, they become very puzzled by the situation. They begin to realize that the situation is not as simple as they had thought. In the car beside them are a cat with Mimi's body and a cat with Kitty's body. However, it can't be right to say that they are Mimi and Kitty. The first cat has Kitty's body, half of Kitty's brain, and Kitty's psychological features; the second cat has Mimi's body, Kitty's half brain, and it too has Kitty's psychological features.

So it seems clear to Mary and her mother that neither of them is Mimi. Mimi's dead. But what to say then about the two cats in the car? Are they both Kitty? But that sounds strange. Is neither of them Kitty? At the same time, the first cat, the one with Kitty's body, seems to be more Kitty than the second, whose body is that of Mimi. What to think? The only thing that seems clear to Mary is that this time, it can't be right to say that the second cat, who has Mimi's body, is more Kitty than the first who has Kitty's body. Beyond that she really doesn't know what to think.

Home, Sweet Home

Not able to solve the puzzle, Mary prefers to feel happy that she again has two cute female cats. Back home, she pours some tuna dry food into two bowls for her two beloved cats and then calls, "Kitty, Kitty, come here!" The two cats come to her. The one with Mimi's body is running almost straight to one of the two bowls and begins to greedily eat the food. However, the other cat, the one with Kitty's body, remains near Mary, apparently bewildered. Mary carries her to the bowl and gently puts her nose in the dry food. The cat doesn't want to eat anything at all. Mary is surprised, but she thinks that the cat with Kitty's body is still disturbed by the operation. She will probably again find her appetite.

The next day, the cat with Mimi's body continues to behave like the old Kitty—she has a strong hunting instinct, very joyful, and purrs little. The behavior of the cat with Kitty's body surprises Mary more and more. She replies when she is called "Kitty," but except for that, her behavior and habits seem different from those of the old Kitty. She is very calm, not very joyful, and purrs a lot and very easily when caressed.

Thinking that perhaps this little cat is ill, Mary goes to the vet and explains the entire story. The vet says that the cat seems in perfect health and he sees nothing abnormal. He is, however, very interested in Mary's story. He has never heard of this private hospital and asks Mary for the address. As to the strange behavior of the cat with Kitty's body, he unfortunately can't offer any explanation.

Wishing to understand the strange behavior of their cat, Mary and her mother make the decision to discreetly go back to the hospital and try to talk to the kind nurse who took care of the two cats. After several hours, this nurse appears and Mary and her mother manage to talk to her in private. At first, the nurse seems reluctant to give them any more information, but after a while, she can't resist. She explains to them that the half brain of the cat with Kitty's body is rightly Kitty's. However, this cat has amnesia. Admittedly, she comes when one calls her "Kitty," but this is just the result of an unfortunate coincidence. The person who took care of her just after the operation decided to give this name to her. So, the little cat with Kitty's body replies when someone calls her "Kitty," but because she's fully amnesiac, she shares no other psychological features with the old Kitty.

Mary is again very disconcerted. She now has two cats. The first has Mimi's body, Kitty's half brain, is not amnesiac, and owns all of the psychological features of Kitty. The second has Kitty's body, Kitty's half brain, is amnesiac, and shares practically no common psychological features with the old Kitty. Therefore, who are her two cats? Is one of them still Kitty? If yes, are both of them Kitty or only one? If only one, which one?

Kitty, Dead or Alive?

Unfortunately and very sadly, Mary does not have a long time to think about the problematic identity of her beloved cats. In fact, when she comes back from her discussion with the nurse, she finds her two cats dead. She's shocked, outraged, and miserable. Why has all of this happened to her? All of her questions are now resolved, but in a very unfortunate way.

The next day, when she again wants to talk to the famous neurosurgeon, there is no one left at the hospital. Apparently, they were alarmed by the reaction of Mary and her mother and, to be on the safe side, decided to switch the location of their research establishment.

Whereas Mary and her mother are still looking for him, the neurosurgeon is already far away. Right now, he's at home; he's relaxing and reading a good novel before his fireplace. The door is half-open; a little tiger cat enters. The neurosurgeon calls her. "Kitty, Kitty! Come, my little darling." The cat springs up on his lap and begins to purr slightly under his caresses.

This little cat is a very playful cat, always ready to run after a butterfly or another insect. She doesn't stop wanting to go in and out. She likes dry tuna food above all and hates chicken. In fact, this little cat has all of the psychological distinctive features of Kitty. However, she has neither Kitty's body nor Kitty's brain. Her brain is an artificial one into which the neurosurgeon has succeeded in "transferring" Kitty's psychological features.

So, is Kitty dead or alive?

Personal Identity through Time

Reading this little story and trying, at each stage, to ask yourself the questions Mary and her mother were pondering, you have been involved in metaphysics—one of the main areas of philosophy. More specifically, you have been interested in the subject of personal identity through time. You have wondered how a little cat like Kitty can be the same cat through the different stages of her life, what is necessary in order to determine whether a little cat like Kitty is the same today as one was in the past or as one will be in the future.

Philosophers, just like the majority of people, are rather preoccupied with their own species, and so most of the time they ask such questions about human beings. However, as we have seen, even if there are some differences, these questions are also relevant when we talk of a little cat, especially when we are very attached to her.

Kitty was first a little kitten; she then grew up, learned a lot of things (how to open the door, how to ask for food, and so on) and stocked up a lot of memories. Later, if the car accident hadn't occurred, she would probably have grown old and even later, she would have died. Furthermore, each second of her life a lot of cells would have continued to die, while others would have continued to be born. Therefore, now, most of her cells would be different from the ones at the moment of her birth. Through all of these stages and changes, we would usually say that the same cat continues to live. But what does this mean? What it is for cat like Kitty to be the same through time?

Science can help us determine whether there is bodily continuity or psychological continuity between two cats at different times. Science cannot really answer the question of what it is for a cat to be the same through time. If a certain religion claims that each cat has a soul and that it is the existence "in" the cat of such a soul through time which makes her the same, we can say that this religion answers the question of the identity of cats through time. But, if it rests "only" on an act of faith without any further reason, this answer can't impose itself upon every rational human being. This is why this answer wouldn't be fully adequate.

In order to answer the question of the identity of cats (or of persons) through time, and in order to discover the different elements which constitute our concept of personal identity, some hypothetical situations have to be considered. This is what we have done in thinking about the story of Mary and her mother. The different cases we have considered can be summarized in the table.

This table allows us to look at the different criteria that philosophers have proposed for personal identity through time. Some of them have claimed that what makes a person the same through time is that there is some bodily continuity. Other philosophers have claimed that the continuity of the whole body is not what matters; brain continuity is sufficient, as the brain is the support of our mental life. Others have maintained that body or brain continuity is not what matters for personal identity through time, but instead, a certain psychological continuity is what matters. Still others have maintained that there is some mysterious extra fact that remains the same through time and backs up the identity of a person. And then some philosophers have claimed that, in reality, there is no personal identity through time at all, even if we do normally think and talk as if there were. According to them, personal identity through time is an illusion.

Cases like the ones in our story have also showed a very strange fact concerning our concept of personal identity through time. The fact that a certain cat is the same as another one at an earlier time or at a later time may depend on the existence of another cat! For instance, in the cases of (4), (5), (6), and (7) above, we have each time a same cat which has the body of Mimi, half of the brain of Kitty and all the distinctive psychological features of Kitty. Whereas

	Number of surviving cats	Body	Brain	Kitty's distinctive psychological features	Which cat is it? (main intuitions)				
(1)	Two	Mimi	Mimi	✓	Mimi				
		Kitty	Kitty	✓	Kitty				
(2)	One	Mimi	Kitty	×	Mimi				
(3)	One	Mimi	Kitty	✓	Kitty				
(4)	Two	Mimi	$\frac{1}{2}$ Kitty	✓	Kitty				
		A third cat	$\frac{1}{2}$ Kitty	×	The third cat				
					a	b	c	d	
(5)	Two	Mimi	$\frac{1}{2}$ Kitty	✓	Kitty	Not-Kitty	Kitty	Not-Kitty	?
		A third cat	$\frac{1}{2}$ Kitty	✓	Kitty	Not-Kitty	Not-Kitty	Kitty	
					d	a	b		
(6)	Two	Mimi	$\frac{1}{2}$ Kitty	✓	Not-Kitty	Kitty	Not-Kitty		?
		Kitty	$\frac{1}{2}$ Kitty	✓	Kitty	Kitty	Not-Kitty		
					c	d	b	a	
(7)	Two	Mimi	$\frac{1}{2}$ Kitty	✓	Kitty	Not-Kitty	Not-Kitty	Kitty	?
		Kitty	$\frac{1}{2}$ Kitty	×	Not-Kitty	Kitty	Not-Kitty	Kitty	
(8)	One	Another cat	Artificial	✓	Kitty				

in (4), this cat is clearly Kitty, it seems possible that this cat isn't Kitty in (5), (6), and (7)!

In philosophy, it is not sufficient to just claim that something is true or that one answer is the right one. In order for a philosophical answer to be satisfactory, it has to be supported by strong arguments with rationally persuasive reasons. Therefore, to be really philosophical, these different answers and considerations regarding the problem of personal identity through time require completion through such arguments.

Now that you have these different pieces of information in hand, try to answer the following questions: How is a cat today the same as another one in the past or in the future? What is it for you today to be the same person you were yesterday, the same person you were in your childhood and the same person you will be in your old age? Perhaps there's no answer to these questions—and that might be the most disturbing answer of all.[1]

---

[1] I want to thank Jiri Benovsky, who helped me by reading and commenting on early versions of this chapter.

17
Cat People?

RANDALL M. JENSEN

Paul Schrader's 1982 horror film *Cat People*—a remake of the 1942 classic film of the same name—tells the story of a strange and seductive species of feline lycanthropes. When these werecats become sexually aroused, they take the form of a ferocious black leopard, which means you really shouldn't date one of them, whether or not she looks like Nastassia Kinski. Even when in their human form, these creatures seem almost inhuman, moving with a preternatural quickness and an uncanny grace and staring into one's eyes directly and intently as only cats can do. Yet the film is aptly named, for in spite of all this, they truly do deserve to be called "people." Under the skin, as they say, we are not so different after all.

Of course, none of us will ever meet a werecat. However, we do share our lives with cats, though they're somewhat more ordinary than these cinematic chimeras. True, our old friend Morris is smaller than we are, and a lot cuter and oranger and far furrier, and he has a much more limited vocabulary, but does that mean he is not a *person*? What is it to be a person, anyway? And why does it *matter* whether some creature is a person or not? If we chase down some of the different ways of answering these questions, we'll have the chance to explore how we think about both our cats and ourselves.

Human People

We sometimes use the words "human" and "person" interchangeably, so that this section heading might strike you as rather redundant. If for some odd reason you were to ask me how many *people* were at a particular showing of the notoriously bad Halle Berry film *Catwoman*, I'd find the answer for you by simply counting the *human beings* present in the theatre. Human. Person. Same thing, right?

Not so fast. Both of these concepts are more complicated than this example suggests. Let's think about the word "human" for a little bit. Sometimes it's a purely descriptive label for a certain terrestrial species: *Homo sapiens*. And it's as clear as day that cats don't belong to that species. Other times, however, the word "human" has a rather different meaning. Consider the way we talk about our cats when they seem most sensitive and in tune with us: "She jumped right into my lap. I swear she knows just how I feel. Sometimes she seems so human!"

Surely this cat-lover's impression has nothing to do with biological classification. She doesn't suspect that her cat is really a very small and very hairy human being who has had lots of very extreme plastic surgery. No, what has struck her is that her cat seems to be thinking and feeling and acting in a certain way, just like one of us would think and feel and act. She's tempted to think of her cat as human for reasons that have nothing to do with biology at all.

Humanity thus seems to be a broadly psychological notion as well as a physiological or genetic one. But that's not all. Sometimes, in referring to something as human, we seem to be talking not about its membership in a certain species or about its mental and emotional life, but rather about its value or its *moral standing*. Consider the following excerpt from St. Thomas Aquinas, the great thirteenth-century theologian and philosopher:

> By sinning man departs from the order of reason, and consequently falls away from the dignity of his manhood, in so far as he is naturally free, and exists for himself, and he falls into the slavish state of the beasts, by being disposed of according as he is useful to others. (*Summa Theologica* II–II, Question 64, Article 2)

Aquinas is in the process of giving his rather frightening justification of capital punishment here. His claim is that *in some sense* a sinner (or the perpetrator of a serious crime, we might say) has become a beast rather than a human being. What kind of claim is this? Obviously, Aquinas isn't saying that a criminal is no longer genetically a human being. And he's also not saying that criminals don't have the same kind of psychological life the rest of us do, that instead they think and feel in some animalistic way. No, his point is rather that a human being who sins no longer has the same moral standing as the rest of us and therefore can be treated *as if* he were not one of us. In this sense, to be human is to be part of the moral community.

Humanity may seem to have as many meanings as a cat has lives, and normally these meanings are all tangled up like a ball of yarn that's been played with for too long. For our purposes, fortunately, three meanings will suffice: *first*, being a member of *Homo sapiens*; *second*, having the same psychology that you and I do; and *third*, having the same moral standing that you and I do. And the notion of personhood has roughly the same range, although we shouldn't go so far as to say these terms are interchangeable. We've already seen that "person" can be used to refer to a member of our species, and it's pretty obvious that it can take on the other two senses as well. For legal purposes we sometimes treat an organization, such as a corporation like Purina, as a person, which means assigning it a particular moral and legal standing without in any way suggesting that it has a real corporate mind of its own.

All of this ambiguity can easily lead to frustrating conversations where we talk past one another rather than to one another. To avoid this, it's best to disentangle the issues and to use terms rather carefully. Accordingly, let's restrict "human" to its biological use, so that a human being is simply a member of *Homo sapiens*. We'll use the term "person" as a psychological label; to call a creature a person is to describe its mental life. And when we want to talk about a creature's moral standing, we'll simply use those very words: "moral standing."

No doubt we use words like these rather promiscuously in ordinary language, but we can get a bit farther if we're a bit more straight-laced when we're trying to do some philosophy. To illustrate: You and I are human persons with moral standing, unless you're an alien feline from outer space or some such thing. Irena, the werecat played by Kinski in *Cat People*, is not a human being, but she is a person and she does seem to have moral standing. Morris the cat isn't a human being, either. Is he a person? Does he have moral standing? We'll need to think on these two questions for a while—about the questions themselves, first, and then about the various possible answers.

Everybody Wants to Be a Cat . . .
Or Is It a Person?

We have a fairly decent handle on what it is to be a human being. But what is it to be a person? A rough answer to this question is pretty easy to come by. As suggested by our recent example of a woman with her feline companion in her lap, a person is someone who thinks, feels, and acts in a certain way—in more or less the way that you and I think, feel, and act.

So what makes you and me persons? Well, here's an obvious place to start: only persons can read and understand this book. Reading and understanding this book (or any book) is therefore what philosophers call a *sufficient condition* of personhood. In other words, such a level of mental acuity is all you need to be a person. But it isn't a *necessary condition* of personhood, since we can easily think of persons who can't read the English language or who can't read at all. A complete and precise definition of person-hood would provide a set of necessary and sufficient conditions that would specify exactly what makes something a person. Such a definition would enable us to divide the universe into persons and non-persons and to see which side of the divide our feline friends might occupy. However, in spite of a lot of trying, it's proven surprisingly difficult for philosophers to reach a consensus about the conditions of personhood.

It may even be a mistake to try. The Austrian philosopher Ludwig Wittgenstein (1889–1951) challenges us to define the more ordinary concept of a game and suggests that we cannot identify a set of conditions that neatly distinguish games from non-games. Why? Well, for any proposed necessary or sufficient condition, we seem able to think of a game that proves the exception to the rule. His point is not that there's something especially paradoxical about the concept of a game but rather that our ability to use concepts meaningfully doesn't seem to depend on our having a complete definition of them. Let's follow his advice and not despair if we don't have a perfect definition of personhood. However, that does-n't mean we don't need to spend a bit of time sorting out how this concept functions in the way we think and talk.

What could a cat do to convince us that it's a person? Talking is probably the first thing to come to mind. A cat that can really con-verse with us has got to be a person. But merely making talking noises isn't enough. A plush Garfield toy that loudly and annoyingly exclaims "Lasagna!" when we push its paw isn't talking in the way people talk, not even if it's programmed with dozens or even hundreds of different sayings. This implies that what's compelling about the idea of a talking cat is that it *understands* something and not the mere fact that it's making certain kinds of sounds. What would really impress us is a cat that could carry on a conversation with us about all the chapters in this book! Only a cat that really understood the chapters could do that.

So perhaps a person is a *rational* animal, to adapt an ancient Greek conception of humanity. Of course, unless you're a mutant Dr. Dolittle who can read animal minds, you can't directly observe rationality or understanding in a cat. Instead, you have to infer something about a cat's inner life from its outer behavior. Different kinds of behavior might be the basis of such an inference, with talking just being the most blatant example.

A cat's behavior might also suggest other characteristics that we associate with being a person. *Emotionality* is the ability to express emotions and to empathize with others. *Self-consciousness* is having conscious experiences and being able to see oneself as the enduring subject of a succession of such experiences. And *moral agency* is the ability to distinguish right from wrong and thus to be held morally responsible for one's actions. Upon reflection, it's hard to deny that we see ourselves as persons on the basis of such *person-making characteristics*, which means that we should feel some pressure to regard other creatures as persons to the extent that they possess them as well. A creature may not need to possess all four of these characteristics to be a person; some science fiction writers have tried to imagine persons without emotion, for example.

The Cat from Outer Space

Speaking of science fiction, please imagine with me that we're exploring the universe in our new spaceship and we've just landed on a planet that's populated by creatures that look an awful lot like terrestrial cats of various kinds: Siamese, Himalayan, Persian, and of course an Abyssinian or two. We're now wondering about their moral standing and about how we should treat these creatures, which we'll call "kats" for the sake of convenience, with no hidden implication that they're in any way "krazy."

Should we treat a kat the way we treat a cat simply because they look rather alike? Probably not. We know we shouldn't decide how to treat other human beings on the basis of their physical appearance, and this is just an extension of that very familiar idea. Is it morally safe for us to treat kats the way most of us treat terrestrial animals, simply because kats aren't human beings? Again, probably not. For imagine that kats are far more intelligent than we are and that they're also so morally advanced that they've created a utopian society and would never seek to deceive or exploit us. Wouldn't it be a moral disaster if we were to herd them up—if herding kats is more easily accomplished than herding cats—and to prepare to use them as research subjects, zoo exhibits, or lunch? We'd be guilty of the moral sin that philosophers call "speciesism," a prejudice that's analogous to racism and sexism. Any of these isms consists in treating some being in a certain way because it falls into a category that just isn't morally significant. The fact that a creature doesn't belong to a certain species no more disqualifies it from having moral standing than the fact that a human being doesn't belong to a certain gender or race means he or she has a lesser moral standing.

So in our investigation into the moral standing of kats, it just isn't helpful to discover that kats look like cats or that kats aren't humans. This is unfortunate, because these facts are obvious and it would be nice if morality could always depend on obvious facts. What would be helpful then? No doubt the answer is about to smack you in the face: Are kats persons? If we're imagining them as more intelligent and also more moral than us, surely they are. And if kats are persons, like we are, then they must have the same moral standing that we have, right? So if we wouldn't put a human being in a cage, then we shouldn't do it to a kat, either. And if we would help a human being in trouble, then we owe the same kind of help to a kat. In short, whatever morality says to and about us, it says to and about kats. Why? Because we're both persons, even though we're not both human.

Our excursion to the planet of the space kats therefore suggests there's a close connection between being a person and having moral standing. And this makes sense, doesn't it? Certain kinds of moral wrongs can only be done to persons. Take lying, for example. You can try to lie to your catnip plant or to your pussywillow tree, but you can't really carry it off. You can only really lie to something that can understand you well enough to be deceived. Furthermore, certain kinds of harms seem much worse, and thus much harder to justify, when done to persons. Killing something before its time nearly always harms it and is often a bad thing. But a person has much more to lose from a premature death than plants or most animals do. A person has a future in a way that non-persons do not.

People have ongoing relationships with each other that are severed when one of them dies. And people invest themselves in projects that take a long time to complete. Some of these projects give meaning to a person's life, so that it's a genuine tragedy when such a project is cut off. In short, persons are invested in their futures in a way that non-persons aren't, which means that death represents a different order of loss for persons. This is all part of why we regard the unjustified killing of a person—which we call *murder*— as one of the worst wrongs there is. And so while it seems arbitrary to connect moral standing with being human (or with being a member of any other species), it doesn't seem arbitrary to connect it with being a person.

Ordinary Cat People?

You may be feeling somewhat impatient with all this talk about extraterrestrial cats and werecats. You may ask why we aren't talking about what's real: the perfectly ordinary cats that live with us, whether they've been invited to do so or not. Yet there's a reason for the foray into fantasy. Sometimes it's difficult for us to look clearly and objectively at what's familiar—like human beings and their cats—because we think we already know the answers to whatever questions might be put to us. If we shift over to something off the beaten path, we may find our minds more able to see the various possibilities.

So, what of our furry feline friends? They're not human. Are they persons? They don't compare so well with our imaginary kats when it comes to our person-making characteristics. Consider rationality. Our cats don't talk, and it isn't just because they haven't yet learned our language or we haven't yet learned theirs. And even if we somehow endowed them with telepathic powers, I doubt we'd be silently communing with them about life, the universe, and everything else. Even if we don't have a complete theory of rationality to work with, it's hard to deny that feline rationality falls somewhere below ours on the rationality scale.

Cats also seem less emotionally sophisticated, less morally responsible, and less aware of themselves and their futures. So things don't look so good for them in the personhood department. We also probably need to confess that we're guilty of a fair bit of anthropomorphism when it comes to the animals we love, meaning that we see them as more like us than they really are. So it'd be pretty easy to conclude that cats just aren't people and that some cat-lovers tend to inflate the qualities of their pets and companions.

However, even if there's some truth in this, we've often erred in the opposite direction, too. The renowned philosopher Rene Descartes infamously seems to have thought of all animals, includ-ing cats, as mere automata, incapable of thinking and unable to feel anything, even pain. Descartes is committed to this point of view because he thinks that we human beings possess our own person-making characteristics in virtue of having an immaterial soul and he does not want to attribute such souls to animals. This actually pre-sents something of a puzzle for *dualism*, which is the view that human beings consist of two distinct parts: an immaterial mind or soul and a body. If human beings are people because they have souls, then what do we say about animals that act very much like they're people—or almost like people, anyway? Dualism seems to establish a radical divide between human beings and the rest of this planet's creatures, and I suspect we're a lot less inclined to main-tain that divide than we once were.

The Cheshire Person

The Cheshire Cat is one of the most memorable characters in Lewis Carroll's *Alice in Wonderland* (although regrettably more people probably remember him from the Disney film version). Alice begins one fascinating exchange by expressing her desire that the Cat quit appearing and disappearing all of a sudden:

> "All right," said the Cat; and this time it vanished quite slowly, begin-ning with the end of the tail, and ending with the grin, which remained some time after the rest of it had gone.
> "Well! I've often seen a cat without a grin," thought Alice; "but a grin without a cat! It's the most curious thing I ever saw in my life!"

What a surprising creature! He can disappear all at once, or he can disappear gradually. Perhaps we should look to him for some inspiration in our thinking about cats and persons, since he's clearly both.

Why should we assume that person-making characteristics are an all-or-nothing affair, that they're either present or not? Perhaps they can make their appearance gradually, just like our friend the Cheshire Cat. After all, these four characteristics come in degrees. Surely the question we need to ask of cats and other creatures is not "Are they rational or not?" but rather "How rational are they?" (and similarly for the other characteristics). Maybe human beings are persons because we're rational *enough*. And what counts as rational enough? That's a hard question. But we don't think that the level of a human being's moral standing corresponds to his or her "rationality quotient," so the benchmark must not be extraordinarily high for our species. But it's still high enough to leave cats behind, I'm guessing. So, what should we say about a creature who just misses the mark? Is a miss as good as a mile?

I don't think so. Let's consider how we think about the personhood of human children. Very young human children probably don't qualify as persons on their own merits. (This means only that they don't possess the four person-making characteristics of rationality, moral agency, emotionality, and self-consciousness to the sufficient degree—and we're not talking about moral standing yet!) In the ordinary course of events, at some later point in their development, we'll gladly proclaim them persons. But we don't want to say that they'll suddenly become a person in one fell swoop, with personhood appearing instaneously like the Cheshire Cat's first favored move. Surely the development of their personhood is gradual, so that there are times where if we're asked if a child is a person what we'll say is neither "Yes" nor "No" but rather "Sort of." If that answer's available for a human child, surely it's also available for a non-human animal. We don't want to be accused of speciesism.

So is a cat a person? We can't reply with a full-fledged "Yes!" no matter how much we might like to. But we don't have to say no, either. We can reply with a confident "Sort of!" Let's see what this might mean in a more specific context. Earlier we saw that you can only lie to a person, because only a person can understand you well enough to be taken in. Can you lie to a cat? Yes and no. I do think it's possible for us to deceive a cat in certain ways, to get a cat to believe something that isn't true and to act accordingly (and often foolishly). Still, I think you'll agree that we can't lie to a cat in the same way that we can lie to each other. So, cats are persons, sort of.

More than One Way to Skin a . . . Dog?

Suppose some people don't like what they may see as a wishy-washy tendency to avoid hard questions, so they try to force us to give a yes-or-no answer as to the personhood of cats. And suppose we feel compelled to say that cats aren't people. Does that automatically mean they have no moral standing? Not at all. The British philosopher Jeremy Bentham (1748–1832) famously argues that when considering the moral standing of animals, "the question is not, Can they reason? nor, Can they talk? but, Can they suffer?" As a *utilitarian*—a moral theorist who believes that the aim of morality is to bring about the greatest happiness of the greatest number—Bentham thinks that suffering is a bad thing and that any creature who can suffer thereby has the only kind of moral standing that matters. Thus, on his view, *sentience* (the ability to experience pleasure and pain) rather than personhood, is what entitles creatures to moral standing.

There's no need for us to feel obliged to decide between personhood and sentience. Instead, we can think that *both* sentience and personhood are morally important creature features. We've already briefly reflected on the distinctive moral importance of being a person. Now we can simply add that being sentient matters morally as well, even if in a different way. The upshot is that a person shouldn't care only about other persons.

If a creature is sentient, Bentham's lesson is that its pain should matter to us. Morality should demand a reason for any suffering at all, and the greater the suffering, the more compelling the reason will need to be. Nevertheless some moral considerations aren't in play for merely sentient creatures. If a creature is sentient and a person to boot, then morality has a lot more to say about how we should treat it. Our cats are clearly sentient. And we've seen that it can be argued that they're sort-of persons. Thus, either way, or both ways, they have some moral standing.

If you were running out of a burning building and you had to choose between saving a cat and saving a human being, you should save the human being, who is a full-fledged person. But if you were running out of that same building and you could save a cat without any serious risk, you should save the cat, who deserves your help. Not to do so would be to fail to acknowledge the cat's moral standing, which would be wrong. Likewise, if you were to rid yourself of an unwanted cat in the same way that you might rid yourself of an unwanted insect, which is in no way a person and perhaps not even sentient, it'd be wrong. A creature's moral standing, which dictates how it should be treated, depends on what it's like to be that creature. What is it like to be a cat? I'm afraid that's a question for another day.

Most of us are no doubt delighted to find that our beloved cats have moral standing. We want people to treat cats the way they deserve to be treated, for they're wonderful creatures and not just objects for our use and entertainment. However, there's a catch: what goes for cats goes for lots of other mammals as well. This means we'll have to answer some tough questions about how we treat other animals: questions about farming, zoos, experimentation, pet ownership, our diets, our attire, and any number of other things. The ethics of animals could easily get really complicated, and all because we started thinking about cats!

From Cats to Humans

As we've been making our way through this conversation, you may have noticed that according to the definitions we've developed, not all human beings are persons. Human embryos, fetuses, and even infants are not persons, for their brains simply aren't developed enough for them to be rational, self-conscious, and so on. A human embryo isn't even sentient. Thus, difficult but all too familiar questions about the moral standing of very early human beings arise. And this creates what for some people is a surprising connection between questions about how we treat animals and questions about abortion and stem cell research. At the very end of their biological lives some human beings cease to be persons as well, due to dementia and other causes, creating a link between animal ethics and the morality of euthanasia and physician-assisted suicide. In the end, thinking about how we should think about and treat our cats is part of the much larger project of trying to answer the biggest question of all: How should we live our lives?

18

Catnesses

CATHY LEGG

Surely the cat, when it assumes the meat loaf position and gazes meditatively through slitted eyes, is pondering thoughts of utter profundity.

—Mij Colson Barnum

Cats' names are more for human benefit. They give one a certain degree more confidence that the animal belongs to you.

—Alan Ayckbourn

In an interview to a local newspaper, I was once asked what was the one thing I would define cat behavior by. My reply was "individuality." Each cat has his or her own particular characteristics and peculiarities. As a cat behaviorist, the issue of cat individuality was always prominent in my mind. Whatever the "rules" for cats are, there will always be the odd cat that will break the rules and display a different behavior pattern.

—Anne Moss

Cats spend a lot of time deep in reflection. People who know and love cats often suspect that those thoughts are profound—profound enough to surprise people who don't know and love cats. Like all of us who think, cats think a lot about *things*. A good example of a 'thing' which cats like to think about is a delicious bowl of milk. Cats love to just lie on the sofa while the thought of a delicious bowl of milk wanders gently in and out of their minds. It's a well-known fact that a mature, mentally alert cat can keep up this delightful activity for over six hours straight.

However, having thought a lot about things, such as delicious bowls of milk, cats sometimes then go on to think about their *thoughts* about those *things*. For example, they may think, "How interesting it is that, just lying here basking in the sun coming through the window, I can fill my head with a thought about a delicious bowl of milk!" This then raises the question, which cats sometimes pursue in their musings, of how it is that these *thoughts* are 'about' actual, drinkable, delicious bowls of milk. Cats are intelligent enough to know that their little furry heads do not contain bowls of milk, so, they wonder, how do they conjure them up just by thinking about them? They know that their thoughts are about delicious bowls of milk, but what makes this so?

Such thoughts can be a bit tiring, and sometimes cats get distracted from them by a bird flying past the window, the need to growl at a passing dog, or even by an actual bowl of milk placed on the floor by their own human. A cat would never confuse a mere thought about a delicious bowl of milk with an actual bowl of milk, and of course a cat much prefers to spend time with the latter.

I know all this because a cat once shared his thoughts on these things with me. This cat's name was Bruce, and his human was a philosopher named David. David wrote many very well-received philosophical papers about issues concerning things and thoughts, such as the question of how the thoughts manage to 'include' or 'talk about' the things. (Some philosophers refer to this issue as 'The Problem of Intentionality'.) Sometimes Bruce would read over David's shoulder when he was writing, and sometimes Bruce would open one furtive eye and peek at David's drafts of philosophical papers while lying spread out across them, to see what ideas David was coming up with about these matters.

David wrote that the world is made up of things and their *intrinsic properties*—in fact, forget the things, the *properties* were the really important part for David. Intrinsic properties are properties which things have quite apart from the properties which any other things have. For example, that the dog down the road, Chuckles, has a head like a misshapen football is an intrinsic property of Chuckles—because it depends solely on the way Chuckles himself happens to be. That he is despised by Bruce, however, is not an intrinsic property of Chuckles, because it depends on the way Bruce is as well as the way Chuckles is. Being despised is thus a *relational* property—it depends how the thing (in this case,

Chuckles) is related to other things (Bruce, and his penchant for despising despisable dogs).

David's Worlds

Still, if Bruce and Chuckles were recreated atom-for-atom, down to the last intrinsic property, the recreated Bruce would despise the recreated Chuckles, because of the way Bruce is and the way Chuckles is ('intrinsically'). In this sense, one might argue that intrinsic properties are more fundamental than relational properties, and that what relational properties exist depends on what intrinsic properties exist. David thought this was true, because of the obviousness of facts such as that if Bruce and Chuckles were recreated atom-for-atom, the recreated cat would despise the recreated dog. He came to believe that if a human were to make a long, long list of *all* the things there are and *all* the intrinsic properties that those things have (it would probably have to be a human as only a human would bother with such a task—a cat certainly would not), then that long, long list would be a total story of everything! There would be nothing else we could say that would be true and not covered by the long, long list. Or in other words:

> all there is to the world is a vast mosaic of local matters of particular fact, just one little thing and then another . . . We have geometry: a system of external relations of spatio-temporal distances between points . . . And at those points we have local qualities: perfectly natural intrinsic properties which need nothing bigger than a point at which to be instantiated. For short, we have an arrangement of qualities. And that is all. (*On the Plurality of Worlds*, p. ix)

Bruce overheard David referring to this view as "Human Supervenience". *['Humean Supervenience'!—ed.]* When Bruce first heard about this, he thought first of all that if Chuckles were recreated atom-for-atom he would despise the new dog-clone *more* than the old one, as to have a *second* one living on the street would be even more annoying. Then, with respect to the general theory, he decided he was skeptical and resolved to think about it.

David pointed out, as many philosophers have, that not all of our thoughts are true—some of them are false. For instance, while lying on the sofa basking in the sun coming in from the window, a cat can think contentedly that his dish on the kitchen floor is full of sardines. If the dish is in fact full of sardines (or, as a philosopher might put it, has the *property* of being full of sardines), then the cat's thought is true. If the dish is empty, or it is only half-full of sardines because the greedy cat next door has sneaked in and eaten some, or if—horrible prospect—the dish is full of jellymeat! (UGH!), then the thought is false. A basking cat might wonder (and some do), *how* do we *manage* to have false thoughts? If the things the thoughts talk about are not part of actuality, where do we get them from to put them in our heads and think about them? We manage this, David thought, because we think in *propositions*, and propositions have some kind of reality, whether they are actually true or false.

What kind of reality do propositions have? David told a story about this in terms of what he called "possible worlds." David pointed out (cleverly, as he was a clever philosopher) that 'The Truth' is not restricted to those things that are *actually* true. It's also true that certain things are *possible*. For instance, although Bruce did not catch the bird which he jumped out of the long grass in front of yesterday, he might have caught it, if he had just been a bit quicker. It was possible for him to have caught that bird. On the other hand, for Bruce to have both four and three legs is not possible. Even if Bruce were unfortunate enough to lose a leg, and so to have four legs at one time and three legs at a later time, he would never have four and three legs *at the same time*. So having both four and three legs is not a possibility for Bruce.

Possibility Is Real

It seems that when we talk about reality, we don't always just refer to the way things actually *are*, we also refer to "ways things might have been." Imagine that I say, "Every cat is cleverer than its owner." We all know that this claim is very arguably true. But it is not just a claim about the many thousands (perhaps millions?) of contented cat-owner pairs which have existed through history and up to the present time (for instance, David and Bruce, Edward Lear and Foss, Sir Walter Scott and Hinx, Matthew Flinders and Trim . . . and so on). It's a stronger claim than that. It says, for instance, that if Bruce had been owned by Edward Lear, Bruce would have been cleverer than Lear, (not to mention clever enough not to mistake him for the Thirteenth Earl of Derby, unlike many humans) and it says that if Trim—the first cat to circumnavigate Australia—had instead accompanied "the author of Waverley" on his fictional journeys, the novelist would at times have felt rebuked beneath an unnerving gleam in the eye of his companion.

One way to think of "ways things might have been" is by imagining them happening. It's as if, for each possible way that things might be, there is a whole world, just as real as ours, where that thing *is* true. There is a world where Bruce caught the bird he jumped for yesterday and missed (but might have caught). There's another world where Bruce caught the bird but it then escaped and flew away, and Bruce was terribly frustrated . . . and so on for all the possibilities for Bruce and the bird—indeed, all the possibilities about anything.

David thought very carefully about these matters and decided that if part of talking about reality involves talking about ways things might have been, *why not say that ways things might have been are part of reality?* Surely this should follow? Thus David wrote (in more or less the following words):

> I advocate a thesis of plurality of worlds, or *modal realism*, which holds that our world is but one world among many . . . absolutely *every* way that a world could possibly be is a way that some world *is*. (*On the Plurality of Worlds*, p. 2)

What makes the world the world it is? What makes two worlds different? It is, David thought, purely the arrangement of the intrinsic properties in worlds. "Just one little thing and then another." If we could ever work out all the possible permutations and combinations of arrangements of intrinsic properties (which is, once again, probably something only a human would think of doing), then we would have a list of all the possible worlds.

Now let's return to propositions. David claimed that we can understand a proposition as a *set of possible worlds*—all the possible worlds where it is true. For instance, consider the proposition, "Bruce lay on the sofa yesterday." That proposition corresponds to a set of worlds which includes the world where Bruce lay luxuriously on the sofa for four and a half hours (which is what actually happened), and other worlds—such as worlds where:

- **Bruce lay on the sofa for five minutes**

- **he lay on the sofa on a golden cushion**

- **he lay on the sofa with a sardine on his head**

- **he lay on the sofa with twelve lions stretched out beside him**

The same thing applies for false propositions. The proposition that Bruce did not lie on the sofa yesterday corresponds to a set of worlds including those where:

- **Bruce sat on the roof all day**

- **he spent the day stalking a sparrow through next-door's garden**

- **he took the bus into town and went to the museum**

Our World and Those Others

The set of worlds that corresponds to a false proposition does not however include the actual world, our world. That is what it is to be false. So when we think about things, really, we are only deciding which possible world-sets include our world, based on the arrangements of intrinsic properties in all the possible worlds, and the specific arrangement of intrinsic properties that exists the actual world. That's all there is to thinking.

Bruce thought about all of this. He had a number of questions. He was very interested in the world where he caught the bird. He asked David how he could get to that world. He hoped that it would not involve a car-journey, or crossing the territory of the white cat who lives in the house with the big pine tree. (That is one very rude cat.) However David told Bruce that he could not go there! Though the worlds are just as real as ours, full of real grass, real birds, real sardines and real sofas, they are "isolated" in space and time. He said (in more or less the following words):

> The worlds are something like remote planets; except that most of them are bigger than mere planets, and they are not remote. Neither are they nearby. They are not at any spatial distance whatever from here. They are not far in the past or future . . . they are not at any temporal distance whatever from now. They are isolated: there are no spatiotemporal relations at all between things that belong to different worlds." (*On the Plurality of Worlds*, p. 2)

Bruce asked, What's a planet? David said it was something like a backyard, only bigger. "How strange," Bruce thought, "backyards totally cut off in space and time from each other! How could one get back for dinner?" Bruce wondered how, given that they were totally cut off in space and time from each other, David was able to know what was going on in them (enough to know for instance, that in one of them Bruce caught the bird he was so close to catching the other day)? Did his human have a special kind of whiskers?

Bruce protested, "If this 'world' is isolated in space and time, how do I get in there to catch the bird, like you said I could?" David replied—there is no need to 'get in there'. You are already there! There is a cat in that world, also named Bruce, who has the same colored fur as you, with the same markings, who likes sardines just like you do, and who behaves in the same naughty way as you do on windy nights. This cat is so like you that he *is* you in that world ("speaking casually"). He is your "counterpart" there. To be more specific, he does not have to be exactly like you to be your counterpart, he just has to be *more like you than any other thing that exists in that world* (as long as the world isn't just full of things which are *totally* different to you, like poached eggs). And it is because *that* Bruce does catch the bird, that we can say that it was possible for you to catch the bird you jumped out of the grass in front of yesterday and just missed.

Bruce's head was hurting a bit so he went and sat on the fence and washed himself very thoroughly. There was something wrong with what David had said. Washing his head was always the best way to straighten out the thoughts in it. Suddenly he put his paw down and sat up straight. He said, I don't care what *that cat* does, whether he catches *that bird.* Just because *that cat* happens to look like me, what should what he did mean about what *I* am able to do? Why does what *that cat* did mean that it was possible for *me* to catch the bird, any more than if that silly black kitten who lives next door by pure dumb luck manages to catch a bird, as he did last Tuesday. *Neither* of those cats is me, so neither of them has anything to do with me!

David replied, what is the *difference* between you and the other Bruce in the other world? What *property* do you have that he doesn't? I told you that he is the same color, he has the same name, he loves sardines like you do, and he behaves exactly the same way you do. For instance, he plays with my fingers but never bites, and he always sits on the pink sofa cushion. What more is there for him to *be* you? Bruce said, "He has to be *me*. *This* cat." David said, "That is not an answer. You are begging the question." Bruce had heard David say that to other humans, "You are begging the question." It usually seemed to make them more inclined to agree with him. He didn't know what 'begging the question' was, it sounded a bit like something a dog might do—they seemed to like to beg for things, undignified supplicating animals. Well he was not a dog!

David said, "I don't believe in-" and then he said a word that sounded like "heck-cat-ies". *['Haecceities'!—ed.]* He said it was Latin for "this cat." He accused Bruce of saying that two possible worlds might differ in non-qualitative properties, and of denying "Human Supervenience" (or at least that is what Bruce thought he said). *['Humean!!—oh never mind' —ed.]* Bruce replied, "No, I'm just saying that *I am me*, and no other cat". Who was this 'Human'? What did he know about cats? Did a cat have him? He paused and rolled around on the ground for two minutes. Then he said, "You human, standing there, my owner, I know what you're thinking. You think that there exists one of your 'total stories' which concerns *me*. Given all the other things you have said, this 'story' will be some incredibly tedious list of boring 'intrinsic properties': my current fur-color, my current food-preference, my recent *behavior*(!) Do you understand what you're saying? You're saying that if another cat came into this backyard, with the same fur color, food preference and behavior, that cat would be your owner, and you would be its human. You would even (and here Bruce growled a little bit) . . . love it the way you love me! I am surprised at you! You don't understand cats! Why don't you get a dog? We know that dog people love their dogs for their "intrinsic properties." Remember how when Mrs Brown's poodle died, she went and bought another one which was the exact same color (which—surprise surprise—matches her living-room rug), liked to eat the same stinky dog roll, had exactly the same expression on its face, and made all the same feeble woofing noises. And she was perfectly happy. I would hate to think that *you* would do that to *me*.

"One day," he said, "you will understand that I and every other cat possesses a magnificent, utterly individual *catness* which underlies any mere 'property' we may choose to display at any given moment." Then suddenly, uttering a miaow which is incapable of being described in words, he bit David on the ankle, which he had never done in his life before (and has not done since). Since that day, I heard that David has behaved a little differently—so differently that given a choice of a roomful of philosophers, people who used to know David would pick out another philosopher than David as the philosopher most similar to the philosopher they used to know. However Bruce sits on David's knee as he has always done.[1]

> The city of cats and the city of men exist one inside the other, but they are not the same city. (Italo Calvino)

> A cat is a cat and that is that. (American folk saying)

---

[1] This chapter draws upon: Robert Adams, "Primitive Thisness and Primitive Identity", *Journal of Philosophy* 76: 1 (1979); Richard Cross, "Medieval Theories of Haecceity," *Stanford Encyclopedia of Philosophy*, http://plato.stanford.edu/entries /medieval-haecceity/ (downloaded September 2007); David Lewis, *On the Plurality of Worlds*, (Blackwell, 1986); David Lewis, "Possible Worlds," in Michael Loux, ed., *The Possible and the Actual: Readings in the Metaphysics of Modality* (Cornell University Press, 1979); Penelope Mackie, "Transworld Identity," *Stanford Encyclopedia of Philosophy*, http://plato.stanford.edu/entries/identity-transworld/ (downloaded September 2007); Ann Moss, "Cats as Individuals", *The Cat Site*, http://www.thecatsite.com/Behavior/195/Cats-As-Individuals.html (downloaded July 2007).

Cool Cats

FELICIA NIMUE ACKERMAN is professor of philosophy at Brown University and adjunct professor at Korea University. Her essays, short stories, and poems have appeared in various venues, including *The Oxford Handbook of Bioethics, Prize Stories 1990: The O. Henry Awards,* and *English Studies Forum.* She is preparing a book of her essays and stories, *Bioethics through Fiction,* in the series, *Explorations in Bioethics and the Medical Humanities.* Felicia's spectacular cat, Palomides, has soft long orange fur and a tlap (tail like a plume). Unlike the cat in the story, fortunately, Palomides is not diabetic.

ROBERT ARP is a postdoc researcher at the National Center for Biomedical Ontology through the University at Buffalo. He works in Philosophy of Mind and Philosophy of Biology and has several papers and books either in print, in preparation, or forthcoming in these areas. His book, *Scenario Visualization: An Evolutionary Account of Creative Problem Solving* is forthcoming, and he talks a little bit about his cute, cuddly, calico, crafty cat named Callie in that work as well.

RANDALL AUXIER is the servant of more than four cats in the environs of Carbondale, Illinois. In this lovely place he has been known to devote himself to fine wines, classic films, edifying books, an occasional chocolate, or a nice cigar, and whatever else the cats permit in their home. He is professor of philosophy at Southern Illinois University, and is addicted to writing chapters in Open Court books. Apart from that, he has no bad habits, except clawing the furniture.

JUDITH BARAD is Professor of Philosophy and Women's Studies at Indiana State University. She is the author of three books and numerous articles on ethics and the philosophy of religion, including such topics as feminist ethics, the role of emotion in moral judgments, the treatment of animals, the philosophy of St. Thomas Aquinas, and the ethics of *Star Trek.* She has given dozens of national and international scholarly presentations, and has been an ethics consultant for Boeing Corporation. Dr. Barad lives in Terre Haute, Indiana, with her grandson, her dog, her husband, and five very precious indoor cats. However, she's working on increasing her relatively small feline family since she's trying to tame three fine feral cats who dine daily in her backyard.

MANUEL BREMER teaches at the University of Düsseldorf, Germany. He specializes in logic and the philosophy of language, with a side interest in animal communication and cognition. Therefore he talks a lot to his two cats Cora and Miezie. They also meow and chatter quite a bit, but sign and non-verbal interaction are more successful with the three of them. Especially since the cats do not care about Manuel's books in logic (like *An Introduction to Paraconsistent Logics*) and semantics (like *Philosophical Semantics*), although they like to sit next to the PC keyboard.

JOHN CARVALHO is Chair of the Philosophy Department at Villanova University where he teaches courses in Ancient Philosophy, French and American critical theory, post-structuralism and aesthetics. He has published essays on terror, power, creativity, fiction as a context for facts, repetition as representation in post-modern photography, time as an image in new wave film and jazz improvisation. He has completed a book length manuscript titled *Thinking with Images.* He has taken in strays and cared for cats in four states for over forty years.

ALLISON HAGERMAN and her husband, Matthew, share a home with five cats and three dogs (yes, dogs) in Albuquerque, New Mexico. Allison has been a graduate student at the University of New Mexico for a long, long time, and the cats have issued an ultimatum that she must finish her dissertation within the next year.

STEVEN D. HALES is Professor of Philosophy at Bloomsburg University. His official interests are epistemology and metaphysics, but he also publishes books like *Beer and Philosophy* and the companion to the volume you are holding, *What Philosophy Can Tell You about Your Dog.* Unfortunately, his wife is allergic to cats, but Steve's young daughter has numerous stuffed, plush felines that she showers with affection.

RANDALL M. JENSEN is Associate Professor of Philosophy at Northwestern College in Orange City, Iowa. His philosophical interests include ethics, ancient Greek philosophy, and philosophy of religion. Recently, he has contributed to *South Park and Philosophy*, *24 and Philosophy*, *The Office and Philosophy*, and *Battlestar Galactica and Philosophy*. The only violent incident of his adult life occurred when he had to defend his family's three-legged Himalayan from a pair of marauding dogs who invaded her yard and attacked her.

DIANE JESKE is an associate professor of philosophy at the University of Iowa. She specializes in ethics and political philosophy, and has published articles on the nature of friendship and its role in the moral life. In 2004 Diane was adopted by a gray and white cat named Pi who has inspired Diane's philosophical work by providing her with a concrete example of a deep and abiding human-feline friendship. In addition to acting as philosophical inspiration, Pi acts as guard of their shared home territory, which she is constantly in the process of redecorating to emphasize the shabby rather than the chic.

JEAN-ROCH LAUPER is a graduate assistant in the philosophy department of the University of Fribourg, Switzerland. He is currently writing a Ph.D. thesis on the issue of vagueness. The name of his cat is "Mimi." Jean-Roch and his wife welcomed her into their home in the winter of 2002 when she was dying of thirst because of the frost. Since her arrival Mimi has changed a lot at the physical as well as the behavioral level. But until now, Jean-Roch and his wife have thought rather confidently—rightly or wrongly?—that the cat who shares their days is the same as the little dehydrated cat they took in some years ago on Christmas Eve.

CATHERINE LEGG holds a B.A. from the University of Melbourne, an M.A. in Philosophy from Monash University, and a Ph.D. from Australian National University, where her thesis ("Modes of Being") concerned realism and Charles Peirce's philosophical categories. After a spell of ontological engineering she returned to academia and now teaches logic and metaphysics at the University of Waikato, New Zealand. Her philosophical researches have been aided through the years by a number of sagacious cats, many of whom have 'personal chairs' (in her home).

BERTHA ALVAREZ MANNINEN is an Assistant Professor of Philosophy at the Arizona State University West Campus in the Department of Integrative Studies. Her main area of research is applied ethics, especially biomedical ethics. When she's not teaching or researching, she likes to relax with her husband, Tuomas, and their five cats: Angel, Uni, Shady, Linus, and Liam—although she still swears she's a dog person.

EVAN MORENO-DAVIS recently completed his M.A. in philosophy at the University of California, San Diego, and is now doing olfactory research at its School of Medicine. His philosophical interests include responsibility, emotion, moral decision-making, and mental illness. His family's cat, Bucket, enthusiastically contributed to the writing of his essay. However, the passages she authored—including "xsd" and ";looooooooooooo"— were redacted for the sake of clarity.

ANDREW PAVELICH is an Assistant Professor of Philosophy at the University of Houston, Downtown. He does research on the Philosophy of Religion, as well as on seventeenth-century philosophers like Descartes and Locke. His cat Yoeshi's research interests include trying to find out what is on top of bookshelves, and learning how to open kitchen cabinetry.

BRYONY PIERCE is a PhD student at the University of Bristol, and an active contributor to current debates on consciousness, rationality and philosophy of action. She directed her own translation company before taking up philosophy, and has also worked as a conference organizer, language teacher, and presenter at a French local radio station. She lives with two cats (one black-and-white and one tabby) and four humans (one husband and three children).

GARY STEINER is John Howard Harris Professor of Philosophy at Bucknell University. He is the author of *Anthropocentrism and Its Discontents: The Moral Status of Animals in the History of Western Philosophy* (2005) and *Animals and the Moral Community: Mental Life, Moral Status, and Kinship* (2008). He is currently being held hostage by his cat Pindar.

JULIA TANNER recently completed her doctorate in philosophy at the University of Durham. Her Ph.D. focused on the moral status of animals and she has written a number of articles on the same topic. It was whilst writing her Ph.D. that she befriended a local cat named Mimi. At around the same time she also discovered she was allergic to cats.

JOSH WEISBERG is an assistant professor of philosophy at the University of Houston. He specializes in philosophy of mind and cognitive science, with a focus on consciousness. He has a cat named Poopy, a dog named Biscuit, and a Ph.D. from the City University of New York.

Felinedex

COMPILED BY L. LEE LAMPSHIRE